Islamic Jurisprudence in the Classical Era

Ten years after his untimely death, Norman Calder is still considered a luminary in the field of Islamic law. At the time he was one among a handful of scholars from the West who were beginning to engage with the subject. In the intervening years, much has changed, and Islamic law is now understood as fundamental to any engagement with the study of Islam, its history, and its society, and Dr Calder's work is integral to that engagement. In this book, Colin Imber has put together and edited four essays by Norman Calder that have never been published. Typically incisive, they categorise and analyse the different genres of Islamic juristic literature that were produced between the tenth and fourteenth centuries, showing what function they served both in preserving Muslim legal and religious traditions and in the day-to-day life of their communities. The essays also examine the status and role of the jurists themselves, and are particularly welcome for giving clear answers to the controversial questions of to what extent Islamic law and juristic thinking changed over the centuries, and was able to adapt to new circumstances. In his introduction to the volume, Robert Gleave assesses the place and importance of Norman Calder's work in the field of Islamic legal studies. This is a ground-breaking book from one of the most important scholars of his generation.

Norman Calder, who died in 1998, was Senior Lecturer in Arabic and Islamic Studies at the University of Manchester. His publications include *Studies in Early Muslim Jurisprudence* (1993) and *Interpretation and Jurisprudence in Medieval Islam* (J. Mojaddedi and A. Rippin, eds.) (2006).

Colin Imber was formerly Reader in Turkish at the University of Manchester.

Robert Gleave is Professor of Arabic Studies at the University of Exeter, UK. He works mainly in the area of Islamic legal theory. His books include *Inevitable Doubt: Two Theories of Shīʿī Jurisprudence* (2000) and *Scripturalist Islam: The History and Doctrines of the Akhbārī Shīʿī School* (2007). He is currently working on an examination of interpretation and linguistic meaning in Islamic jurisprudence.

Islamic Jurisprudence in the Classical Era

NORMAN CALDER

Edited by

COLIN IMBER

Introduction and Afterword by

ROBERT GLEAVE

University of Exeter

CAMBRIDGE
UNIVERSITY PRESS

CAMBRIDGE
UNIVERSITY PRESS

32 Avenue of the Americas, New York NY 10013-2473, USA

Cambridge University Press is part of the University of Cambridge.

It furthers the University's mission by disseminating knowledge in the pursuit of education, learning and research at the highest international levels of excellence.

www.cambridge.org
Information on this title: www.cambridge.org/9780521110808

First published 2010

A catalogue record for this publication is available from the British Library

Library of Congress Cataloguing in Publication data
Calder, Norman.
Islamic jurisprudence in the classical era / Norman Calder, Colin Imber.
p. cm.
Includes bibliographical references and index.
ISBN 978-0-521-11080-8
1. Islamic law – History – To 1500. I. Imber, Colin. II. Title.
KBP55.C348 2010
340.5′9–dc22 2010000034

ISBN 978-0-521-11080-8 Hardback

Contents

Editor's Preface

At the time of his death in 1998, Norman Calder was working on a book that was to form a sequel to his brilliant and controversial *Studies in Early Muslim Jurisprudence*. The four chapters presented here are the outcome of his research on this project, and although they are only part of the book that Norman had envisaged, they nonetheless make a substantial addition to the scholarly literature on classical Islamic jurisprudence. Their importance and position within this literature is the subject of Professor Robert Gleave's Introduction, while his Afterword provides a conspectus of Norman's intellectual and academic development as reflected in an important but easily overlooked part of his *oeuvre*.

The chapters were complete at the time of Norman's death, and my role has been strictly editorial, little more than incorporating hand-written material into the body of the text and providing full source references. I am particularly grateful to Robert Gleave for undertaking to write the Introduction and Afterword, and I must also record my thanks to Mustafa Baig for his bibliographic and technical help.

Introduction

Robert Gleave

It is unfortunate that these four studies, the final reflections of Norman Calder on classical Muslim jurisprudence, cannot be presented here in their intended context. The chapters are clearly part of a larger, unfinished project, but Calder left no suggestion of a 'structure' into which these studies might be slotted. There are no 'introductory remarks' that might ease the reader into the work, preparing him or her for the rigours to come. They were given to Norman's friend and colleague, Colin Imber, for editing as individual files (a task for which he is owed much thanks). Mercifully, and almost as a concession to a less initiated audience, Calder does (at least) open each chapter with an introductory passage. He also makes frequent reference to how a specific point is related to a (perceived) general characterisation of classical Muslim legal literature. These topical comments are buttressed by a few asides and correctives concerning contemporary and past Islamic legal scholarship. Notwithstanding these hints at a more general 'thesis' into which the four chapters fit, greater detail of the stage on which the Calder's analysis was to be set would have been useful. Calder was a structured thinker, and each chapter (both those written and those that perhaps never were) would have had a role. These roles can only be estimated through deduction and inference, and even then with varying degrees of conviction on my part. Principal connecting themes can be identified, but without an idea of the larger context presupposed for these studies, any identification will inevitably be partial at best, skewed at worst. Hence, the following account is presented with more than a little apprehension.

Fortunately, there are other immediate contexts that can do some of the work of the absent plan. First, there are Calder's other writings and the approach exhibited therein.[1] Employing these as a source comes with the inescapable caveat of

[1] All bar one of Calder's journal articles and book chapters have been collected in Norman Calder, *Interpretation and Jurisprudence in Medieval Islam*, J. Mojaddedi and A. Rippin, eds. (Aldershot,

Calder's own intellectual development. Undoubtedly his methodology developed and changed over the nineteen years between his first publication and his death. This development prevents any hard and fast linkages between different pieces of writing. Nonetheless, there are obvious commonalities between the arguments Calder presents in this volume and those he developed elsewhere. The second context that may aid our assessment of these four studies is the field of Islamic legal studies more generally, spanning not only the period up to when these studies were composed (i.e., the year or so before Calder's death in 1998), but also developments in the field since then. The discipline provides the intellectual context in which Calder was writing, and a broader view of the debates within the discipline enables us to picture (albeit imperfectly) how Calder envisaged his approach being applied to other debated topics. With these tools at our disposal, we can present both a (potentially forced) coherence within these four studies and a set of salient themes.

Calder's four final studies could be described as a request to the participants in the then emerging discipline of Islamic legal studies to take the literary quality of the sources they utilise seriously. He is concerned by the growing popularity among researchers of what (in his view) was a rather mercenary use of classical Muslim juristic literature. This literature generally, and two of its genres in particular – *fiqh* (or *furūʿ al-fiqh*) and *fatāwā* collections – are seen as sources of legal practice, or of social conditions, without a proper examination of their generic, stylistic and religious features. His concern is that little attention is being paid to the overarching relationship between literature and reality, and, more specifically, this particular legal literature and its contemporary legal/social reality. Before the economic or social historian can use this corpus of literature (with its internal logic and its genres and sub-genres), it needs to be understood on its own terms, and within the intellectual tradition in which it was composed. Only once this preliminary assessment has been carried out can the utility for the (legal or social) historian of these potential sources be assessed. Calder's studies (both here and in his other writings in the 1990s) are first steps in delineating elements in a robust intellectual methodology.

Now, it seems unlikely that Calder would have felt compelled to embark on this analysis and issue this request without the prevalence of an alternative approach within the field. It, therefore, becomes important to examine the disciplinary developments which, I believe, prompted his response. Calder, in this

UK: Ashgate, 2006). His encyclopedia articles are listed in G.R. Hawting, J.A. Mojaddedi, and A. Samely (eds.), *Studies in Islamic and Middle Eastern Texts and Traditions in Memory of Norman Calder*, (Oxford: Oxford University Press, 2000), 10. Calder's book reviews are listed and analysed in the Afterword to this volume.

volume and elsewhere, names some of the proponents of the position he is kicking against: Hallaq, Libson,[2] the editors of the important volume *Islamic Legal Interpretation* (Masud, Messick and Powers)[3] and to a lesser extent Reinhart.[4] With the rapid increase of writings in the field in the 1990s (spurred on, from 1994 onwards, by the publication of the specialist journal *Islamic law and Society*), these named individuals were, perhaps, the more prominent of a growing cadre of expertise within the field. Of these, Hallaq's publications have been particularly influential, and it is his work, in particular his important article 'From *Fatwās* to *Furūʿ*', that receives the greatest proportion of Calder's explicit comment. That article is, then, an appropriate place from which to begin. As with Hallaq's previous work, the initial focus in 'From *Fatwās* to *Furūʿ*' is on the inadequacies of established scholarship on Islamic law. Hallaq's target is the (previously) widespread view in Islamic legal studies, illustrated by citations from the writings of Coulson and Schacht, that Islamic law, after the tenth century, was not subject to significant change. Islamic law, according to this old view, was rigid and unchanging after its formative period, and therefore divorced from the exigencies of developing Muslim society. This may or may not be an accurate characterisation of the views of Coulson and Schacht, but the method is familiar to readers of Hallaq's published writings in the 1980s and 1990s. Hallaq's task, as he conceives it, is to disprove this widespread view, and indicate that change did occur in Islamic law and it was certainly not rigid and unchanging in the later centuries. His criticism of Coulson and Schacht here jigsaws nicely with his rejection of the notion that an individual jurist's interpretive activity (*ijtihād*) was theoretically restricted in the post-formative period, most adroitly expressed in his much-cited article, 'Was the Gate of *Ijtihād* Closed?'[5] *Ijtihād*, an individual jurist's effort to discover a legal ruling in a particular case, is associated with independent reasoning and the potential for a jurist to discover new solutions to (both novel and established) issues. If *ijtihād* ceased to be practised

[2] Calder refers to Gideon Libson, 'On the Development of Custom as a Source of Law in Islamic Law', *Islamic Law and Society*, 1 (1994): 131–55, but similar statements can be found in his *Jewish and Islamic Law: A Comparative Study of Custom during the Geonic Period* (Cambridge, MA: Harvard University Press, 2003), 249–50, n. 7.

[3] Muhammad Khalid Masud, Brinkley Messick, and David S. Powers (eds.), *Islamic Legal Interpretation: Muftis and Their Fatwas* (Cambridge, MA. and London: Harvard University Press, 1996), particularly their 'Muftis, Fatwas, and Islamic Legal Interpretation' in that volume, 3–32.

[4] A. Kevin Reinhart, 'Transcendence and Social Practice: *Muftis* and *Qadis* as Religious Interpreters', *Annales Islamologiques*, 27 (1993 [1994]): 5–28.

[5] Wael B. Hallaq, 'Was the Gate of *Ijtihād* Closed?', *International Journal of Middle East Studies*, 16 (1984): 3–41. Johansen's view was that this remained a primarily theoretical issue and did not have much to do with actual legal change. See B. Johansen, 'Legal Literature and the Problem of Change', in *Islam and Public Law*, ed. C. Mallat (London: Graham and Trotman, 1993), 29–31 (and in B. Johansen, *Contingency in a Sacred Law*, Leiden: Brill (1999), 446–8.

(i.e., its 'gate' was closed), then the potential for change in the law was minimised (possibly even eliminated). The phrase *insidād bāb al-ijtihād* ('the closing of the gate of *ijtihād*') can be found in some mediaeval sources, and these infrequent references, Hallaq argues, are elevated to historical fact by the contemporary generation of Islamicists (including Schacht, Anderson, Gibb, Tritton, Coulson, Watt, Khadduri and Rahman). The gate, according to Hallaq, was never closed, and the phrase *insidād bāb al-ijtihād*, used by a handful of Muslim jurists, has been misunderstood by these Islamicists. Once *ijtihād* is restored as an element of post-formative Islamic law, legal change becomes possible.

In 'From *Fatwās* to *Furūʿ*', Hallaq asserts not only that change occurred, but also that the principal mechanism of change was the fatwa. While readers can, of course, refer to Hallaq's article itself, it is perhaps worth pinpointing those elements of the article that Calder found problematic. A description of the institution of the fatwa need not be rehearsed here (Calder gives such a description in Chapter 4, as do Hallaq[6] and others). Hallaq's argument is that a fatwa (or rather the legal opinion or doctrine asserted by an individual mufti in a fatwa) has the potential to become incorporated into the body of authoritative legal doctrine (*madhhab*) in the post-formative period. This authoritative doctrine is expressed in works of *furūʿ* within a particular legal tradition (Ḥanafī, Shāfiʿī, Mālikī, etc).

There is plenty of evidence that this potential was realised on occasions, and Hallaq provides the reader with a barrage of references to *furūʿ* works in which the authors explicitly state that they are incorporating the fatwas of past (and perhaps even contemporary) learned scholars into their works. The incorporation happened, according to Hallaq, through a process which, given the available sources, is not always entirely recoverable. Nonetheless, sufficient examples of the end result of the process (together with many secondary accounts of it happening), are known to construct a skeletal description of the mechanism. First, the fatwas of either a prominent mufti, or a number of prominent muftis, are collected in a single work. These fatwas (which Hallaq calls 'primary' fatwas) include dates, places, names and other socially specific data that can be an important source to the social historian, but also indicate that the mufti concerned was engaging with reality when practising his legal reasoning. In some collections, the details, present in the original fatwa, are removed by the collator of the fatwa collection (these fatwas, stripped of details are, for Hallaq, 'secondary' fatwas, subjected to a technique known as *tajrīd*). The collections of fatwas then became a source for subsequent *furūʿ* writers. Some of the original wording of the fatwa may survive its incorporation into the *furūʿ* work, though it is also

[6] Hallaq, 'From *Fatwās* to *Furūʿ*', *Islamic Law and Society*, 1:1 (1994), 29–65.

possible that only the doctrine (or mufti's opinion) survives in the *furūʿ*. Hallaq provides examples of this process from the Mālikī school (including fatwas of Ibn Rushd al-Jadd (d. 520/1126) and their incorporation by al-Kinānī (767/1365) and al-Ḥaṣṣāb (d. 954/1547)).

The fatwas deemed worthy of inclusion, according to Hallaq, were those which ensured that the *furūʿ* works were up to date, including the latest developments in legal doctrine by the most prominent muftis, and with the most direct relevance to the *furūʿ* writers' contemporary Muslim society. New legal doctrines, the origins of which can be traced to real fatwas, were incorporated; in parallel, obsolete, irrelevant, 'strange' (i.e., minority) and 'weak' (i.e., unsubstantiated and unsupported) doctrines were removed. The new opinions take their place in the hierarchy of authoritative opinions, and their position depends on a variety of evaluation processes that subsequent scholars carry out (the exact details of this evaluation process need not be repeated here). Since the aim of *furūʿ* works was to provide a comprehensive expression of the law as proposed by a particular *madhhab*, this expression had to be of some use to the legal functionaries (and consequently, it had to be of relevance to the developing Muslim society). Hallaq concludes that 'the fatwa, reflecting the exigencies of the social order, was *instrumental in the ongoing process of updating and indeed amending* the standard legal doctrine as expressed in the *furūʿ*'.[7] '[T]he juridical genre of the fatwa was chiefly responsible for the growth and change of legal doctrine in the schools, and our current perception of Islamic law as a jurists' law, must now be further defined as a muftis' law. Any enquiry into the historical evolution and later development of substantive legal doctrine must take account of the mufti and his fatwa.'[8]

I have taken some time to outline Hallaq's presentation in 'From *Fatwās* to *Furūʿ*' not only because it has proved influential in subsequent Islamic legal scholarship, but also because it encapsulates a number of assumptions and conclusions that Calder considers either mistaken or at least in need of serious modification. For Calder, Hallaq's erudition and command of the sources was not in doubt. Furthermore, Hallaq is laudably eager to demonstrate (contra the 'orientalists') that post-formative Islamic law is not a mere recapitulation of past glories, but a phenomenon of interest in its own right, with an internal dynamic that demonstrates impressive originality and a level of sophistication which is arguably higher than that found in the early period. Calder's own reading of post-formative Muslim tradition is similarly positive.[9] Rather, Calder's concerns

[7] Ibid., 31 (emphasis in original).

[8] Ibid., 33.

[9] See N. Calder, 'The Limits of Islamic Orthodoxy', in *Intellectual Traditions in Islam*, ed. F. Daftary (London: I.B. Tauris, 2000), 66–86 (especially p. 84, where he describes the 'rich, complex and

were, in part, with the precision (or rather, the lack of it) with which Hallaq had formulated his conclusions:

> It is possible to agree with Hallaq's thesis at its most general – that in some sense or another Islamic law was capable of responding to social change – without feeling that he has characterised well either the basic structures of the Islamic legal system or the modality of its accommodation to change.[10]

Now, challenging the idea that Islamic law did not change between the tenth and nineteenth centuries was a preoccupation of a number of scholars in the 1980s and 1990s. However, the identifications of the mechanisms of 'change' and its relationship with *ijtihād/taqlīd* were topics on which there was little scholarly consensus.[11] A particularly productive line of enquiry has been to focus on legal and social practice, and examine its relationship with legal doctrine. Perhaps the most extensive work in this area has been carried out by David Powers.[12] However, Powers makes only occasional reference to the development of legal doctrine in works of *furūʿ*. When practice diverged from doctrine, he makes pertinent remarks, but in the end, his analysis is of legal practice and social reality, and how legal doctrine was one (and not always the dominant one) which influenced that practice/reality. One example of his method will suffice: The concentration in Islamic legal studies on doctrine untempered by practice has led scholars to certain conclusions about the practical implications of, say, the rules concerning inheritance. Powers demonstrates (through an analysis of fatwas, legal documents and other social-historical sources) that an examination of legal practice reveals that the range of means whereby an individual's wealth could be distributed after death was not limited to the inheritance rules themselves. Other mechanisms (including the family *waqf*) were available. This gives us a richer notion of the practicality of Islamic law, and certainly mitigates the conclusions of some early orientalists (Hurgronje, in particular) for whom Islamic law was a mere deontology, and not a law

varied tradition' of classical, post-formative, Muslim thought, and that 'the needs of the 20th century hardly indicate that [this tradition] should be restricted'.). See also, N. Calder, 'History and Nostalgia: Reflections on John Wansbrough's *The Sectarian Milieu*', in *Islamic Origins Reconsidered: John Wansbrough and the Study of Islam:* Special Issue of *Method and Theory in the Study of Religion: Journal of the North American Association for the Study of Religion*, 9;1, ed. Herbert Berg (Berlin: Mouton de Gruyter, 1997), 43–73.

10 See chapter 3, p. 160.

11 In the period when Calder was composing these chapters, the most significant advance was made through a special issue on *ijtihād/taqlīd*, guest edited by Hallaq, of the journal *Islamic Law and Society*, 3;2 (1997). Calder's contribution was his article, 'Al-Nawawī's Typology of *Muftīs* and Its Significance for a General Theory of Islamic Law', 137–64.

12 See in particular his collection of studies, *Law, Society and Culture in the Maghrib, 1300–1500* (Cambridge : Cambridge University Press, 2002).

as such.[13] Now Powers's work here operates to an extent in the opposite direction to much Islamic legal scholarship: his aim is to identify practice and relate it to doctrine (and not, or at least only occasionally, vice versa).

A more strident, and perhaps less subtle presentation of the practice-doctrine relationship can be found in the work of Haim Gerber. Gerber, with a focus on the Ottoman period, aims to discover the extent to which Islamic law was rigid and not subject to change or influence in the post-classical period. In his various writings, he aims to demonstrate, in a manner not dissimilar to that of Hallaq, that in the late classical period (on the eve of the intrusion of modernity), Islamic law was not the inflexible system characterised by the old orientalists (Schacht in particular, but Coulson and Gibb also). These scholars were also the targets of Hallaq's criticism in many of his articles in the 1980s and 1990s, and like Hallaq, Gerber's prime piece of evidence against this assumption is fatwas. Whatever the soundness of Gerber's methodology, his conclusions were that the legal decisions of the muftis (such as the famous Ḥanafī Khayr al-Dīn al-Ramlī (d. 1081/1671)) were heavily influenced by their school doctrine, and that they do exhibit *taqlīd*. However, their legal activity is characterised by an openness to change which can be recognised when examining their fatwas:

> Islamic law was not sealed off from full-fledged innovations, which took place under the banner of *istiḥsān*, local custom (*'urf*), necessity (*ḍarūra*), and public interest (*maṣlaḥa*). It cannot be proven, nor do I claim, that it was al-Ramlī who introduced these innovations. It is sufficient that he acknowledged innovations by others, and that the channels of Islamic law, as reflected in his thought, remained open to change.[14]

Also prominent in the field is Baber Johansen, whose writings are (perhaps surprisingly) not referenced by Calder in these pages. Johansen had approached the issue of change in Islamic law as early as 1979 in his assertion that certain elements of Ḥanafī penal law were developed and changed in response to and under the influence of legal practice.[15] He developed his conceptions of the modalities of legal change in a series of articles, the most relevant here being his 'Legal literature and the problem of change: the case of the land rent'.[16] There Johansen distinguishes between the core texts of the *madhhab* (*mutūn*), in which authoritative doctrine was declared, and the commentaries and fatwas

[13] D. Powers, 'The Mālikī Family Endowment: Legal Norms and Social Practices', *International Journal of Middle East Studies* 25 (1993): 379–406.

[14] Haim Gerber, 'Rigidity Versus Openness in Late Classical Islamic Law: The Case of the Seventeenth-Century Palestinian Muftī Khayr al-Dīn al-Ramlī', *Islamic Law and Society*, 5; 2 (1998): 194–95.

[15] See B. Johansen, 'Eigentum, Familie und Obrigkeit im hanafitischen Strafrecht', *Die Welt des Islams*, 19 (1979): 1–73 (also in Johansen, *Contingency in a Sacred Law*, 349–420).

[16] See n. 5.

which drew on that doctrine, often tangentially. Johansen's example of land rent in the Ḥanafī school indicates that the law as practised was subject to (often) volte-face change, and these changes were often justified in religiolegal terms by muftis and jurists. However, the expression of the most radical challenges to the established *madhhab* doctrine were restricted to commentaries (*shurūh*) and fatwas. The sacred core of the *madhhab* was preserved in the *mutūn*, while legal change and development, in response to social need, were permitted elsewhere. The task of characterising the modalities of change in Islamic law requires, for Johansen, an awareness of where innovative opinions can be introduced and how the opinions move from being peripheral to less marginal in the authority structure:

It is, therefore, relevant to be aware of the many layered structure of the genres of the legal literature that we study and the different functions assigned to them, if we are to avoid misleading simplifications concerning the content, the meaning and the historical development of Islamic law.[17]

Now Hallaq's account, in which social and legal reality influence legal doctrine (*furūʿ*) through the institution of *iftāʾ* has undoubtedly received more attention than that of Johansen's distinction between the dynamics of change in different genres of legal literature. The most sustained critique of Johansen's views is that of Lutz Wiederhold, who argues that

Furūʿ-manuals, commentaries (*shurūḥ*) on the *furūʿ*-manuals, *uṣūl*-books, or *fatwā*-collections are all normative sources because they reflect what their authors considered to be a norm. Although normative sources may contain descriptive passages that include elements of contemporary social reality, we cannot regard their normative content as a description of social reality, in general, or of legal practice, in particular.[18]

However, it does not follow from the fact that normative works of the genres listed here cannot be used to construct social reality or legal practice that they are uneffected by the said reality/practice. It is merely that the effect, generally speaking, cannot always be identified (I doubt Wiederhold would mean to imply that it can never be identified). More specifically, Wiederhold argues against the simplistic notion (implied in Hallaq's line of reasoning) that *ijtihād* never ended, and this means that change in Islamic law was a continuous possibility (and, in innumerable instances, an actuality):

The sources that I have consulted treat *ijtihād* neither as a method – in the sense of a set of tools – nor as a mechanism of legal change. Rather, the *uṣūl*, *furūʿ* (including *shurūḥ*),

[17] Johansen, 'Legal Literature and the Problem of Change', 31, in *Contingency in a Sacred Law*, 464.

[18] Lutz Wiederhold, 'Legal Doctrines in Conflict', *Islamic Law and Society* 3;2 (1997): 249.

adab al-qāḍī, *adab al-muftī*, and *fatwā* literatures raise questions as to whether a legal scholar may activate the mechanisms of legal change and, if he may, what qualifications are required to utilize the methods that are expounded in legal theory in solving a legal question.[19]

The theoretical question of whether (and which) scholars are qualified to exercise *ijtihād* is, for both Wiederhold and Johansen, distinct from the notion of legal change, and though there may be a link between *ijtihād* and change, it is difficult to prove (or, as Wiederhold points out, to disprove). Wiederhold develops Johansen's argument by pointing out that choice between competing solutions to a problem (one of the mechanisms for legal change identified by Johansen) was itself an element in *ijtihād* for many scholars. This, for Wiederhold, increases the likelihood of a direct linkage between the theoretical discussions concerning *ijtihād* and legal change. Notwithstanding this conclusion, both scholars argue that any account of change must concentrate on the 'evolution of new legal ordinances'.[20] As we shall see, for Calder, the evolution of new legal ordinances (which should be distinguished from a jurist's choice to emphasise an ordinance that has already been proposed but considered marginal) is unusual in the central *furū*ʿ texts of a *madhhab*. When change does occur, it is best described as an extension of existing opinions to new cases, brought on by casuistic reasoning during scholastic exchange. For Calder, the influence of social or legal practice here is minimal.

These citations, and the views expressed therein, represent the contours of the scholarly debate over the possibility of change in Islamic law when Calder composed these four chapters. His notes do not take into account all the views developed here (only Hallaq and Powers are explicitly cited), and it is possible that Calder hoped to make further citation and adjustment to future versions of these chapters. In any case, one may speculate on what Calder's initial comments might be on the general direction of the discussion within these works. He would probably wish to apply his comment on a citation from Libson more generally within the field. When Libson states that Islamic law, or the 'Islamic legal system', influences and is influenced by social circumstance (i.e., is subject to change), Calder comments:

> What, in an Islamic context, could be the referent of 'a legal system' or even 'law'? It does not seem possible to make that kind of assertion either of *sharīʿa* or *fiqh*; but nor can the writer [i.e., Libson] be assumed to be talking merely about the actual practice of this or that Muslim community at a particular place and time.[21]

[19] Ibid., 267.
[20] Ibid., 268.
[21] See Chapter 1, p. 72.

The citation from Libson ('chosen more or less at random') exemplifies what for Calder is the most problematic element in the then current debate over the potential for change. What, exactly, is meant by the term 'Islamic law' when scholars say, for example, that 'Islamic law, after its formative period became increasingly rigid and set in its final mould'?[22] As is evident in the present volume, the imprecision of the formulation clearly frustrates Calder. 'The problem is that "the law" is radically ambiguous in an Islamic context, since it might refer to literature or to practice'.[23] Elsewhere, he had expressed his frustration with the widespread use of the term 'Islamic law' without any explanatory gloss or comment:

> The connotations of the phrase 'Islamic law' are in part a product of western perception and have been introduced now to Muslim societies through linguistic calques like Arabic *al-qānūn al-islāmī*. There is no corresponding phrase in pre-modern Muslim discourse. There, the two terms which expressed the commitment of the Muslim community to divine law were *fiqh* and *sharīʿa*.[24]

We can begin with the presumption that what is meant by the term Islamic law' in the above analyses is actually the theoretical legal system described in works of *furūʿ al-fiqh* (this Calder clearly suspects is the most likely intention). Such a presumption, however, immediately excludes other possible contenders for the referent of 'Islamic law'. A list could be made of the other possible contenders, including (1) divine law (which is known only to God, normally associated with the term *sharīʿa*); (2) the law of any state that claims to be 'Islamic' (the notion of an 'Islamic state', like *al-qānūn al-islāmī*, is, of course, an anachronism when applied to the pre-modern period); (3) the actual practice of a past Muslim governmental body (such as the law emerging from *maẓālim* courts); (4) the law as it is described in court records (which are, after all, a professional representation of the procedure within the court); (5) the law as it was actually applied in a particular context by a governmental agency (which may not be identical with that found in court records); (6) the personal doctrines (in the form of norms and ordinances, found in fatwa-collections) of academic jurists or indeed jurists drafted in as legal functionaries (under Hallaq's analysis at least, these are not in themselves 'Islamic law' but are attempting to become so by influencing the *fiqh*) and (7) the law, as it is practised by a Muslim community (that is, its 'custom'), which it believes to be religiously grounded, but in fact has no textual or juristic support. The list of potential referents could be extended, but

[22] Hallaq, 'From *Fatwās* to *Furūʿ*', 1.

[23] See Chapter 3, p. 162.

[24] N. Calder, 'Law', in *History of Islamic Philosophy*, eds. S.H. Nasr and O. Leaman (London: Routledge, 1996), 2, 988.

Calder's concern is that very few authors use the phrase without discrimination, a tendency that prevents an important topic (such as 'change in Islamic law') from being discussed systematically, or with any scholarly nuance. This does not mean that such studies are without merit; rather the authors, in Calder's view, have failed to capitalise on the potential of their insights. If, as I suspect, the chapters in this volume are partly (but not entirely) an extended examination of the presumptions, method and conclusions found within the studies of Hallaq, Powers and others, then this, in itself, is Calder's assessment of their contribution. Of the previously cited works, only Johansen's analysis appears to have the potential to sit squarely with that of Calder.[25]

With this background, it is possible now to relate, seriatim as it were, Calder's chapters to the field of Islamic legal studies more generally. The overarching aim of the four studies is to establish a working typology of classical Muslim legal literature, and to explore the function (in literary as well as societal terms) of the various genres and subgenres. In the first chapter (The Ḥanafī Law on Fornication), Calder sets out a typology of *fiqh* works, employing as an example the law of *zinā* within classical Ḥanafī works of *fiqh*. His technique is reasonably consistent – the (often extensive) translation of a representative passage is followed by a comparison of this presentation with others usually on the same topic. The initial focus is on the difference between *mukhtaṣar* and *mabsūṭ* works of *fiqh*. This distinction is, in some ways, more informative than the standard *mutūn/shurūḥ* distinction. The latter refers to formal structure, while the *mukhtaṣar/mabsūṭ* distinction is not merely about volume, but about the techniques of legal presentation and reasoning displayed in the different texts. Calder is quite willing to make quality assessments of the various *mukhtaṣars*: al-Qudūrī's (d. 428/1037) *mukhtaṣar* is 'the finest';[26] al-Mawṣilī's (d. 682/1283) text is 'a search for greater precision and refinement of expression'; [27] al-Marghinānī's (d. 593/1197) 'falls short of the balanced, formal, concise, organised elegance of Mawṣilī', [28] though with some 'organisational success'; al-Nasafī (d. 710/1310–11) displays 'grammatical control, extensive ellipsis and achieved concision'.[29] Calder feels able to make these judgements as he is viewing the texts within a purely literary analysis, and he is measuring them against literary qualities that are almost scientific in their propensity to be quantified.

Such comments, perhaps, appear initially out of place, but Calder's critique is akin to an evaluation of an author's achievement in character formation in a novel,

[25] Calder's assessment of Johansen's scholarship more broadly is described in my Afterword, in this volume.

[26] See Chapter 1, p. 23.

[27] See Chapter 1, p. 28.

[28] See Chapter 1, p. 32.

[29] See Chapter 1, p. 33.

or the employment of metaphor within poetry. The development is not with the basic content of rules, but with their stylistic expression – from rough beginnings to classicism and then to mannerism. This process can be marked by (among other factors) the increased concision of expression, the emergence of technical vocabulary, and heightened precision and refinement of presentation. The characteristics of a good *mukhtaṣar* are contrasted with the development of the *mabsūṭ* subgenre, mostly (but not always) presented as a commentary (*sharḥ*) on a *mukhtaṣar*. The defining characteristic of a *mabsūṭ* is not its size, but its literary telos: 'to provide arguments (causes) for the basic proposition of a *mukhtaṣar*'.[30] The *mukhtaṣar*, so he argues, is almost constructed to 'mark a difference and invite elucidation of the difference' with a set of cases. The *mabsūṭ* is the arena in which this elucidation takes place, particularly in the case of Sarakhsī (d. 490/1097). Calder relates the emerging structure of the juristic discipline (in the argumentative distinctions between *mukhtaṣar* and *mabsūṭ*, but also in the logical and rhetorical features of the texts themselves) to the Aristotelian tradition, and in particular the idea of a science. For Aristotle, a science achieves permanent value 'only in so far as it dealt with species and not with individuals'.[31] This emphasis within the *fiqh* is, ultimately, linked in Calder's mind to the discipline's 'resistance and indifference to social reality'.

In the final section of the chapter, Calder examines the rules concerning *zinā* within Qāḍīkhān's (d. 592/1196) *al-Fatāwā*. His purpose here is to distinguish this sort of *furū'* work from the *mukhtaṣar* and *mabsūṭ* subgenres. His intention is to demonstrate that, despite its title (which might encourage the reader to think that here we have some record of social practice mediated through fatwas), the sources for the text are literary, the link with social practice is oblique (perhaps non-existent). The general feature of the *fiqh* tradition is to avoid the implementation of the drastic *ḥadd* penalties through the postulation of the appearance of legitimacy (*shubuhāt*), which excuses the perpetrator's transgression. For example, as with the other genres of *fiqh*, the *Fatāwā* of Qāḍīkhān is not obviously more practical. Once the *ḥadd* is evaded, there is 'no comment on local practice' and no 'guidance on what to do'.[32] The same can be said of other Ḥanafī works with *Fatāwā* in the title (such as *al-Fatāwā al-Hindiyya*). These are not collections of fatwas (*pace* Hallaq) but works of *furū'*. Fatwa here means simply a juristic view (uncoupled from the literary genre of fatwa).[33] This tradition of *fiqh*

[30] See Chapter 1, p. 39.

[31] See Chapter 1, p. 47.

[32] See Chapter 1, p. 68.

[33] Hallaq, From *Fatwās* to *Furū'*, 19 (in reference to Qāḍīkhān) and 14. In this view, Calder is concurring with Schacht's conclusions in his 'On the Title of the *Fatāwā 'ālamgīriyya*,' in *Iran and Islam: in Memory of the Late Vladimir Minorsky*, ed. C. E. Bosworth (Edinburgh: Edinburgh University Press, 1971), 475–8.

(*mukhtaṣars*, *mabsūṭ*s, *fatāwā* – the last term being used in a particular Ḥanafī manner) is contrasted with an eminently practical document – the Ottoman Criminal Code (of ca. 1540). Some of the categories within *fiqh* are transferred to the Code and there may be signs of influence. In the main, the Criminal Code does not derive its legitimacy from any supposed origin within the *fiqh*. Rules within the Code can also be justified by an examination of the *ikhtilāf* within the Ḥanafī tradition. In a note that comes very close to Johansen's own formulation of the theory-practice dynamic, Calder states, 'theoretically, the governor can exploit elements of *ikhtilāf* in devising a practical system'.[34] The legal historian may be able to find specific instances of this happening, but this would not mean, for Calder, that the *fiqh* has suddenly taken on a more practical character.

While the first chapter exemplifies the possibilities in a diachronic analysis of a literary tradition, in Chapter 2, Calder turns his attention to a single jurist's oeuvre. The famous *Shāfiʿī* jurist, al-Nawawī (d. 676/1277), had previously been the focus of Calder's attention.[35] The study here is more wide-ranging, but also more particular in its conclusions. He begins with a study of al-Nawawī's *Majmūʿ*, itself a commentary on the *Muhadhdhab* of al-Shīrāzī (d. 476/1083). The *Majmūʿ* is, as Calder demonstrates, a *mabsūṭ* (though not a commentary on a *mukhtaṣar*, but on a *mabsūṭ*). Hence, the *Majmūʿ* is an attempt to expand the reasoning processes within the *Muhadhdhab*, bring in additional evidence, examine certain linguistic and stylistic matters relevant to the legal texts under examination, outline the *ikhtilāf* among the learned scholars, and acknowledge, with humility, the limited nature of the achievements of the *fiqh*. In order to compensate for this paucity of knowledge, al-Nawawī foregrounds the authority of the *madhhab*. The copious material in the *Majmūʿ* was trimmed down for al-Nawawī's *Rawḍa*. The *Rawḍa* is not quite a *mukhtaṣar*, not quite a *mabsūṭ*. Calder recognises that his typologies might need to be refined here. As with the Ḥanafī texts in Chapter 1, it is possible to approach the text with the hope of a clear, single rule to aid one in legal practice (as a mufti or a *qāḍī*). But it is 'not the most obvious' approach; instead, it is 'one of the most trivial approaches to such books'.[36] In its place, Calder proposes that authors in the *fiqh* tradition were not only performing an act of worship through the exercise of their intellectual capabilities, they were developing an art form. Their discussion of *zakāt*, for example, discusses the categorisation of different types of camel and the varying levels of *zakāt* on them. The discussion is

> An exploration of a purely notional world: a complete model of a pastoral economy, exquisitely detailed and absolutely autonomous, expressing in terminology that is fossilised and

[34] See Chapter 1, p. 68, n. 59.
[35] N. Calder, 'Al-Nawawi's Typology of Muftis'.
[36] See Chapter 2, p. 93.

in normative sentences that express layers of hypothetical possibilities .... This is art, and it reminds this reader of nothing so much as a medieval miniature.[37]

The same can be said of the extensive discussion in the *Rawḍa* concerning hermaphrodites. Hermaphrodites receive quite extensive attention in the *fiqh* works; and in a manner similar to the different categories of camel, are equally irrelevant (or of limited relevance) to judicial practice. 'A work of law offers its readers a literary experience – diverse, various profound. It is not like a manual of instruction.'[38] This line of analysis is extended by an examination of al-Nawawī's *mukhtaṣar*, the *Minhāj al-Ṭālibīn*, with an added emphasis on the way in which al-Nawawī's works, the *Minhāj* in particular, provide a core of texts for the *madhhab*. Finally, for the sake of completeness and contrast, Calder examines al-Nawawī's commentary on the hadith collection of Muslim. While the *fiqh* works begin with the *madhhab*, and provide its elaboration in the most impressive of terms, the commentary on Muslim's collection of hadith is more direct. It takes revelation as its focus, and because of this, al-Nawawī can offer more commentary and comment on the other *madhhab*s. However, when examining the juristic reports, al-Nawawī slips into a juristic presentation, and the *madhhab* appears as an outcome of the process. Al-Nawawī's presentation of a linear process from revelatory text to *madhhab* rule is not as crass as other examples within the genre of hadith commentary, but the end result is still a text of intellectual justification.

In Chapter 3, Calder turns his attention to a view that he considers widespread in Islamic legal studies: that change and development in Islamic law is 'intimately related' to the process of giving legal opinions (*fatāwā*) on demand (the activity known as *iftā'*). The proponents of this view (Hallaq, but also Powers, Messick and Masud) base their conclusions (in part) on the extant collections of fatwas by the jurists of the past. In this and also the following chapter Calder takes one such collection (the famous *al-Fatāwā* by Taqī al-Dīn al-Subkī (d. 756/1355)) and subjects it to detailed analysis in order to discover the relationships between the various functionaries in the Islamic juristic enterprise (whom he names as the writing jurist, the mufti and the qadi), the interplay between practice (reality) and doctrine as evidenced within the fatwas, and the broader role of *iftā'* in medieval Muslim society. In a sense, the two chapters form a single line of argument, extracted from a single text, and hence can be taken together.

A fatwa by al-Subkī on the proper operation of a religious endowment (*waqf*) and the distribution of its income enables Calder to illustrate some broad

[37] See Chapter 2, p. 94.
[38] See Chapter 2, p. 99.

conclusions concerning internal distinctions among those skilled (to whatever level) in the study of Muslim jurisprudence. Al-Subkī distinguishes writing jurists (and their students) from muftis, and muftis from qadis. This distinction is also an evaluative hierarchy (with writing jurists at the head), and this evaluation is, in part, related to an increasing level of involvement in particulars (*juzʿiyyāt*) as one moves down the hierarchy. When discussing the task of the mufti, al-Subkī (Calder claims) makes it clear that the fatwa is 'unsuitable as a direct expression of the law, that is, of the *madhhab*',[39] because it is contingent not only on juristic opinion (the whole *fiqh* exercise could be described in this manner), but on the specific facts of a case. The role of the qadi is yet further sullied by being overwhelmed, if you like, by the particulars of the case. The stratification of legal activity is linked to the relationship between universals and particulars (once again, the Hellenistic categories, albeit rudimentary, creep into the juristic presentation). The scholar-jurist deals in universals, and his is the highest calling. The mufti is involved in making these universals 'descend' (*tanzīl*) into the world of particulars, through his issuance of a fatwa. The qadi similarly may be involved in the application of doctrine, but the effect of the realia of community life is felt more keenly in his operations making his judgement more restricted, and hence less memorable. Calder does not consider scholarship to date to have taken the scholar jurist/mufti distinction seriously enough.

For Calder, the fatwas selected and analysed in Chapters 3 and 4 reveal not only the tripartite distinction (scholar jurist/mufti/qadi) in explicit terms, they also reveal something about fatwa collections and their contents. Many of the fatwas in al-Subkī's collection have a juristic quality. They are preserved, Calder argues, because of this quality not because of a desire to preserve historical facts. This characteristic may bear the marks of a fatwa's origin (not only in a question, but also in lively oral debate, presumably in a pedagogic setting). The collection as a whole is not supposed to be representative of al-Subkī's *iftāʾ* activities (most of his fatwas were not recorded, being of limited juristic interest and remaining on the paper *ruqʿat al-istiftāʾ*). For Calder, those who use these collections for the reconstruction of social history (particularly in any quantitative analysis) will do well to recognise the literary characteristics of the genre:

> None of the standard collections of fatwas is merely a collection of fatwas, repeating the quality and the mix of socially realised fatwas. The collection necessarily involves selection, organisation and transformation.[40]

This may, indeed, be common sense, but it is a view that had not (yet) sufficiently moderated contemporary analysis of these important legal texts.

[39] See Chapter 3, p. 123.
[40] See Chapter 4, p. 199.

Al-Subkī's fatwa collection also reveals certain elements of the relationship between secular power and religious (judicial) authority. There was a clear conception of different spheres of activity (both practically and intellectually), and there was a terminology to accompany this distinction. The law, or at least the literary expression of the law, is not required to change in response to the activities of a secular justice system (even when staffed, in part, by a religious judiciary). Judicial activity will be subject to negotiation with governors, administrators and the organs of government under the sultan. A question such as the supervision of waqfs and whether the sultan is qualified to carry out this duty, leads into a discussion of the relationship between a judge and the governor who has appointed him. The distinction between spheres of legal activity (as was discussed in relation to *zinā* law and the Ottoman Criminal Code) is expressed also in al-Subkī's fatwas, and any discussion of how the legal practice influenced literary expression needs to be aware of these category differences. A qadi is bound to express the opinion of the *madhhab* on a particular issue. A highly qualified qadi might be able to decide between different *madhhab* views on an issue (*tarjīḥ* as an element in *ijtihād*). But the qadi, even if he was in other guises a scholar-jurist or a mufti, could not rule according to an ordinance that was outside the *madhhab*. In this way, the doctrine remained extremely stable, but this did not mean that a brake was applied to creativity. Real creativity, the informed development of novel opinions was (nearly) always presented as the discovery of 'lost', 'forgotten,' or previously unknown *madhhab* opinion.

In Chapter 4, Calder uses al-Subkī's fatwas to present a different set of conclusions about the activity of *iftā*ʿ. The ideal conception of *iftā*ʿ (as proposed in the manuals of *uṣūl al-fiqh*, and in much of contemporary scholarship) is contrasted with the 'social function of fatwas' as evidenced by the examples in al-Subkī's collection. Looking at the items within the collections, Calder develops a typology of fatwas, and the four types developed here (with examples provided) are dependent on the questioner-recipient. The central feature of the fatwas is not their practicality (though some undoubtedly had practical consequences). Indeed, 'the only element which can, consistently, with security, be discovered sometimes to be absent is the practical'.[41] Al-Subkī's collection demonstrates, for Calder, that the conception of the fatwa as a primarily practical legal instrument is misconceived (or, perhaps, unjustifiably narrow). Instead, he proposes that those wishing to open up the fatwa collections to analysis should consider how the process (from requesting a fatwa, to receiving a demand for one, to considering the problem, to issuing a response, to receiving the mufti's assessment)

[41] See Chapter 4, p. 198.

forms a manifestation of the divine presence within the Muslim community. The actual content (which may be irrelevant to circumstances or even beyond the ken of the recipient) is of secondary importance in such an analysis:

> To mediate what was superfluous (because already known to the recipient), or useless (because it was an unattainable ideal), or incomprehensible (because the recipient had only a partial understanding of the message) was still to enact the formal affirmation of the divine command in the community.[42]

This perspective, which has rarely (if ever) been acknowledged in the secondary literature on fatwas to date reinforces what is clearly a central emphasis within Calder's four studies here. That is, in classical Muslim jurisprudence, the motives for an individual scholar's involvement may be hazy, but the discipline as a whole is designed to serve a primarily religious and/or aesthetic purpose. Those who write works of *fiqh* (in whatever subgenre), or act as muftis (at whatever level), or collate their own fatwas or those of others into ordered and organised collections, all are fulfilling a religious obligation. The products of this activity, the literary works themselves, are, at one time, an encoded theological message and examples of literary artifice. To try to use such works to predict practice, or as a contrast to practice, or as a means of modifying practice is to adopt the 'least interesting' of the available approaches. For Calder, these commonplace methodologies in Islamic legal studies do an injustice to the literature that has formed the core of the learned discipline of *fiqh*. As he stated elsewhere:

> Western scholarship (even when written by Muslims) has rarely presented Islamic law in such a way as to demonstrate its values rather than the values of the observer.[43]

Calder, in these chapters, wishes to indicate alternative approaches within the discipline, or at least prompt a reconsideration of the (usually unacknowledged) assumption that the term 'law' can be applied in an Islamic context in an unproblematic manner.

Calder's exposition of classical Muslim jurisprudence, and his critique of current Islamic legal scholarship have lost none of their relevance in the intervening decade. Certain observations posed here have been developed by others. In other areas, Calder, I am sure, would continue to be dissatisfied with the formulation of the dynamics of Islamic law presented in the explosion of publications in Islamic legal studies. Examples, taken more or less at random, you might say, from the deluge of recent studies, demonstrate the pervasive influence of the

[42] See Chapter 4, p. 199.

[43] Calder, 'Law', 479.

approach that troubled Calder:

> [The paradigm of a static rigid inflexible Islamic law] continues to prevail to a large degree, although increasingly attempts are being made to dislodge it. A characteristic feature of these attempts has been the effort to show that at certain points and in certain places *the law* did undergo change … [Ibn ʿĀbidīn's (d. 1252/1836)] idea of the employment of custom in legal practice is eloquent testimony to the ability of *Islamic law* to transform itself and adapt to significant change.[44]

> A fatwa is a story in which a Muslim tells a jurist a problem concerning the law … . All in all there is no doubt that the input of particular stories in the corpus of Islamic jurisprudence has been enormous.[45]

Having said this, there have also been significant contributions in Islamic legal studies with which (I suspect) Calder would feel more at ease. In the course of an examination of al-Qarāfī's (d. 684/1285) fatwa on the custody of children for divorced mothers (an opinion that was counter to the Mālikī *madhhab*'s position), Sherman Jackson writes:

> It is not possible at present to tell whether al-Qarāfī was successful in his attempt to retain custody for the divorced mothers in the present dispute. Based on subsequent Mālikī manuals, his arguments do not appear to have had any permanent effect on school doctrine … . While this seems to indicate that al-Qarāfī failed in his attempt to change school doctrine … to look at the matter from this perspective is perhaps to miss the point. … What matters, in other words, is not whether al-Qarāfī was able to sway the school regarding the status of this particular precept as a whole, but whether the school tradition, in tandem with his acumen as a jurist, provided enough material and mechanisms for him to be able to challenge the finality of the status quo.[46]

Jackson's analysis (both here and in his other publications) would appear (at first blush) to conform to Calder's description of the mechanisms of change and the relationship between *furūʿ* and fatwas. It undermines, albeit mildly, the increasingly commonplace identification of fatwas as the primary mechanism of any change to legal doctrine.

The problematic issue of change in Islamic law (whether by fatwa or any other mechanism) forms a (not so hidden) subtext in much of Calder's presentation here. One recent study that has extended Hallaq's identification of *iftāʿ* as the primary mechanism for change is Miriam Hoexter's article 'Qadi, Mufti and Ruler: Their Roles in the Development of Islamic Law'. She argues that Hallaq's

[44] W. B. Hallaq, 'A Prelude to Ottoman Reform: Ibn ʿĀbidīn on Custom and Legal Change', in *Histories of the Modern Middle East: New Directions*, eds. I. Gershoni, H. Erdem and Ursula Woköck (Boulder, CO, and London: Lynne Rienner, 2002), 37 and 56. Emphasis added.

[45] A. Zomeno, 'The Stories in the *Fatwā* and the *Fatwās* in History', in *Narratives of Truth in Islamic Law*, eds. D. Dupret, B. Dreskens and A. Moors (London: I. B. Tauris, 2007), 25.

[46] S. Jackson, 'Kramer versus Kramer in a 10th/16th Century Egyptian Court: Post-formative Jurisprudence Between Exigency and Law', *Islamic Law and Society*, 8 (2001): 50–51.

exclusive identification of the mufti as the agent of change is in need of modification. By producing a series of examples in which qadi judgements influenced legal doctrine, she claims to have demonstrated that qadi's role was in 'the initiation of change, that is, at the starting line of the process of change', whereas the role of rulers 'was at the closing end of the same process … . The development of *Islamic law* was a result of a joint effort by qadis, muftis and rulers.'[47] Calder's reaction to such a conclusion would be, I suspect, to question what, exactly was meant by 'Islamic law' in such a context, and if it was the legal doctrine of *furūʿ* works, one would expect the authors of those works (the scholar-jurists) to figure somewhere within this supposed process of change.[48]

Calder's three-fold typology of scholar-jurist, mufti and qadi is, to an extent, a prefiguring of Hallaq's typology in his *Authority, Continuity and Change in Islamic Law*. There, Hallaq recognises the importance of the scholar-jurist category, terming it the 'author-jurist'. Hallaq would probably not have described it as a 'hitherto overlooked juristic category' had he had access to Calder's analysis here.[49] Now, much could be said about Hallaq's examination of *madhhab* formation in his important book, but I shall restrict myself to the points relevant to Calder's analysis. Hallaq, as we have already discussed, emphasises both the structural potential for change in Islamic law, and the actual instances of change in legal doctrine (by which, one presumes he means the legal views put forward in *furūʿ* works).[50]

This 'change', which Hallaq makes the subject of his enquiry, is approached from various angles; the most pertinent to the studies presented here is the various actors in the process proposed by Hallaq. In identifying the 'type' of the author-jurist, Hallaq claims he has identified an important participant in the process of legal change, which supplements his previous analysis in 'From *Fatwās* to *Furūʿ*'.[51] First of all, Hallaq identifies four types, his additional figure being law

47 Miriam Hoexter, 'Qadi, Mufti and Ruler: Their Roles in the Development of Islamic Law', in *Law, Custom, and Statute in the Muslim World: Studies in Honor of Aharon Layish*, ed. R. Shaham (Leiden: Brill, 2006), 85. Emphasis added.

48 The study of Ahmad Atif Ahmad (*Structural Interrelations of Theory and Practice in Islamic Law*, Leiden: Brill, 2006), notwithstanding its title, addresses the important question of the relationship between *furūʿ* and *uṣūl*. While the *furūʿ* clearly had a link to religious and legal practice, Calder's point here is that it cannot, as such, be considered representative of, or appropriately termed 'practice'.

49 Hallaq, 'A Prelude to Ottoman Reform', 37.

50 Calder's comments on imprecision could equally apply to some of Hallaq's phrasing in this work. 'It is not our primary concern to show that *Islamic law* underwent change … although there is sufficient justification to do so.' 166, emphasis added.

51 A section of chapter 6 is a reproduction of parts of this earlier article, though the insertion of the author-jurist into the process (whose absence from the analysis Calder criticises in this volume) alters the thrust of the original article somewhat, as does the inclusion of lightly

professor. However, the contribution to change of both the law professor and the qadi is minimal.[52] It is the mufti and the author-jurist who hold centre stage in Hallaq's depiction of the process of change. The author-jurist sees in the mufti's fatwa a new legal opinion at variance with the *madhhab*, and is able to include it within the *furūʿ* as an optional, minority opinion (which could in time gain support and become the *mashhūr* of the *madhhab*). The skill with which an author-jurist did this was, for Hallaq, an indication of his importance and his legal acumen.[53] The contrast between the two scholars' analyses could not be greater. For Calder, the scholar-jurist is the guardian of the *madhhab*, and ensures its stability, its permanence and its religious authority. The mufti (and, at a lower level, the qadi) are involved in legal practice, and hence their activities, even when specific instances of change can be identified by the modern critical historian, are quite separate. For Hallaq, there is a flow of ideas and influence between the various agents that enables change to be effected on a continuous basis. The differing conclusions may, of course, be due to the two scholars selecting different texts, but I doubt it. The difference is, in my view, more fundamental, perhaps even methodological. Hallaq approaches the texts, seeking room for innovation and change in order to deconstruct a paradigm of Islamic law as suffering from a 'rigidity which ultimately led to paralysis'. The paradigm is part of an orientalist agenda, which needs to be 'dislodged'. Calder, perhaps influenced by Gadamer, emphasises the importance of the intellectual tradition of Muslim jurisprudence, and views the modern scholar's task as examining how it has been maintained and developed. Originality is not denied, but it operates within boundaries, and the general momentum of scholarship is conservative.

Each chapter in this work exemplifies a different mode of scholarly and textual analysis. There is a diachronic examination of a literary tradition (Chapter 1);

edited material from Hallaq's article '*Qāḍī*s Communicating: Legal Change and the Law of Documentary Evidence', *Al-Qantara*, 20 (1999): 437–66. Much of the section on the author-jurist comes from Hallaq's perceptive article on Ibn ʿĀbidīn (see n. 46). In that article, in a section not included in the book, Hallaq states that he hopes to demonstrate 'not only that the mechanisms of legal change constituted a structural feature of the law but that the discourse of the author-jurist – a manipulator of the discursive tradition – was necessarily an integral part of these structural mechanisms. More specifically … [Hallaq attempts] to show that through these mechanisms – of which one tool was the discursive strategies of the author-jurist – a fundamental reformation of legal methodology and theory was effected.' Hallaq, 'A Prelude to Ottoman Reform', 38.

[52] Hallaq's comments that the qadi's contribution could only have been 'at the embryonic stage' are, to an extent, the same point made by Hoexter (see n. 49), though with less exuberance.

[53] Ibn ʿĀbidīn's view that custom can, on occasions, overrule Ḥanafī *madhhab* doctrine does not, to me at least, appear to be an indication of change in Islamic legal doctrine (except insofar as it represents a principled emphasis on custom). Instead, it represents a recognition of the different cogs of legal practice and legal doctrine, which are not always interlocked. See Calder's analysis in Chapter 3.

an investigation into the oeuvre of a single author (Chapter 2); a detailed analysis of single work (Chapter 3); and a positioning of a work within a wider social-cultural milieu (Chapter 4). The studies are models of scholarship in more than one sense. Calder avoids extensive or prolix footnotes, focussing on a particular text, in a particular context, as evidence for his conclusions. I see Calder's work here as (at least partially) a reaction to existing approaches within the field. The presumptions that were becoming dominant in the discipline, to a greater or lesser extent, control his response. This is sometimes implicit in his work, but it is often also explicitly stated. It is quite likely, in my view, that the primary explanation of why Calder carried out these investigations in the manner that he did was his concern that a new emerging orthodoxy in Islamic legal studies had been adopted rather too easily. Scholarship since Calder's death has not seen a widespread challenge to this orthodoxy, though there have been occasional voices of dissent. Calder may have been critical of some of the assumptions operative within the discipline over the past century or so, but his technique is always to engage with that disciplinary tradition, to draw out elements that can be confirmed, and to isolate points that need refinement. In this sense, his attitude is one of critical engagement with past Islamic legal scholarship. Such an approach contrasts with a common *modus operandi* in modern scholarship in which previous scholarship is often classed as irretrievably infected by 'orientalist' assumptions, and therefore, by implication, of little academic value in a (post) modern context: useful as a straw man, but misleading (perhaps even pernicious) for researchers of Islamic law. It is with this perspective in mind that I offer in the Afterword a commentary on Calder's approach to Islamic studies generally, and Islamic legal studies in particular. Rather like the *fiqh* authors he studies here, Calder recognises his position within a tradition of Western scholarship of Islam (and specifically Islamic law). He is no less innovative for allowing the state of the discipline to control his presentation, as innovation does not always mean denying either what is current or what has gone before. In this way, these chapters retain an undiminished freshness of approach that will, I am sure, continue to enliven the field of Islamic legal studies.

1

The Ḥanafī Law on Fornication

Introduction

The analysis and presentation of divine law, in an Islamic context, took place primarily in the literary genre known as *furūʿ al-fiqh* (branches of jurisprudence). There, the law was presented as, essentially, a permanent system of norms and values, unchangingly valid. Since the historical reality of Muslim societies included change and diversity, it is necessarily the case that the relationship between the law as an intellectual structure and the law as realised in social practice was oblique. It was a matter of degrees and kinds of difference.[1] Works of *furūʿ* can be classified as of two major types, *mukhtaṣar*s or epitomes of the law, and *mabsūṭ*s or expansums. The *mukhtaṣar* characteristically contains a succinct and highly compressed sequence of norms, loosely bundled under topical headings: a structured framework or skeleton of the law. The *mabsūṭ* justifies and explains the law and multiplies its details. In its most characteristic form, it is a commentary on a *mukhtaṣar*. There are other types of *furūʿ* literature (notably the treatise or *risāla* on a single topic or bundle of topics of the law), some of which will be identified in the following pages; and it is possible to distinguish different tendencies within the broad typology of *mukhtaṣar* and *mabsūṭ*. The conditions that govern the genre as a whole include the fundamental condition of loyalty to school tradition. The earliest extant works of Islamic law, the foundational works of the four major schools, already display the standard organisational and presentational patterns of *furūʿ* literature.[2] But

[1] See below for Subkī's use of the terms *ʿurf*, *ʿāda* and *marsūm* to designate a world of legal practice that was not covered by the *sharīʿa*. For the Ottoman period, Colin Imber has suggested separate origins for legal practice and legal theory; Imber, *Ebuʿs-Suʿud: The Islamic Legal Tradition* (Edinburgh: Edinburgh University Press, 1997), 24–62.

[2] Norman Calder, *Studies in Early Muslim Jurisprudence* (Oxford: Oxford University Press, 1993).

the special qualities of the early works will not be considered in the following pages, which are concerned with the period from about 400/1010 to 1300/1883. This chapter and the one that follows it present and analyse passages from *furūʿ* literature, across different schools and literary types, and through the centuries, with a view to identifying and describing the conditions of the genre. The subject matter of the present chapter is the juristic topic of *ḥudūd* (sing., *ḥadd*), or penalties, and specifically the *ḥadd* for fornication, and its expression within the Ḥanafī school of law.

Section 1. Four *mukhtaṣars*

1. The finest of the early Ḥanafī *mukhtaṣars* is that of Aḥmad b. Muḥammad al-Qudūrī (d. 428/1037). It was not the first. There had been at least two significant earlier efforts to summarise the school tradition: those of Aḥmad b. Muḥammad al-Ṭaḥāwī (d. 321/933) and Muḥammad b. Muḥammad al-Ḥākim al-Marwazị (d. 334/945). Of these, the *Kāfī* of al-Hākim retained a constant authority because it was so obviously, and painstakingly, close to the foundational works of the school, essentially those of Muḥammad b. al-Ḥasan al-Shaybānī (d. 189/804).[3] Qudūrī, working in Baghdad, benefited from (and certainly also transcended) these works, and benefited also from a continuous teaching tradition which had confirmed the needs and sharpened the perceptions of those involved. His work is a presentation of Ḥanafī law, based on selection, summary and organisation of norms, under the broad, loosely organised topical headings which had already served for the management of material in the foundational texts. His achievement can be measured, and was recognised, precisely in relation to selection, summary, organisation and expression. The norms that he adduced had already been weighed and established. More contentious norms were necessarily eliminated by the constraints of the *mukhtaṣar* genre. The broad acceptance of Qudūrī's text, which made it for centuries a teaching tool, a point of reference and a focus of commentary, was due to its security and reliability as an expression of the basic norms of the Ḥanafī tradition; his literary skills would not have compensated for error or deficiency in his account of the law. *Mukhtaṣars* which were larger and aspired to embrace more and more of the law were, inevitably, more suspect; and so, *a fortiori*, were *mabsūṭs*. Hence, Ibn ʿĀbidīn (d. 1252/1836), looking back over almost a thousand

[3] See Norman Calder 'The *ʿUqūd rasm al-muftī* of Ibn ʿĀbidīn', *Bulletin of the School of Oriental and African Studies*, 63 (2000): 215–28, for a late Ḥanafī assessment of the school and its origins. Ibn ʿĀbidīn, writing in the nineteenth century, still uses the work of al-Ḥākim as representing a decisive statement of the school tradition.

years of literary production within the Ḥanafī school, articulated what he had learned from his teachers, that *mukhtaṣars* (with some exceptions) were superior to commentaries, and commentaries superior to *fatāwā*. This last, in a Ḥanafī context, was a type of *furūʿ* literature, similar to a *mabsūṭ* but devoid of justificatory argument.[4] The authoritative *mukhtaṣars*, by contrast, had a secure orientation towards tradition and the literature that contained and expressed it.

Qudūrī's *mukhtaṣar* (also called his *matn* or 'text'), directly or indirectly, dominated all subsequent efforts to express, in epitome form, the structure of Ḥanafī law. More than 250 years after the production of this work, ʿAbdallāh b. Maḥmūd al-Mawṣilī (d. 682/1283), whose teaching career was also spent mostly in Baghdad, produced another *mukhtaṣar*, entitled *Al-Mukhtār li-'l-fatwā*. Describing it as a new statement of the *madhhab* of the Imam Abū Ḥanīfa, he indicated that he would follow in it the juristic preferences (the *fatwā*) of the Imam himself. But what he most obviously followed was the selections and summaries, indeed the precise expression, of Qudūrī. Here is Mawṣilī's introduction to the *kitāb* (or topic) of *ḥudūd*, and the whole of his section on fornication (*zinā*).

1. *Kitāb al-ḥudūd*. *Ḥudūd* are a punishment, fully specified, and mandatory as a right due to God. *Zinā* means penetration by a man, of a woman, in the front part, without ownership (*milk*) or appearance of ownership (*shubhat milk*).

2.1. It is established by testimony or confession. Testimony means that four men bear witness to *zinā* on the part of a man and a woman. When they testify, the qadi asks them about what, how, where, when, and the identity of the woman. When they have testified, and mentioned that she was prohibited to him in every respect, and borne witness to the event like the mascara-stick in the mascara-pot, and been established as upright both secretly and publicly, then the qadi passes judgement.

2.2. If they are less than four, they are slanderers. If they go back on their testimony prior to a stoning, the penalty lapses and they are subject to the *ḥadd* of slander. If after a stoning, they are liable for the *diya*.[5] If only one of them, then a quarter of the *diya*. If they testify to a prior act of *zinā* and were not prevented from testifying [earlier] by their distance from the imam, their testimony is not accepted.

3.1. Confession means that one who is sane and mature testifies four times, on four different occasions, being dismissed by the qadi on each occasion so as to be out of vision, and is then questioned by the qadi as he

[4] See Section 4.1, below.

[5] Financial compensation, of specified value, incurred for deliberate killing or injury.

questions witnesses, except for the question when. If he testifies to all that, the *ḥadd* is due.

3.2. If he goes back on his confession before the *ḥadd*, or in the process, he is set free. It is recommended that the imam should prompt him to recant, using words like, 'Perhaps there was a *shubha*,[6] or you only kissed, or touched her.'

4.1. The *ḥadd* of a fornicator, if he is *muḥṣan*,[7] is stoning until death. He is to be taken out to open ground. If it was established by testimony, the witnesses begin, then the imam, then the people; if the witnesses refuse, or one of them, he is not stoned. If it was established by confession, the imam begins, then the people. If he is not *muḥṣan*, the *ḥadd* is beating, a hundred lashes for a free man, fifty for the slave. He is to be struck with a lash, free of knots, the strikes to be of medium force and distributed across the body excluding the head, face and private parts. A man is to be stripped of his clothes, except the *izār*.[8] A woman is not to be stripped save of padding and stuffing. In case of stoning, if a hole is dug for her it is permitted. A man is beaten standing in all *ḥudūd*.

4.2. Stoning and beating are not combined for a *muḥṣan*; nor beating and banishment for a non-*muḥṣan* unless the imam considers [banishment] a benefit, in which case he may act as he sees fit.

4.3. A slave-owner does not carry out a *ḥadd* on his slave except with the permission of the imam.

4.4. If the fornicator is sick, then if *muḥṣan*, he is stoned, otherwise he is not beaten till he recovers. A pregnant woman is not subject to the *ḥadd* until she gives birth, and, if the *ḥadd* is beating, until she recovers from parturition. If stoning, immediately after giving birth. If there is no one to bring up the child, then not until the child has no need of her.

5.1. The quality of being *muḥṣan* (the *iḥṣān*) for the stoning penalty depends on freedom, sanity, maturity, Islam, and penetration of the front part in a valid marriage, where both partners have the quality of *iḥṣān*.

5.2. *Iḥṣān* is established by confession, or by the testimony of two men, or one man and two women; likewise if they have a child known to be theirs.

6.1. If a man has intercourse with the slave-girl of his son, or his descendants, and says, I knew it was forbidden; or with the slave-girl of his father or his ascendants, or of his mother, his wife, or his master; or with his

[6] That is, a *shubhat milk* as defined in para. 1. The term means a factor of doubt that may render the accusation of *zinā* invalid.

[7] See para. 5.1 for a definition of this term.

[8] In this context, evidently a loin-cloth.

thrice-divorced wife during the *ʿidda*, and says, I thought it was permitted, he is not subject to the *ḥadd*; but if he says, I knew it was forbidden, he is. As to the slave-girl of a brother or an uncle, he is subject to the *ḥadd* in all cases.

6.2. If a man hires a woman to fornicate with her and does so, or has intercourse with a woman from outside the household but not in the vagina, or if he has homosexual intercourse, he is not subject to the *ḥadd* but is subject to *taʿzīr* (discretionary punishment).

6.3. If a woman other than his wife is brought to him after a wedding ceremony, and he has intercourse with her, he is not subject to the *ḥadd* but he must pay the *mahr* (bride-price). If he finds a woman other than his wife in his bed and has intercourse with her, he is subject to the *ḥadd*.

6.4. *Zinā* in *dār al-ḥarb* [the abode of war, i.e., non-Muslim territory] and in *dār al-baghy* [the abode of rebellion, i.e., land controlled by dissident Muslims] does not entail the *ḥadd*.

6.5. One who has intercourse with an animal is subject to *taʿzīr*.

6.6. If a man fornicates with a child, or with an insane woman, he is subject to the *ḥadd*. If a woman who is sane and mature seduces a child or an insane man there is no *ḥadd*.

7. *Taʿzīr* means at most 39 lashes, and at least three. The strokes are most severe for *taʿzīr*, then for the *ḥadd* of *zinā*, then for the *ḥadd* of drinking, then for the *ḥadd* of slander.[9]

This is a neat, well-organised exposition. It begins with two definitions at para. 1, and moves on to the two modes of proving *zinā*, namely testimony or confession, at paras. 2 and 3. Para. 4 distinguishes and describes the two types of punishment and the processes and conditions of execution. Para. 5 defines the quality of *iḥṣān* (adj. *muḥṣan*) and its mode of proof. Para. 6 is a list of problematic instances of intercourse which may or may not entail the *ḥadd* penalty. And para. 7 offers a few remarks about *taʿzīr* (discretionary punishment). Every rule here can be discovered in the foundational texts of the Hanafī school and most of them had already been chosen and expressed by Qudūrī in the precise terms and phraseology used also by Mawṣilī.

Qudūrī's *kitāb al-ḥudūd*[10] began in fact with the material of Mawṣilī's para. 2.1. That paragraph follows Qudūrī precisely, but the material of 2.2, though verbally derived from Qudūrī, is brought up from later in Qudūrī's text (where its elements had been dispersed). Likewise para. 3.1 follows Qudūrī precisely,

[9] Mawṣilī, *al-Ikhtiyār li-taʿlīl al-mukhtār* (Beirut: Dār al-Maʿrifa, 1975), 79–92.

[10] Qudūrī, *Matn* (Cairo: Muṣṭafa al-Bābī al-Ḥalabī, 1957), 94–5.

and 3.2 brings up material that had been later in Qudūrī's text. The result is two neat and comprehensive paragraphs, bundling in a coherent manner material that had been separated in Qudūrī. Because of his superior organisation (his coherent bundling of material), Mawṣilī's paras. 4 and 5 are neater and more unified than the corresponding material in Qudūrī. Para. 6 corresponds to a similar bundling of material in Qudūrī, but includes extra material and attempts a loosely principled ordering. The material, however, is obviously casuistic and resistant to any structural principle. Mawṣilī's para. 7 introduces material which had been presented by Qudūrī towards the end of his discussion of the *ḥadd* of slander. In relation to *taʿzīr* and in relation to homosexual intercourse, Quduṛị had briefly indicated the existence of dispute between Abū Ḥanīfa and his pupils, but these and all other indications of dispute have been removed by Mawṣilī, in accord with his stated intention of giving the rulings only of Abū Ḥanīfa. The whole passage represents a clear effort to improve the presentation and organisation of material that had originally been selected and presented by Qudūrī. This is accompanied by minor syntactic variation designed to improve the clarity and flow of the sentences.

There are some substantive differences between Qudūrī and Mawṣilī. The material of paras. 2 and 3 is derived in its entirety from Qudūrī, except, in para. 3.1, the explicit omission of the question when (implicit in Qudūrī[11]), and, in para. 3.2, the generalising reference to a *shubha* in the imam/qadi's promptings. Para 4.1 shows a minor refinement in the words, not in Qudūrī, 'or one of them': if the witnesses refuse, or one of them, he is not stoned. (The principle had been established in the earliest texts.[12]) Also at 4.1, the rule that a man is beaten standing is not in Qudūrī, though it can be found in al-Ḥākim's summary of Shaybānī.[13] The last phrase of 4.4 ('If there is no one to bring up the child ...') is not in Qudūrī, but had been produced and attributed to Abū Ḥanīfa earlier.[14] The material of 5.2. is also not in Qudūrī, but can be discovered in al-Ḥākim, embedded in more detail.[15] The materials of para. 6 are slightly expanded by Mawṣilī. Qudūrī's text does not contain a reference to the thrice-divorced wife (6.1); nor comment on

[11] The printed text of Qudūrī, *Matn*, 94, in fact includes the question 'when?', but this seems to be an error, as the commentary tradition assumes that he omits it. See Ḥaddādī, *al-Jawhara al-nayyira* (Istanbul: Maṭbaʿa Maḥmūd Beg, 1884; repr. Multan: Maktaba-ye Ḥaqqāniyya, n.d), vol.2, 237. [This edition of *al-Jawhara al-nayyira* includes the question 'when?', with the implication that it exists already in Qudūrī's text. There appear to be discrepancies in the printed versions of *al-Jawhara*. Ed.]

[12] See Sarakhsī, *Mabsūṭ* (Beirut: Dār al-Maʿrifa, 1986), IX, 46 and IX, 62, both references derived from al-Ḥākim's summary of Shaybānī's works.

[13] Sarakhsī, *Mabsūṭ*, IX, 73; cf. IX, 51.

[14] Marghinānī, *Hidāya* (Cairo: Muṣṭafa al-Bābī al-Ḥalabī, 1970), V, 245–6.

[15] Sarakhsī, *Mabsūṭ*, IX, 42–3.

hiring for fornication (6.2); nor the case at 6.6. Conversely, Qudūrī contains one sentence, in this section, which is omitted by Mawṣilī: A man who marries a woman whom he may not legally marry and has intercourse with her is not subject to the *ḥadd*. All of the cases introduced by Mawṣilī, and of course all of the material originally contained in Qudūrī, can be traced back to the foundational texts of the Ḥanafī school, those attributed to Shaybānī.[16]

The changes that Mawṣilī introduced to his text demonstrate, in part, a search for greater precision and refinement of expression; in part, an extension of detail. All his extra material can be accounted for by reference to the tradition, and all his refinements of expression by reference to juristic logic or linguistic elegance. The same of course is true of Qudūrī's material: it too was an attempt to summarise and clarify the principles behind a larger and less organised bundle of rules contained in the foundational texts of the Ḥanafī tradition. Neither in Qudūrī nor in Mawṣilī is it possible to discover any reference to the legal or penal practice of their time or any intermediate time. Their work, their aims and intentions, can be analysed entirely in terms of the literary tradition which they inherited and continued.

The definitions introduced by Mawṣilī (para 1.) were already established[17] and constitute perhaps a sign of scholastic formalisation, reflecting the establishment of *fiqh* as a school discipline with aspirations to being a formal science. A casuistic tone dominates both texts. It is particularly marked at para. 6, where the listing of cases shows no tendency towards the discovery or acknowledgement of generalising principles. It is nonetheless possible to detect principles. The juxtaposed, antithetical, rules of paras. 6.3 and 6.6, for example, cry out for a logical explanation, something that would be provided only in the *mabsūṭ* tradition. No doubt the capacity of some rules (or cases) to prompt fruitful reflection was one of the factors that made them suitable (amongst the much larger body of cases presented by al-Ḥākim, in his summary of Shaybānī) for inclusion in a *mukhtaṣar*.

2. Approximately one century before Mawṣilī produced his *Mukhtār*, and about one hundred and fifty years after Qudūrī produced his *Matn*, another effort had been made at the production of a *mukhtaṣar*: this was the *Bidāyat al-mubtadiʾ* of ʿAlī b. Abī Bakr al-Marghinānī (d. 593/1197). Like the other two, this text was commended in the early nineteenth century by Ibn ʿĀbidīn as an authoritative account of the *madhhab*. As an independent work, it did not have the success of the other two. Embedded within its more famous commentary

[16] Pending the complete editing and publication of Shaybānī's works, it is convenient to use al-Ḥākim's summary, which is contained within the published edition of Sarakhsī. For the hiring of a woman for purposes of fornication, Sarakhsī, *Mabsūṭ*, IX, 58; the thrice-divorced wife, IX, 88; fornication with children and the insane, IX, 54–5.

[17] Sarakhsī, *Mabsūṭ*, IX, 36.

(the *Hidāya*, also by Marghinānī), it was probably more influential than either. Marghinānī described his aims as follows:

1. It appeared to me in my early days that there should be a work of *fiqh* containing [an account of] every topic, small of compass, large of meaning; a book informing of agreement amongst the meandering paths. I found the *mukhtaṣar* of Qudūrī the finest of books, presenting the highest degree of skill and delight. And I observed that the great ones of the age, old and young, desired to memorise *al-Jāmiʿ al-ṣaghīr* [of Shaybānī]. So I formed the intention of combining them, in such manner as not to go beyond these two texts, save where necessity demanded. And I called my book the *Bidāyat al-mubtadiʿ*.[18]

The description is accurate. Marghinānī's *kitāb al-ḥudūd* at first follows broadly the order, the terminology, and the phraseology of Qudūrī. There is some syntactical refinement, and some movement of material to create better structure, but this becomes significant only where the intention is to permit the incorporation of material from *al-Jāmiʿ al-ṣaghīr.* For example, the casuistic listing of types of intercourse that may or may not entail the *ḥadd* (corresponding to para. 6 of Mawṣilī's text) is neatly introduced by the definitional phrase, 'Intercourse that entails the *ḥadd* penalty is *zinā*' (derived from a chapter heading in the *Jāmiʿ ṣaghīr*) and this is followed by material from both sources. The first case is as follows:

2. He who divorces his wife three times and then has intercourse with her during the *ʿidda* period, and says, 'I knew she was prohibited to me', is subject to the *ḥadd*. If he said to her, 'You are free, or acquitted', or, 'Your affair is in your own hands', and she chooses her freedom, and he then has intercourse with her during the *ʿidda* period, and he says, I knew she was prohibited to me, he is not subject to the *ḥadd*.[19]

This is derived from the *Jāmiʿ ṣaghīr*. Like the other juxtaposed, antithetical, pairs of rules identified above (paras. 6.3 and 6.6 in Mawṣilī's text), it hints at the existence of a principle which is not actually articulated. It might be thought a useful or principled introductory case, but the following list simply follows Qudūrī, then adds the following from the *Jāmiʿ ṣaghīr*.

[18] This passage is found in the biographical tradition and described as being a part of the introduction to the *Bidāya*, Laknawī, *Al-Fawāʾid al-bahiyya* (Beirut: Dār al-Maʿrifa, n.d.), 140. It is not present in the version of the *Bidāya* incorporated into the printed versions of the *Hidāya*; it is however a nice expression of the aims and intentions of the genre and accurate in its depiction of the contents of the *Bidāya*.

[19] Marghinānī, *Hidāya*, V, 253–4.

3. If a *ḥarbī*[20] enters our territory with a safe-conduct and commits fornication with a *dhimmī*; or if a *dhimmī* commits fornication with a *ḥarbī* woman. … If a child or one insane commits fornication with a woman who seduces him. … He whom the sultan forces to commit fornication. … He who confesses four times on four different occasions that he has committed fornication with so-and-so, and she says, 'He married me'; or if she confesses and he says, 'I married her'. … He who commits fornication with a slave-girl and kills her. … Everything done by an imam [political authority] who has no imam above him cannot be subject to a *ḥadd* penalty; but he is subject to *qiṣāṣ* [retaliation for deliberate killing] and to financial claims.[21]

The effect is one of trailing and slightly disorganised thought, falling short of the effort at meaningful selection and suggestive neatness that had already been achieved by Qudūrī and was enhanced in Mawṣilī.

Material related to testimony (of the type represented in para. 2.2 of Mawṣilī's ṭext) is bundled towards the end of Marghinānī's presentation of *zinā*, and massively expanded with cases derived from the *Jāmiʿ ṣaghīr*. Here are the first nine of sixteen cases.

4. If the witnesses testify to a prior *ḥadd* and were not prevented from bearing witness by their distance from the imam, their witness is not accepted, except only in the case of slander. In the *Jāmiʿ ṣaghīr*: if the witnesses testify against him in respect of theft, drinking wine, or *zinā* after a lapse of time, it is not accepted, but he is liable [for the value of goods stolen] in the case of theft.
5. If they testify against a man that he committed fornication with such and such a woman, who is absent, he is subject to the *ḥadd*. But if they testify that he stole from so-and-so, who is absent, he is not subject to amputation.
6. If they testify that he committed fornication with a woman they did not recognise, he is not subject to the *ḥadd*. But if he confesses, he is.
7. If two testify that he committed fornication with so-and-so and that he forced her, and another two that she submitted willingly, the *ḥadd* is averted from both, according to Abū Ḥanīfa. His two companions say that the man only is subject to the *ḥadd*.

[20] A *ḥarbī* is a non-Muslim resident of *dār al-ḥarb*, a *dhimmī* a non-Muslim resident of *dār al-islām*.

[21] Ibid., 278–89.

8. If two testify that he committed fornication with a woman in Kūfa and two that he committed fornication with her in Basra, the *ḥadd* is averted from both. If they differ as to where in a single house, the man and the woman are subject to the *ḥadd*.
9. If four testify that he committed fornication with a woman in Nakhīla at sunrise, and four that he committed fornication with her at sunrise in Dayr Hind, the *ḥadd* is averted from both.
10. If four testify to fornication by a man and she is a virgin, the *ḥadd* is averted from both, and [the *ḥadd* of slander] from them.
11. If four testify to fornication by a man, and they are blind, or have been subject to the *ḥadd* of slander, or one of them is a slave, or has been subject to the *ḥadd* of slander, they are subject to the *ḥadd* [of slander], and the man is not subject to the *ḥadd*. But if they testify thus being immoral, or if it appears they are immoral, they are not subject to the *ḥadd*.
12. If the number of witnesses is less than four, they are subject to the *ḥadd* [of slander].

All these are derived from the *Jāmiʿ ṣaghīr* and are presented, generally, in the order found there. Some minor displacement and the movement of some material from a different section of the *Jāmiʿ* suggests that Marghinānī was conscious of a small need for reorganisation and coherent bundling, but it does not amount to much. The cases trail onwards, a loosely bundled but generally unprincipled sequence of if-clauses. Only numbers 4 and 12 were also found in Qudūrī, and the delay in presenting the fundamental rule at number 12 is not helpful. The task of conjoining the material of Qudūrī and the material of the *Jāmiʿ* has produced a book much less structured than Qudūrī's.

But this material has its own interest and excitement. The cases are significant and challenging prompts to reflection. The technique of presenting antithetical pairs of rules (already noted) which demand articulation of a principle of difference is evident at numbers 5, 6, 8 and 11. A similar demand for a principle of difference is created by the statement of dispute at number 7, and the peculiarity of theft at number 4. All of the material helps towards a general appreciation of the rules of testimony, and all of it has a direct, concrete, lively, realistic feel which both reflects and engenders a fascination with precise, hard-edged detail. The realistic feel, however, is literary realism, not a reflection of the real world: Marghinānī found everything here either in Qudūrī or in texts which had come into existence some three centuries or more prior to his own time (the texts where Qudūrī too had found his norms).

In spite of the unorganised feel of these trailing casuistic passages, derived from the *Jāmiʿ*, Marghinānī also had some organisational successes. Whereas

Qudūrī had attempted to bundle information about *taʿzīr* at the end of his section on slander, and Mawṣilī had moved it up to the end of the section on *zinā*, Marghinānī took it all to the end of the chapter on *ḥudūd* and created a separate section, making it easier to bundle and expand material related to this topic.

Marghinānī's text falls short of the balanced, formal, concise, organised elegance of Mawṣilī (who benefited perhaps from Marghinānī's work) and indeed has less formal elegance than Qudūrī. Nonetheless it was a reliable account of the tradition (in the sense that it drew on two established texts) and it had the merit of greatly expanded detail. In combination with the commentary written by its author, the *Hidāya*, it acquired great fame and had considerable influence. It is possible that its deficiencies (mostly the undigested trailing casuistry derived from the *Jāmiʿ*) were a part of its success, both because the detail charmed, and because the loose structure prompted new efforts at summary and organisation. In succeeding centuries, two works emerged which were directly based on the *Bidāya/Hidāya*, namely the *Wiqāya* of Maḥmūd b. Aḥmad al-Maḥbūbī (seventh/thirteenth century) and the *Nuqāya* by ʿUbaydallāh b. Masʿūd al-Maḥbūbī (d. 747/1346). Equally dependent on Marghinānī's work were the two great independent *mukhtaṣars* of the later Ḥanafī tradition: the *Kanz al-daqāʾiq* of ʿAbdallāh b. Aḥmad al-Nasafī (710/1310–11) and the *Multaqā al-abḥur* of Ibrāhīm b. Muḥammad al-Ḥalabī (956/1549). There were other *mukhtaṣars*, but those mentioned in this paragraph are those listed by Ibn ʿĀbidīn (in the early nineteenth century) as the most authoritative texts of the Ḥanafī *madhhab*: the *Mukhtaṣar* of Qudūrī, the *Bidāya*, the *Mukhtār*, the *Wiqāya*, the *Nuqāya*, the *Kanz*, and the *Multaqā*. Ibn ʿĀbidīn described them as the most authoritative texts of the Ḥanafī *madhhab*, superior in status to commentaries and to *furūʿ* works called *fatāwā*.[22]

3. ʿAbdallāh b. Aḥmad al-Nasafī, born in Nasaf in Soghdia, was trained in Central Asia, and arrived in Baghdad in 710/1310–11 only to die there the same year. This was only thirty years after Mawṣilī's death, and yet his *mukhtaṣar*, the *Kanz al-daqāʾiq*, represents a different literary world. The quality of his achievement is easily discovered in his presentation of the rules of *ḥudūd*.

1. *Kitāb al-ḥudūd*. A *ḥadd* is a punishment, fully specified, for the sake of God. *Zinā* is intercourse in the front part devoid of *milk* or *shubhat milk*. It is established by the testimony of four to *zinā*, not to intercourse or relations,[23] and the imam then asking about the what, how, where, when and who with; if they bear witness that they saw him have intercourse with her like the mascara-stick in the mascara-pot, and are established to be

[22] See Calder, 'The *ʿUqūd rasm al-muftī*'.

[23] Cf. Sarakhsī, *Mabsūṭ*, IX, 85.

> upright secretly and publicly, he gives judgement for the *ḥadd*. And [it is established] by confession. …

The link to Qudūrī and Mawṣilī is obvious. Not so obvious, because lost in this effort at translation, is the combination of elegance and compression achieved in the syntactic control of this material. Strictly speaking, there is only one sentence here: 'It is established by the testimony of four … and by confession … (*yuthbatu bi-shahādati arbaʿatin … wa-bi-iqrāri-hi …).*' The conditions of valid testimony and valid confession are expressed in a tight sequence of subordinate clauses, very imperfectly represented in my translation.

The typology of intercourse, that which does and that which does not entail a *ḥadd* penalty, is introduced under a new chapter heading.

> 2. Chapter on intercourse which entails and does not entail the *ḥadd*. There is no *ḥadd* in the case of a *shubhat maḥall*, even if he thinks it is prohibited, like intercourse with the slave-girl of his son or his son's son, or a woman in her *ʿidda* divorced by equivocal expression; nor in a *shubha fīʿl-fiʿl* if he thinks it is permitted, like a thrice-divorced woman in her *ʿidda*, or the slave-girl of his parents or his wife or his master. Lineage is established in the first type only. He is subject to the *ḥadd* for intercourse with the slave-girl of his brother and his uncle, even if he thinks it permitted; and with a woman found in his bed. Not [for intercourse with] a strange woman brought to him in marriage ceremony, he being informed she is his wife, but he must pay the *mahr*; nor a woman of prescribed degree whom he has married; nor a strange woman in other than the front part; nor for homosexual intercourse; nor an animal; nor in the case of *zinā* in the abode of war or the abode of rebellion; nor the case of a *ḥarbī* with a *dhimmī* woman, in his case; nor the *zinā* of a male who is under age or insane with a fully responsible woman, but not the converse; nor a hired woman; nor under compulsion; nor a confession if the other denies it. …[24]

What is remarkable about this passage is its grammatical control, extensive ellipsis and achieved concision. There is no new rule here. (The rule about lineage is found in the *Bidāya* and can be traced back to the foundation texts.[25]) A new terminology has emerged to distinguish intercourse that is not subject to the *ḥadd* even if one confesses to knowing it is prohibited and intercourse that is not subject to the *ḥadd* only if one claims one thought it was permitted. But the cases are familiar (the emergence of this terminology will be considered later).

[24] Text in commentary on the *Kanz* by Zaylaʿī, *Tabyīn al-haqāʾiq* (Beirut: Dār al-Maʿrifa, 1975), III, 163–95.

[25] The question is discussed in Sarakhsī, *Mabsūṭ*, IX, 96.

Casuistic listing is still the fundamental mode of presentation, albeit subject to stringent syntactical control. A full appreciation of the syntax depends on considerable acknowledgement of ellipsis. The density of expression is sometimes breathtakingly achieved, as notably in the phrases, 'in his case' and 'but not the converse'.

A similar grammatical and syntactical virtuosity is evident in the next section, which again has a chapter heading.

3. Chapter on testimony to *zinā* and recanting. They testify to a prior *ḥadd* other than slander, he is not subject to the *ḥadd*, but is liable for property. If they establish his *zinā* with an absent woman, he is subject to the *ḥadd*, unlike theft. If he confesses to *zinā* with an unknown woman, he is subject to the *ḥadd*, but if they testify to that, not. As also if they differ on her willing submission, or the place, even if there are four for each act; but if they differ within one house the man and the woman are subject to the *ḥadd*. If they testify to the *zinā* of a woman who is a virgin, or the witnesses are immoral, or they testify to the testimony of four, even if the original four subsequently testify, there is no *ḥadd* for anybody. …

All of this material derives from the *Bidāya* and still reflects the order that Marghinānī chose to present his material. Some cases however have been relegated and some brought forward. The rule about testimony to the testimony of four witnesses, and so on, derives from Marghinānī and can be traced back to the foundation texts.[26] Breathtakingly condensed and splendidly virtuoso is the last phrase 'there is no *ḥadd* for anybody' (*lam yuḥadda aḥad*) for it refers back to three different cases (or four if the subordinate case of late testimony by the original four is counted) and it indicates that there is no *ḥadd* in these cases either for the person accused or for the accusers.

In the thirty years from Mawṣilī to Nasafī, something extraordinary had happened. Mawṣilī's concern for elegant structure and clear expression, for an unshowy perspicuity of style had given way to a virtuoso linguistic performance in which syntactical control, grammatical ellipsis and organisational dexterity were on display. The style is foregrounded: It draws attention to itself, and leaves the meaning correspondingly obscured. Obscured but not obscure; for every clause is a precise, clear, objective and stringently correct articulation of the norm aimed at. Only, for those who wish to know the law, it is certainly convenient to have read Qudūrī or Marghinānī first; and for many, the exact significance of those packed clauses may only become clear after a backward glance at Marghinānī's text. The transition can be defined as a move from a classical to

[26] Sarakhsī, *Mabsūṭ*, IX, 66; also in *al-Jāmiʿ al-ṣaghīr*.

a mannerist style. The titles of the two books reflect the same transition. Mawṣilī wrote *Al-Mukhtār li-ʿl-fatwā*, an account of the rules chosen (*mukhtār*) to be promulgated as fatwas – that is, chosen by Abū Hanīfa and authoritative within his school. Nasafī wrote a *Kanz al-daqāʾiq*, a treasure trove of subtleties. The metaphor works, for his prose is as glittering and precious as his meaning (once discovered) is precise, secure and authoritative.

As far as can be easily ascertained, a mannerist style dominated all subsequent *mukhtaṣars* of the Ḥanafī school, and had corresponding effects on the form and the subject matter of *mabsūṭs*. It did not, however, displace the classical style: Qudūrī remained a standard textbook and continued to generate commentaries long after 700/1300–01.

It is useful here to stress two conclusions about the *mukhtaṣar* tradition. First, it is a literary tradition, abstracted from reality. There is no evidence that any of these writers allowed the actual processes of social reality to affect their descriptions of the law. Everything in their works can be accounted for in terms of examining and exploring the foundational texts where all the major decisions about concepts and norms within the law had already been established; or in terms of studying and exploiting earlier works of the *mukhtaṣar* genre. (This does not mean of course that the jurists did not in their practical and professional lives try to establish relationships between reality and literature; but those relationships do not constitute a part of the subject matter of a *mukhtaṣar*.) Secondly, the only process of development that can be securely identified within the tradition is the move towards classicism (from the *Kāfī* of al-Ḥākim al-Marwazī, through Qudūrī and Marghinānī, to Mawṣilī) and then from classicism to mannerism (from Mawṣilī to Nasafī and beyond). The rules do not change, though later *mukhtaṣars*, by virtue of their conceptual and stylistic refinement, capture more detail than earlier ones. Given the conditions of the genre, it is inconceivable that a rule, once established clearly, could change or that a new rule could be introduced that contradicted a previously acknowledged rule. Logical development from known rules seems possible, though no clear example has been found. We have seen a single example of a refinement of terminology designed to capture an already established and fundamental distinction (the *shubhat maḥall* and the *shubha fī ʿl-fiʿl*). Real measurable development, implying a process that is more or less continuous through time and in a definable direction, can be distinguished only in relation to organisational technique, linguistic presentation and syntactical virtuosity. There, the process is from a sufficiency, or a text, or a beginning, or a selection (*Kāfī*, *Matn*, *Bidāya*, *Mukhtār*) to a treasure-trove, and, beyond that, to a meeting of seas (*Kanz*, *Multaqā al-abḥur*). The taste for the mannerist phase may take time to acquire, but neither the reality nor the nature of the development is in doubt.

Section 2. Four *mabsūṭs*

0. The earliest, perhaps the most captivating, and certainly the most influential of all Ḥanafī *mabsūṭs* is the *Mabsūṭ* of Muḥammad b. Aḥmad b. Abī Sahl al-Sarakhsī (490/1097), a commentary on the *Kāfī* of al-Hākim al-Marwazī. It is not, however, the most convenient introduction to the genre. It will be easier to appreciate the qualities of this *Mabsūṭ*, if we work backwards, from the works of Mawṣilī and Marghinānī, to that of Kāsānī, and then to the *Mabsūṭ* itself.

1. Mawṣilī wrote a commentary on his *Mukhtār* which he entitled *Al-Ikhtiyār li-taʿlīl al-mukhtār*. The subtitle reveals his major preoccupation: He wished to justify the rules of the *Mukhtār* by providing them with an *ʿilla* or reason. The provision of reasons (*taʿlīl*) was the central, but not the only, condition of his *mabsūṭ*.

> When my book [the *Mukhtār*] circulated in the hands of the learned and was studied by some jurists, they requested that I should write a commentary to indicate the reasons (*ʿilal*) for the rules and their meanings; to explain their forms and reveal their structures; to mention further rules that were required and could be relied on; and to report on areas of dispute amongst our companions, providing reasons (*ʿilla*) for the dispute, while aiming at brevity and fairness.[27]

He was to provide justification for the rules, while explaining their forms and structures; he was to add further rules, subject to good authority; and he was to give an account of disputes, also grounded in justification (*taʿlīl*).

Here are the first few paragraphs of the *kitāb al-zinā*. The text of the framework *mukhtaṣar* is highlighted.

1. *Kitāb al-ḥudūd*. *Ḥudūd* is the plural of *ḥadd*. Linguistically, it means prohibition (or prevention: *manʿ*). Derived from it is *ḥaddād*, meaning gatekeeper, because he prohibits the people from entry. The *ḥudūd* (boundaries) of land prohibit or prevent the emergence of common ownership. A divorced woman in her *ʿidda* is subject to bounds (*uḥiddāt*) because she has prohibited herself pleasure and delight, as is known. A phrase which gathers and prohibits [sc. the meaning of something] is a *ḥadd* [definition], because it gathers the meanings of a thing and prohibits the entry of something else. The *ḥudūd* of the Law are prohibitors and deterrents in relation to the committing of their causes.[28] In the Law, **they are a punishment, fully specified, and mandatory as a right due to God**, in which, as we have shown, the linguistic meaning is present. *Qiṣāṣ* is not

[27] Mawṣilī, *Ikhtiyār*, I, 6.
[28] The cause (*sabab*) of a *ḥadd* penalty, in Ḥanafī discourse, is the sinful act itself.

called a *ḥadd* because it is a right between men (*ḥaqq al-ʿibād*). Likewise *taʿzīr*, because it is not specified.

2. The legitimacy (*sharʿiyya*) of *ḥudūd* is established by Book and Sunna. As to Book: *al-zāniyya wa-ʾl-zānī* (Q23:2); *al-sāriq waʾl-sāriqa* (Q5:38); *wa-ʾlladīna yarmawna al-muḥṣanāt* (Q24:4); the *muḥāraba* verse (Q5:33) and others. As to Sunna: the hadith of Māʿiz, that of the woman of Ghāmid, the hadith of the hireling, and other famous hadith, as will be evident in the course of the chapters. And [*ḥudūd* are also established] by rationality (*al-maʿqūl*): namely, that human nature and base desire are inclined towards the fulfilment of desire, the seizure of pleasures, and the acquisition of things they aim at or love, such as alcohol, fornication, revenge for killing, taking the property of others, and vaunting oneself over others by invective or blows; especially the strong against the weak, and the high against the low. Hence, wisdom requires the laying down of these *ḥudūd* as a guard against this corruption, and a deterrent against its perpetration, so that the world may remain in an order of righteousness. For, to deprive the world of these deterrents would lead to its destruction, wherein would be manifest corruption. There is an indication of this in God's word, *wa-la-kum fi-ʾl-qiṣāṣ ḥayātun* (Q2:179); and in the words of the Arab sages, 'Killing is the surest purifier of killing.'
3. He said: **Zinā means penetration by a man, of a woman, in the front part; without ownership (*milk*) or appearance of ownership *(shubhat milk)*.** As to the first [element], it is because of the general occasions of the use of the word *zinā*. When one says, 'So-and-so committed *zinā*', one knows that he had intercourse with a woman in the front part, under illegal conditions. For example, when Māʿiz explained *zinā* as meaning intercourse in the front part, illegally, like the mascara-stick, then the Prophet imposed the *ḥadd*. As to the stipulation of ownership, it is because ownership is a cause (*sabab*) of permission, and so the act is no longer *zinā*. As to the appearance of ownership, it is because of the Prophet's words, 'Evade *ḥudūd* by appearances' (*idraʾu ʾl-ḥudūd bi-ʾl-shubuhāt*).
4. *Zinā* must include passing the place of circumcision (*mujāwazat al-khitān*), because copulation is established thereby; anything less is foreplay, not subject to the rules of intercourse as they effect major ritual pollution, or atonement, or fasting, or pilgrimage.
5. He said: **It is established by testimony or confession**. Because these are proofs within the Law, and by them judicial decisions are established, as we have explained in the section on judicial claims. God's words, 'Those who accuse upright women, and fail to bring four witnesses, beat them' (Q24:4), are evidence that the *zinā* they implied is established if they

bring four witnesses, so as to avert from themselves the *ḥadd* of slander. This is testimony. As to confession, truth in this circumstance is preponderant (*rājiḥ*) because it is a confession against oneself, and constitutes a harm to oneself; and on the basis of confession the Prophet imposed the *ḥadd* on Māʿiz. Definitive knowledge is impossible for us, and so there is a sufficiency in preponderant appearance (*al-ẓāhir al-rājiḥ*).

6. **Testimony means that four men bear witness to zinā on the part of a man and a woman.** Because of the verse we have given. And because of God's words, 'Those of your women who commit fornication, bring four from your midst to testify against them' (Q4:15). He specified four for the reason given earlier.
7. **When they testify, the qadi asks them about what, how, where, when, and the identity of the woman.** Because this is a device (*iḥtiyāl*) for the evasion recommended by the Prophet when he said, 'Evade *ḥudūd* as far as you are able'. ...[29]

Para. 1 expands on the meaning of *hudūd* contrasting its meaning linguistically (*fīʾl-lugha*) with its meaning in the law (*fīʾl-sharʿ*). The legal definition identifies a genus (punishment) and two differentia (specified, and a right due to God). The point of these distinctions is brought out by explicit contrast: *qiṣāṣ* (retaliation) is also a punishment, but it is a right (or claim) between men, and *taʿzīr*, also a punishment, is not specified as to form or quantity. The Aristotelian nature of this definition with classification of difference is apparent. Para. 2 is a generalised introduction to the justification of *ḥudūd*. It refers, synoptically, to all the major items of Book and Sunna that are brought into play in this context and it identifies an argument of rationality which justifies and explains the *ḥudūd* by identifying a social need. The substance of this argument is also Aristotelian, and the addition of two generalising sententia (one from the Book of God, and one from the Arabs) which stand as authority for the argument may reflect Aristotelian rhetorical method.

Para. 3 establishes the fundamental technique of a *mabsūṭ*: lemma and comment. The words, 'He said', introduce a passage of the *mukhtaṣar*, which is then followed by reasons for the law. 'As to *a*, it is because of *b*, and *c* etc.' or, simply, 'Because of *b*, and *c* etc.' The pattern is repeated at paras. 5, 6 and 7 above, and in paras. 8 and 10 below. The whole of the *mukhtaṣar* is eventually incorporated into the commentary, functioning as a framework or skeleton for the new book. The type of cause that emerges to justify rules is varied. There are many examples of reference to specific verses of the Qurʾan, or to specific hadith from the Prophet.

[29] Mawṣilī, *Ikhtiyār*, IV, 79–80.

But arguments that refer to linguistic usage and to general principles of coherence are also used (para. 3). Arguments of reason are juxtaposed to arguments of Prophetic authority, and may even be allied to generalisation about the law (coherence), as at para. 5. Para. 4 contains an extra rule, adorned with analogical cross references to other topics of the law where the same rule is effective. There is a consistent tone to the arguments on this topic, one already established in the material and expression of the *mukhtaṣar* tradition, namely a tendency to ensure that the *ḥudūd* will not be put into effect. This tone is grounded in a Prophetic hadith, of which two versions are mentioned, respectively, in para. 3 and in para. 7.

The discovery that the primary (not the exclusive) aim of a *mabsūṭ* is to provide arguments (causes) for the basic propositions of a *mukhtaṣar* prompts a reformulation of what a *mukhtaṣar* is. A *mukhtaṣar* provides a basic pattern of norms which define the discipline of the law. A *mabsūṭ* demonstrates the truth and validity of those norms by grounding them in argument: arguments of authority (divine and prophetic) predominate, but arguments of reason and general coherence are also brought into play, as are definitions and linguistic usage. All of this is consistent with an Aristotelian notion of a science or discipline. The justificatory material in a *mabsūṭ* represents an attempt to assert the status of the core rules (the *mukhtaṣar*) as a demonstrative science. The validity of the law as a whole depends on a hierarchy of arguments: those that ground the *mukhtaṣar* in reasons, and those that extrapolate from the *mukhtaṣar* new rules.

One of the characteristics of Mawṣilī's *mukhtaṣar* was that he removed all mention of dispute, giving only the rule that represented the main tradition as it was attributed to Abū Ḥanīfa. In the introduction to his *Ikhtiyār*, he had promised to re-introduce items of dispute and to provide them with their reasons; as in the following example.

8. He said, **The *iḥṣān* of stoning depends on freedom, sanity, maturity, Islam, and penetration of the front part in a valid marriage, where both partners have the quality of *iḥṣān*.** As to freedom, it is because of God's words, 'They are subject to a punishment which is half that of free women' (Q4.25). He has imposed upon them a punishment which is halved, but stoning cannot be halved so it is not binding on slaves. As to sanity and maturity it is because there is no commission (*khiṭāb*) without them. As to Islam, it is because of the Prophet's words, 'He who is an idolater is not *muḥṣan*.' The narrative that he stoned a Jewish couple relates to the law of the Torah. The story is well-known. As to valid marriage and entry, it is because of the Prophet's words, 'The virgin with the virgin a hundred lashes'; the word 'virgin' is applied to one who has not married.

Also because it is a means of achieving legitimate intercourse. Entry is made a condition only by virtue of the Prophet's words, 'The non-virgin with the non-virgin a hundred lashes and stoning.' The word non-virgin means one who has intercourse in a legitimate marriage in the front part.

9. Further, these are bounties, abundant and perfected and tending to restrain one from licence; hence one's crime, given these bounties, is more vicious. A crime and a sin when the bounties of the Bountiful are perfected is more wicked and more vile and merits the viciousness (*taghlīẓ*) of the penalty for the perpetrator.
10. As to both parties having the qualities of *iḥṣān*, it is because every act of intercourse which does not entail the *iḥṣān* of one of the two parties does not entail the *iḥṣān* of the other, like two slaves or two who are insane. Its result is as follows: if he marries a slave-girl, or a child, or one who is insane, or an unbeliever, and secures entry, he does not become *muḥṣan*. Likewise if she is free, sane, and mature and he is a slave, or a child, or insane, she does not become *muḥṣan*. Unless he enters her after becoming a Muslim, or emancipation, or maturity, or recovery, in which case she becomes *muḥṣan* by virtue of this act of intercourse, not any previous one. This is because the bounties of the married state are not perfected with these people. For these qualities are repellent to human nature either because of the enmity between religions, or the baseness of slavery, or absence or deficiency of sanity, or because a child has no inclination towards [a sexual partner], with the result that the crime is not made more vicious.
11. From Abū Yūsuf: 'Penetration while having the quality of *iḥṣān* is not a condition.' Also from him: 'If intercourse takes place before emancipation and then the two parties are emancipated, they become *muḥṣan* on the basis of the prior intercourse.' Reply to the first: every act of intercourse that does not entail the *iḥṣān* of one party does not entail the *iḥṣān* of the other, as we have explained. To the second: every act of intercourse that does not entail *iḥṣān* when it takes place does not entail it at a subsequent time, like the intercourse of a slave.
12. Also from Abū Yūsuf: 'If he enters his wife and subsequently becomes insane or demented and later recovers, he is not *muḥṣan* until he enters her again after recovery', because the first *iḥṣān* became void and there is no renewal of *iḥṣān* save with renewed entry.[30]

The passage is a good example of the precise and controlled formality that characterises this *mabsūṭ*. In para. 8, for each of the first six conditions of *iḥṣān*, in

[30] Ibid., IV, 88–9.

turn, Mawṣilī offers a characteristic statement, As to *a*, it is because of *b* and *c*, and so on. Only for the condition of Islam is there a slight expansion of argument in order to identify and explain away a counter-argument, namely the hadith of the Jewish couple. The words 'virgin' and 'non-virgin' apply equally to males and females, and the argument at this point is very compressed and elliptical: One can become a non-virgin without marriage. But Mawṣilī was aiming at a schematic and streamlined presentation of arguments. Para. 9 refers to these six conditions as a single block, representing a combination of bounties which, by virtue of their combination, serve as a special restraint against fornication. Para. 10 takes up the final condition of *iḥṣān*, namely that both parties should have all the qualities of *iḥṣān*. The results of this rule are worked out in some detail so as to clarify what is at issue, and include a logical extension of rules: If an unbeliever becomes a Muslim, he becomes *muḥṣan* by the next subsequent act of intercourse. The motif that *iḥṣān* is a combination of bounties, representing a special kind of perfected state, is introduced again, with the concomitant notion that an act of transgression when so many bounties are conjoined deserves a particularly vicious punishment. The arguments are offered in a highly reduced, elliptical, schematic fashion: There is enmity between different religions, baseness in slavery, deficiency in insanity, absence of reciprocal desire in children, and each of these factors represents a qualification of the perfected state, such that the more vicious of the two possible penalties is not justified. Though the motive for this discussion is ultimately *ḥadd* penalties, the immediate subject of discussion has become the nature and qualities of perfectedness in a sexual relationship; as much philosophical as juristic.

When he has neatly dealt with each of the conditions of *iḥṣān*, Mawṣilī introduces, at para. 11, two opinions from Abū Yūsuf which differ from the main tradition. For each opinion, he indicates, as succinctly as possible, the mode of reply. (A really effective reply to Abū Yūsuf's views would certainly have to expand on this; but a really effective statement of his views would also require expansion.) Finally, at para. 12, Mawṣilī introduces a view from Abū Yūsuf which is not identified as different from the main tradition; it is rather an extra finesse within the law, a logical extension of known rules.

Mawṣilī's work then is a point by point demonstration of the grounds for the law. He offers systematic arguments based on definitions, language use, authority, reason and structural coherence. He works neatly, and with a precise and suggestive concision, which is also perhaps an invitation to exploration and expansion. Further, he identifies major areas of dispute, and provides the arguments that undermine opinions which are opposed to the main tradition. He derives (or reports) extra items of the law where opportunity offers; 'where they were required and could be relied on' was his own assessment of the matter. At least in respect of the great stress he lays on the formal qualities of organisation and structure, his commentary mirrors the qualities of his *mukhtaṣar.* The special concern for the reasons and justification of the law which is signalled in the subtitle of his work (*taʿlīl*) is evident in the detail of his exposition, and in the repeated use of causal phrases, throughout the main exposition, and throughout exploration of dispute.

2. Marghinānī wrote two commentaries on his *Bidāya*. The first he called the *Kifāyat al-muntahā* which, as implied by the title, was an aspiration towards the furthest degree of explanation and elucidation. Unfortunately, it was wordy and prolix (*tabayyantu fī-hi nubadhan min al-iṭnābi*), and, before completing it, he turned his efforts and his concern towards a shorter work which he called the *Hidāya*. It is in the introduction to this that he tells about his two efforts at commentary, promising to avoid, in the *Hidāya*, the excessive detail that had marred his *Kifāya*. The two works serve as a useful symbol of the possibilities of a single literary type. The basic qualities of a *mukhtaṣar* and a *mabsūṭ* are sufficiently clear to justify the distinction between these types within the overall genre of *furūʿ*, but the content of a *mabsūṭ* was almost infinitely expandable. Some *mabsūṭ*s were small and neat, some were not. The distinction is exemplified in Marghinānī's two efforts at commentary, and indeed, outside the Ḥanafī tradition, in such sequences of works as Ghazālī's *Basīṭ*, *Wajīz* and *Wasīṭ* (*The Expanded*, *The Succinct* and *The Intermediate*). However, as we shall see, for the period under discussion (prior to ca. 700/1300), the formal components of a *mabsūṭ* did not vary as between large and small: A large *mabsūṭ* simply contained more of everything that was contained in a small *mabsūṭ*.

Here is the passage from Marghinānī's *Hidāya*, in which he deals with the conditions of *iḥṣān*, the conditions we have just seen expounded so neatly by Mawṣilī.

1. He said: **The *iḥṣān* of stoning is that he is free, sane, mature, Muslim, married by a valid contract of marriage, and has entered his wife, both of them having the quality of *iḥṣān*.** Sanity and maturity are a condition of legal competence (*ahliyya*) for the penalty, for there is no commission (*khiṭāb*) without them. The other conditions are laid down so that the crime becomes perfected by virtue of the perfectedness of the bounty. For the neglect of a bounty becomes more vicious when the bounties are multiplied, and these qualities are great bounties. Further, stoning has been decreed when these qualities are conjoined and is dependent on their conjunction; this is different from noble lineage and knowledge [also bounties] because the Law has not specified that these be taken into consideration, and to declare the law on a basis of opinion is impossible.

2. Also because freedom enables a valid marriage; and a valid marriage enables legitimate sexual intercourse, and the aim [in this context] is that one gain full satisfaction (*shabʿ*) with a legitimate partner. Islam makes possible marriage to a Muslim woman, and strengthens the belief in the prohibition [of *zinā*]. Hence all of them together constitute a deterrence against *zinā*. A crime when the deterrents are many is more vicious.
3. Shāfiʿī opposes us on Islam as a condition, and likewise Abū Yūsuf, in one transmission. They argue on the basis of the narrative that the Prophet stoned a Jewish couple who had fornicated. We reply: That was on the basis of the Torah, which was abrogated. This is confirmed by the Prophet's words, 'He who is an idolater is not *muḥṣan*.'
4. Taken into consideration for entry is penetration of the front part to the degree required for major ritual ablution.
5. The condition that both parties should have the quality of *iḥṣān* at the time of penetration means that if he entered an unbeliever wife, or a slave, or someone insane, or a child, he would not be *muḥṣan*. Likewise if the husband had any of these qualities and she was free, Muslim, sane and mature. This is because the bounty does not become perfected in these circumstances. Indeed [human] nature abhors the company of the insane, and rarely does one desire a child because of her lack of desire for oneself, or desire a wife who is a slave, in order to avoid the slave status of a child, and there is no personal harmony when there is difference of religion. Abū Yūsuf was opposed to his two companions on the question of the *kāfir*, but the proof against him is as we have mentioned, and also the Prophet's words, 'A Muslim is not made *muḥṣan* by a Jew or a Christian, nor a freeman by a slave-girl, nor a free woman by a slave.'[31]

In a number of different ways this is not so neat, not so formally achieved, as Mawṣilī's text. Marghinānī, does not approach the list at para. 1 systematically, dealing with each item in turn. He jumps straight to sanity and maturity. He then turns abruptly to the idea of perfectedness which lies in the conjunction of all these qualities. Towards the end of para. 1, he mentions noble lineage and knowledge. For a reader completely unfamiliar with the argument, this must be puzzling (though an assiduous reader might work it out). The reference is to a dispute that had been recorded in Sarakhsī. Abū Yūsuf, defending his view that Islam was not one of the conditions of *iḥṣān*, noted that noble lineage and knowledge were also bounties whose presence made particularly vicious an act of fornication by one who possessed them. But they were not made conditions

[31] Marghinānī, *Hidāya*, V, 236–40.

of *iḥṣān*; and therefore Islam should not be a condition of *iḥṣān*. Marghinānī's casual reference scarcely provides the information needed to understand the point. The Law, he tells us, has not specified these particular bounties. But Marghinānī has not shown us how the Law has specified the other bounties, those that really are to be taken into consideration. His argument is not fully explicated.

It is easy, however, to overstress the difficulties of reading this passage. Most of those who read it would recognise the reference, and would mentally rebuild from Marghinānī's allusions the argument that lay behind them. Works of this kind were never intended to be read in isolation. They existed as part of an ongoing tradition of literary production, in which the various literary products contained different expressions of the same laws and the same arguments. And they existed as a part of an ongoing teaching tradition, in which the norms and arguments of the law were also taught orally by a teacher, at various levels, and on numerous occasions. Those who came to Marghinānī's text did not, even if they came to it for the first time, come to its arguments for the first time; they possessed a prior framework of reference which could deal with allusions and obscurities. And if they could not, they knew that arguments were not usually the preserve of one writer. They could expect to find them repeated, perhaps better formulated, in another context. In these circumstances, it is by no means clear that the merits of order and structure, so evident in Mawṣilī, outweigh the merits of loose structure and allusion that are evident in Marghinānī. Certainly there is little sign within the tradition of a general preference for Mawṣilī over Marghinānī; rather the reverse.

At para. 2, Marghinānī deals with the qualities of freedom, valid marriage and Islam, but only with reference to the idea that they permit of a perfected bounty which makes transgression a particularly vicious act, deserving a vicious punishment. Para. 3 identifies Shāfiʿī and Abū Yūsuf as holding an opposed view on the question of Islam in particular, and there is a brief indication of their argument and the reply. This is repeated with extra detail at para. 5. Para. 4 provides a definition of sexual penetration and a cross-reference to the law of purity. Para. 5 deals with the requirement that both parties have all the conditions of *iḥṣān*. It follows the same set of arguments as were adduced (later) by Mawṣilī. The whole is a variation on a theme, a re-expression of a conventional and established set of justificatory arguments. There is nothing here that had not been expressed before, nothing that would not be expressed again.

We have already seen that Marghinānī's *Bidāya* contains more rules than Mawṣilī's *Mukhtār*, and that they have a loose and lively disarray which does not lack charm. In fact, just as Mawṣilī's commentary shows features and characteristics which parallel those of his *mukhtaṣar*, so too does Marghinānī's commentary: a loose and lively disarray could be as much a comment on his *Hidāya* as it is on his *Bidāya*. The two *mabsūṭ*s differ in organisation, style and in selection of material, but reflect a common reservoir of possible content. That content consists primarily of arguments that explain, justify and extend the law. The fundamental pattern of reference is to Qurʿan and Sunna (not much in evidence in this passage, but that is because the broad pattern of reference to Quranic passages and familiar hadith is established elsewhere). To this is added arguments of reason and general principles of coherence, some exploration of dispute and the recording (or, rarely, generation) of new rules where they can be usefully included. The typology of materials is exactly the same in both works. Marghinānī's text, because of its looser structure, offers perhaps greater incentives to analysis and enjoyment. And he had his analytical successes.

6. He said: **Intercourse entailing the *ḥadd* is *zinā*.** *Zinā* both in the law and in linguistic usage is intercourse by a man, with a woman, in the front part, without ownership or the appearance of ownership. This is confirmed by the Prophet's words, 'Evade *ḥudūd* by *shubuhāt*.' A *shubha* is of two types: a *shubha* in the act, called a *shubha* of confusion (*shubhat ishtibāh*); and a *shubha* in the rule (?*maḥall*), called a classificatory *shubha* (a *shubha ḥukmiyya*). The first is realised in respect of one who is confused [about the act]. Its meaning is that he thinks something that is not evidence is evidence, and that thought must be present for the full realisation of confusion (*ishtibāh*). The second is realised by virtue of evidence which negates the prohibited nature of the act in its essence. This *shubha* does not depend on the thought or the belief of the perpetrator. The *ḥadd* penalty lapses for both types, in virtue of the absolute expression of the hadith.
7. Lineage is established in the second type if he claims the child, but not in the first type even if he claims the child. Because the act in the first type gave rise directly to *zinā*, and the *ḥadd* lapsed only because of something incidental, namely his confusion. But the second type did not give rise to *zinā*.
8. A *shubha* in the act has eight instances: the slave-girl of his father, his mother, and his wife; a thrice-divorced woman in her *ʿidda*; a wife irrevocably divorced on the basis of financial compensation, while she is in her *ʿidda*; the slave-girl of his master in the case of a slave; the slave-girl held in pledge in the case of the pledge-holder, in a transmission from the *Kitāb al-ḥudūd*. In these instances, there is no *ḥadd* if he says, 'I thought she was permitted to me'; but if he says, 'I knew that she was prohibited', he is subject to the *ḥadd*.

9. A *shubha* in the rule has six instances: the slave-girl of his son; a wife irrevocably divorced by allusive speech; a slave-girl who has been sold, in the case of the seller, prior to delivery; a wife who is due a dowry, in the case of the husband, prior to her receiving it; a slave-girl held in common; the slave-girl held in pledge in the case of the pledge-holder, in a transmission from the *Kitāb al-rahn*. In these instances there is no *ḥadd* even if he says, 'I knew that she was *ḥarām* to me'.

Something has been achieved here. The casual listing of two types of fornication, one requiring the *ḥadd* only if the perpetrator says, 'I knew it was *ḥarām*', the other not requiring the *ḥadd*, has been abandoned in favour of a classificatory terminology. It was to be a boon for later *mukhtaṣars*, and it seems that Marghīnānī did not know it when he wrote his *Bidāya*. It may be a personal development. Mawṣilī knew the terminology and extended it slightly: He distinguished three types of *shubha*: a *shubha* in the act, a *shubha* in the rule (*maḥall*), and a *shubha* in the contract. This enabled him to gather a coherent bundle of cases under his third heading (e.g., a man who had married his wife without witnesses, or a slave-girl without the permission of her master), and he gave more cases and detail under the headings already provided by Marghīnānī. His book continues the process of classificatory refinement and management of detail.

In other respects the text of Marghīnānī is rather wordy; and he proceeded to discuss numerous cases, as they had been presented in his *mukhtaṣar*, separately and in relative disorder, since that was how they had been listed there. But he put the effort to good use by providing arguments of authority and reason for each of the cases individually.

The references in para. 8 to the *Kitāb al-ḥudūd* and in para. 9 to the *Kitāb al-rahn* are to the books with those titles contained within the *Aṣl* or *Mabsūṭ* of Shaybānī. Here, as elsewhere, Marghīnānī derives his material from the tradition in which he writes and not from consideration of social reality. The essential nature of his work, as also of the work of Mawṣilī, is conservative and expository, not innovatory, or responsive to social reality. The task of these writers, as it emerges in their works, was to present a basic pattern of rules. The rules were selected from those that had already come into existence and been expressed in the foundational texts of the Ḥanafī *madhhab*,[32] or were restated in the ongoing tradition of *furūʿ*.

A *mabsūṭ* provided the rules with patterns of justificatory argument, whether of authority (Divine, Prophetic and, more rarely, Companion) or of definitions,

[32] These were eventually classified as the six books of Shaybānī, plus a number of other works attributed to Shaybānī and Abū Yūsuf, and the works of the immediately succeeding generations; the whole came to be known as *ẓāhir al-riwāya* or the 'manifest transmission'. Cf. Calder, 'The *ʿuqūd rasm al-muftī*'.

language use, reason and coherence. Much of the justificatory argument can also be traced back to the foundational texts, though much too must be related to the teaching tradition which led up to Sarakhsī's *Mabsūṭ*, where we find the first expression of many justificatory arguments that were to be repeated and developed through the centuries. By placing the rules within a body of justificatory argument, the jurists gave them a certain status, approximating to that of a science: They were not merely propositions but justified propositions. A *mabsūṭ* has the qualities of a scientific demonstration. While much of the organisational technique of the tradition might have emerged by natural development, without any reference to Aristotelian logic or rhetoric, the fact is that the works of Aristotle's *Organon* (usually mediated through other works of logic) were, potentially, a part of the subject matter of the juristic curriculum, and played their part in confirming or moulding techniques of presentation and argument. The *Analytics* provided theories about demonstrative proof and the place of definitions within a structure of proof; the *Topics* provided a loose bundle of types and modes of argument, and a theory of dialectic; the *Rhetoric* provided hints about the overall management and presentation of argument.

Amongst the theoretical factors which may have affected the jurists was Aristotle's general theory of what a science is. It is a permanent body of fully justified propositions, derived by appropriate argument (perhaps at more than one remove) from unmediated first principles. It is intrinsic to the nature of a real science that its propositions are eternally true; and, conversely, there is no real science of contingent matters. Whether this idea was mediated directly to the Muslim jurists from a reading of Aristotle's texts, or those of his commentators, or was mediated indirectly through educational technique or ancient tradition, it tended to confirm and stabilise what was also a theological conviction, namely that the law was eternal and unchanging. The general methodology of juristic writing, discovered in all these jurists, confirms that their literary purpose does not include reference to the contingent world of social events. They dig into the foundational texts in order to establish the permanent norms of a fully justified legal system: It is permanent because it is God's law, and it is permanent too because that is an essential attribute of any system that lays claim to being a real science. For Aristotle, a science which related in some sense to contingent reality would achieve its permanent value as a science only in so far as it dealt with the species and not with individuals. It is just possible that some such idea existed for the jurists, whose resistance and indifference to social reality is as remarkable (for us) as it is (for them) unproblematic. An account of the law was an account of concepts and rules that had been discovered and expressed generations or centuries beforehand, irrespective of the degree of concinnity that existed between the rules and social structures.

The idea of the law as a pure structure, a pure science, having its ultimate origins in the words of God and his Prophet, its immediate origins in the works of Shaybānī and other followers of Abū Ḥanīfa, is absolutely integral to the style and technique of Mawṣilī. His technique betrays his aims, namely to depict the unchanging norms of the Ḥanafī tradition, embedded in a pattern of justificatory argument. In Marghinānī too, the general principles of presentation show that the law is to be depicted in terms that were evolved, and norms that were established, a long time ago. He is likely to surprise only by citing a book or a rule that is rare or unexpected. It is inevitable, in these circumstances, that the relationship between the law and real contemporary social practice will be oblique (variously so): a space requiring a hermeneutical bridge. The law could not be simply a template for social practice.

3. Kāsānī died only six years before Marghinānī (in 587/1192). His great work is entitled *Bada'i' al-ṣanā'i' fi tartīb al-sharā'i'* (*Innovations of artifice in the organisation of the rules*).[33] The title says much about his aims, but it will be useful to come to it after some appreciation of his style. This book is a *mabsūṭ*, but unlike the others we have looked at, not based on a *mukhtaṣar*. In the section on *iḥṣān*, Kāsānī, having introduced a basic definition, goes through each item in turn: 'As to sanity, it is because ...'; 'as to maturity, it is because ...'; 'as to Islam, it is because it is a bounty that gives perfection, and entails the giving of thanks; therefore it prohibits (or prevents) *zinā*, which means putting neglect where thanks is due.' The dispute that surrounds the issue of Islam is introduced only after the list has been completed.

1. There is no dispute on these conditions except in reference to Islam. It is related from Abū Yūsuf that Islam is not one of the conditions of *iḥṣān* ... According to Abū Yūsuf, a Muslim becomes *muḥṣan* by marrying a *kitābī* woman, and a *dhimmī* is stoned under these conditions. Shāfi'ī holds the same view.
2. They argue: i. It is related that the Prophet stoned a Jewish couple, and if Islam had been a condition he would not have done so. ii. Making Islam a condition serves as a restraint from fornication. But religion in an absolute sense is sufficient as a restraint from fornication since fornication is prohibited in all religions.
3. We reply: i. With regard to fornication by a *dhimmī*, God's words, 'The fornicatress and the fornicator, beat each of them a hundred times' (Q24:2). By these words God has made it mandatory to beat every fornicator or fornicatress (or the fornicator and the fornicatress absolutely) irrespective

[33] Kāsānī, *Badā'i' al-ṣanā'i' fi tartīb al-shara'i'* (Beirut: Dār al-Kitāb al-'Arabī, 1982).

of whether they are believers or unbelievers. Since beating is mandatory, stoning is excluded necessarily. ii. The fornication of an unbeliever is not the equal of fornication by a Muslim in respect of being a crime. Therefore it is not its equal in requiring punishment. (It is like the fornication of a virgin and a non-virgin.) This is explained by the consideration that fornication by a Muslim involves a special increase in evil which does not affect a non-Muslim, namely that he has put neglect where thanks is due, because Islam is a bounty, whereas the religion of unbelief is not. iii. With respect to the fornication of a Muslim with a *kitābī* woman, the Prophet's words to Hudhayfa when he wanted to marry a Jewish woman, 'Leave her, for she does not make you *muḥṣan*'. iv. Also, the Prophet's words, 'He who is an idolater is not *muḥṣan*'. (The *dhimmī* is an idolater in truth so he is not *muḥṣan*.) v. Also what we mentioned before, namely that the satisfaction of sexual desire with an unbelieving woman is not perfected. Hence the bounty is not perfected, and, as a restraint, it is not perfected.

4. As to their claim that the restraint is in place simply by virtue of a religion, we reply, Yes, but the restraint is not perfected except by the religion of Islam, for it is a bounty, and therefore fornication on the part of a Muslim means to place neglect where thanks is due; whereas the religion of unbelief is not a bounty, and is not so effective as a restraint. As to the hadith of the Jewish couple, it is possible (*yaḥtamilu*) that it happened before the revelation of the beating verse and [the rule] was abrogated thereby, and it is possible (*yaḥtamilu*) that it happened after the revelation of the beating verse. But abrogation of a *khabar wāḥid* is a lighter thing than abrogation of the Book.

Kāsānī's argument is frequently obscured because marginal glosses have been incorporated into the printed edition. I have omitted some untidy writing in para. 1 and I have put into brackets in para. 3 and elsewhere other items which I suspect were originally marginal. Absolutely characteristic of Kāsānī is the dialectical presentation of dispute items. Here, para. 2 identifies the arguments of the opponents, para. 3 those of the Ḥanafī tradition, and para. 4 takes up unexplained items of the opponents' argument. The central argument (para. 3), that of the Ḥanafī masters, is remarkably detailed and its elements carefully differentiated. Much of this detail can be found in, or derived from, Sarakhsī, but not all: argument i cannot be found there. This passage too is a variation on a theme: more sharply dialectical than Mawṣilī or Marghinānī, more rigorously organised than Sarakhsī, and displaying a strong bias towards structured formality in presentation of argument (see also argument ii at para. 2, argument ii at para. 3 and the first part of para. 4).

The perception of the law as a sequence of dialectical aporias is one feature of Kāsānī's text. The concern with precisely differentiated argument and formal expression is also uniquely his. More difficult to convey is his concern with organisation and structure at a higher level. The introductory paragraphs of his *Kitāb al-ḥudūd* may be suggestive.

5. *Kitāb al-ḥudūd*. Muḥammad (al-Shaybānī) conjoined the problems of *ḥudūd* and *ta'zīr* [in one *kitāb*]. He began with the problems of *ḥudūd*, so we will begin as he did. Therefore, seeking help from God most high:
6. Discourse on *ḥudūd* falls into topoi (*mawāḍi'*): on its meaning, linguistically and juristically; on the causes and the conditions of the necessity of *ḥudūd*; on how their necessity becomes manifest before a qadi; on their qualities; on the specified details; on the conditions of the permissibility of their being put into effect; on the manner and the place of implementation; on what causes them to lapse after they have become *wājib*; on the rules governing a situation where *ḥudūd* are conjoined; on the status of those punished.
7. As to the first [topos]: *Ḥadd* in language is an expression for prohibition, hence the gate-keeper is called *ḥaddād* because he prohibits the people from entry. In the Law, it is an expression for a punishment, fully specified, and mandatory as a right due to God. It is different from *ta'zīr* which is not specified, and may be by beating, imprisonment, or something else. And [it is different] from *qiṣāṣ* which, though it is a fully specified punishment, is a right of men, subject to forgiveness and negotiation. This punishment is called a *ḥadd* because it prohibits the one punished, if he is not actually killed, and it prohibits others, by their witnessing it ...; and it helps the latter ... to conceive of it happening to him were he to commit that crime. ...[34]
8. As to [the second topic,] the causes of its being necessary, these can only be explained after establishing its types. The *ḥudūd* are of five types: theft, fornication, drinking, drunkenness, and slander. ... As to the *ḥadd* of fornication, it is of two types: beating and stoning. The cause (*sabab*) of the necessity of each type is *zinā*, and they differ by virtue of a condition, which is *iḥṣān*. *Iḥṣān* is a condition for the necessity of stoning but not a condition for the necessity of beating. It is necessary to consider therefore the meaning of *zinā* and *iḥṣān* in the usage of the Law. *Zinā* is a word signifying illegal intercourse, in the front part of a living woman, with freedom of choice, in the Abode of Justice, by one subject to the rules of

[34] I have emended the text slightly to omit elements of repetition which are probably due to gloss or to dittography.

Islam, in a manner devoid of the reality of ownership, or the appearance of it, (or the right of ownership,) or the reality of marriage, or the appearance of marriage, or the appearance of confusion (*shubhat al-ishtibāh*), where that is possible, in regard to both ownership and marriage.

9. The basis for taking appearance (*shubha*) into account here is the famous hadith, 'Evade *ḥudūd* by *shubuhāt*'. Also because the *ḥadd* is a punishment which is perfected and it requires a crime which is perfected; and intercourse in the front part without either ownership or marriage is not perfected as a crime, except in the absence of all *shubuhāt*.

10. Once *zinā* is known according to the usage of the Law, we will now explore a number of problems.

11. A male who is a child or insane, if he has intercourse with a strange woman, is not subject to the *ḥadd*. This is because the act perpetrated by these two [males] does not have the quality of prohibition, and intercourse by them is not *zinā*. It follows that there is no *ḥadd* for the woman, even if she submits willingly. This is according to our three companions. But Zufar and Shāfi'ī said that she is subject to the *ḥadd*. There is no dispute in the case of a mature and sane man who has intercourse with a female who is a child or insane: he is subject to the *ḥadd* and she is not.

11.1. They argue: That which prevents the act being *zinā* [in the first case] affects only one party, and so its result is unique to that party. It is like the case of a mature and sane man who has intercourse with a female who is a child or insane: he is subject to the *ḥadd* but she is not. The same applies here.

11.2. We reply: The necessity of a *ḥadd* in respect of a woman, in the context of *zinā*, is not because she is a *zāniyya* (fornicatress), for *zinā* cannot be realised on her part, for *zinā* is intercourse and she is the object of intercourse not the agent. That she is named in the Holy Book as a *zāniyya* is metaphoric usage. The *ḥadd* becomes binding on her because she is the object of an act of *zinā*. But the act of a male who is a child or insane is not an act of *zinā* and so she is not the object of such an act, and is consequently not subject to the *ḥadd*. Conversely the act of *zinā* is fully realised on the part of a male who is mature and sane, and so a female who is a child or insane becomes the object of an act of *zinā*. However she is not subject to the *ḥadd* because of absence of legal competence (*ahliyya*), whereas the man is competent and the *ḥadd* is therefore mandatory for him.

12. Intercourse in the back part of a female or a male does not entail the *ḥadd* according to Abū Ḥanīfa. ...[35]

[35] Kāsānī, *Badā'i'*, VII, 33–4.

I have interrupted this passage in the midst of a structure that is unfinished. At para. 10, Kāsānī indicated that, having established a definition of *zinā*, he would now explore a number of problems. The first of these is contained in para 11. The second begins at para. 12. Going further back, it is clear that Kāsānī had introduced, at para. 8, two terms requiring exploration, namely *zinā* and *iḥṣān*. I have interrupted the passage in the midst of the discussion of *zinā*. Kāsānī has more than three pages of discussion of *zinā* before he returns to the definition of *iḥṣān*, promised in para. 8. At para. 8, he had entered on the topos, causes of *ḥudūd*, which is the second of ten topoi (or *mawḍiʿ*) which he had identified in para. 6. Kāsānī, in other words, has the general structure of his argument completely under control. Its parts (topoi or *mawḍiʿ*) have been analysed, ordered in a logical manner, structured and boxed, with sections and subsections, and he never loses control.

Nor does he manifest fatigue. The problem discussed at para. 11 is the first case set out to elucidate the definition of *zinā*. It is an aporia – a case of dispute, or a puzzle – in which the two sides can be clearly identified and their arguments set out dialectically: they say, we say. Para. 12 introduces the next case, which is also an aporia, a dispute between Abū Ḥanīfa and his two companions, and here too the argument is given in full, the various points of Abū Ḥanīfa's case fully differentiated and set out in a clear, formal manner. In subsequent cases Kāsānī continues to list types of intercourse that will cast light on the meaning and definition of *zinā*: intercourse with a dead body, intercourse under compulsion, intercourse in *dār al-ḥarb*, intercourse by a *ḥarbī*, and so on. The cases are familiar, their organisation in this manner, to this end, within this structure, new. For each one, he either gives a brief demonstrative reason why the case does or does not come under the heading *zinā*, or he indicates the presence of a dispute and sets out the arguments, at greater length, dialectically.

Kāsānī's work then is characterised, at the level of chapter (*kitāb al-ḥudūd*) by a strong sense of structure, combining, organising and distributing hierarchically the various parts (topoi or *mawḍiʿ*) that require to be discussed; and, at the level of individual item, or case, or norm, by a search for aporias and a display of dialectical argument. The dialectical quality is derived from Sarakhsī, though, in all cases, Kāsānī's arguments benefit from sharper, clearer expression, from refinements of argument, or new arguments, or from deletions of untidy or ineffective arguments. The organisational skill which Kāsānī deploys for a single argument is deployed at a higher level to organise and bundle the parts (*mawḍiʿ*) that constitute a topic.

The word *mawḍiʿ*, introduced by Kāsānī at para. 6 to designate the broad subject areas which seemed to him to require discussion under the general heading of *ḥudūd*, is the normal Arabic translation for Aristotle's *topos*, the subject matter of his *Topics*. We can be fairly sure that the reference is deliberate. The neatness, formality and precision that Kāsānī brings to the expression of argument may be assumed to derive in part from his knowledge of demonstration derived from study of Aristotelian logic. The dialectical format of his arguments too may be related to Aristotle's theory of dialectic and to the supposition that a student should be able to deploy proofs on both sides of a question. And finally, both the *Topics* and the *Rhetoric* offer processes of invention and division which are intended to enable a structured and organised presentation of knowledge. It should be noted, however, that Kāsānī does not introduce anything new. All the subordinate topoi that he identifies within the broad subject matter of *ḥudūd* could be derived from Sarakhsī's *Mabsūṭ*. What he has done is to divide and bundle rules and information that were provided in a less organised manner by Sarakhsī (or by some intermediate thinker). The process of dividing and bundling is not to be dismissed as merely a trick of organisation, for effective organisation gives things a place and an importance which might be missed in some less structured system. The topic, for example, identified by Kāsānī as, 'The conditions of the permissibility of *ḥudūd* being put into effect', enables him to create a space for a discussion of political authority as a necessary condition of *ḥudūd*. It is possible to detect the roots of this discussion in some of the problems discussed by Sarakhsī, but neither he (nor any subsequent writer in this context) gave it the clear, generous and structured expression of Kāsānī. It is a case where structural concern precipitates a kind of progress, a clearer and more refined articulation of something that had been only dimly present earlier in the tradition.

Kāsānī's interest in structure is obvious and it dominates his mode of organisation and expression. He had in fact acknowledged and explained this in the introduction to his work. There he noted that, though Ḥanafī scholars had produced many books on the law, none had shown a real concern for structure (*tartīb*) except his own teacher, Muḥammad b. Aḥmad al-Samarqandī (d. between 373/983–4 and 393/1002–3). Following the model of Samarqandī's work, he, Kāsānī, had produced this work and called it *Badāʾiʿ al-ṣanāʾiʿ fī tartīb al-sharāʾiʿ* (*Innovations of artifice in the organisation of the rules)*, in order to stress his concern with literary artifice (*ṣanʿa badīʿa*) and exquisite organisation (*tartīb ʿajīb wa-tarṣīf gharīb*).[36]

It is worth stressing again the conservative and literary qualities of this juristic tradition. I do not mean that we might not find, with appropriate analysis, either new rules or rules that have changed slightly as the tradition develops. But to foreground these, or to describe the system as one that accommodates itself to time and social reality, would be radically to falsify the tradition.

[36] Ibid., I, 1–2.

Kāsānī's raw material, like that of all the other writers we have discussed, is literary. He has developed it and made it his own, not by changing the norms, but by expressing the norms and their attendant arguments in a distinctive manner, one which reflects his personal concern for literary refinement. It is certain that he gave to some norms a new clarity and refinement of expression, and that he developed justificatory arguments towards levels of expression and refinement that had not existed before. But he does not, in the context of this work, seek to establish the relationship between this structure of rules and the social practices of his own time. The law is a permanent structure of concepts and arguments, requiring constantly to be explored and expressed, and independent of social reality.

4. Sarakhsī's *Mabsūṭ* is the largest of the *mabsūṭ*s discussed in these pages. This is in part a result of the qualities of the *mukhtaṣar* on which it is a commentary. Al-Ḥākim al-Marwazī produced his *Kāfī*, as far as can be easily ascertained, by studying and summarising the work known as the *Mabsūṭ* or *Aṣl* of Shaybānī, and adding to it elements either of rules or of dispute from other books of Shaybānī. Since the works of Shaybānī were massive, complex and very untidy (products of school redactions over generations), so too was al-Ḥākim's *mukhtaṣar*. His notion of a *mukhtaṣar* did not include radical reorganisation, nor radical pruning of contents; he simply followed where Shaybānī's text led, summarising, omitting formal and stylistic features, occasionally rearranging items, mostly simply restating what he found before him. Characteristically, his study of a topic of the law (e.g., *ḥudūd*) begins with some attempt at presentational coherence but is transformed rapidly into a list of norms, items and cases, revealing of course, for that was why they had been preserved in the first place, but straggling along more or less incoherently, and with greater or lesser degrees of repetition, and some contradiction, depending on the state of the original texts, or the mood and capacity of the author. Sarakhsī's *Mabsūṭ* is built on and round this material and so shares many of its qualities.

For example, it is also a characteristic of the *Mabsūṭ* that Sarakhsī will attempt some kind of generalised and coherent thinking near the beginning of a topic, but gradually revert to piecemeal discussion of individual items as these become the material he has to deal with. There is a very fine example of structured thinking at the beginning of the *Kitāb al-ṣarf*, which then becomes a long list of illustrative cases – the loci of analysis and argument. The same is true of the *Kitāb al-ḥudūd*. This begins with a flurry of definitions. 'The word *ḥadd* in language means prohibition, hence *ḥaddād* meaning gatekeeper … and *ḥadd* meaning definition … ; in Law it means a punishment, fully specified and mandatory as a right due to God, etc.' Much of what we have already seen in the tradition has its origin, or its earliest known appearance, in Sarakhsī. Sarakhsī begins the subject proper, the *ḥadd* of *zinā*, by distinguishing the two punishments; this allows a brisk identification of the main Quranic props for this *ḥadd*, the major hadith and the patterns of abrogation that subsist between them. He then identifies two areas of *ikhtilāf*: whether stoning is an established *ḥadd* and whether the penalties may be combined. Each of these permits a further exploration of relevant hadith. Sarakhsī then makes the general point that a crime requiring the *ḥadd* may be established either by testimony or by confession and introduces in that context the first words of his base text: *zinā* is alone amongst claims in that it is established only by the testimony of four witnesses.[37] This leads into a general discussion of how the qadi is to deal with the witnesses, a discussion of *iḥṣān*, a discussion of banishment as a possible addition to the punishment of stoning and, thereafter, a long sequence of if-clauses, most of them derived directly from Marwazī. It is probably the case that there are more details of rules, cases and arguments in Sarakhsī than in any text discussed so far – but considerably less order and coherence.

Sarakhsī's basic approach is the same as that of the other commentators. He gives the rule as he found it in his base text, and immediately plunges into a sequence of causes or reasons for the rule. However, he is more interested in establishing dialectic than in merely giving demonstrative arguments that justify known rules. Wherever possible, Sarakhsī relates a rule to a dispute, identifies the authorities behind the dispute and provides a sequence of arguments for and against each side of the dispute. In Aristotelian terms: he identifies aporias or puzzles, re-states them as opposing opinions or *endoxa*; and provides arguments for both sides, indicating clearly which side is to win (invariably that of the Ḥanafī tradition). In the case of Sarakhsī (as also for Aristotle) there were real dialectical games behind the textual evidence. Scholars and students engaged in public dispute in order to practice and demonstrate their facility in the manipulation of argument.

Sarakhsī's concern for dispute and dialectic is evident from his first plunge into the topic of *ḥudūd*. His first aporia relates to the *ḥadd* of stoning which is denied by the Khawārij and affirmed by the Sunnis. Then there is the question of combining the two punishments of beating and stoning. This is affirmed by the Ẓāhirīs, denied by the Ḥanafīs. The institution of four witnesses for *zinā* had led some to make the claim that the standard two witnesses were required for each of the two participants in the act.

1. But this is weak, for the testimony of two, just as it establishes the act of one person, can also establish the act of two people. We say: God loves

[37] Sarakhsī, *Mabsūṭ*, IX, 36–7; the first quotation from Marwazī, I take to be at 37, l.15.

> concealment (*sitr*) for his servants, and this he recommended, while blaming those who spread slander. It is to establish concealment that there is an increase in the number of witnesses for this crime. The Prophet indicated this when he said to Hilāl b. Umayya: 'Bring four to testify to the truth of what you say, otherwise the *ḥadd* is on your own back.' ʿUmar indicated the same when Abū Bakra, Shubul b. Maʿbad and Nāfiʿ b. al-Azraq testified before him that al-Mughīra b. Shaʿba had committed *zinā*. ʿUmar said to Nāfiʿ, the fourth witness, 'What is your testimony?' He said, 'I saw naked feet, panting breaths, and a vile thing'; or, in another transmission, 'I saw them both under one blanket, they were heaving up and down and quivering like reeds'; or, in another transmission, 'I saw a man on top, a woman below, two hennaed feet, and a man who came and went – nothing else'. And ʿUmar said, 'God is great, praise be to Him who has prevented the humiliation of one of the Prophet's Companions'. This is proof that the condition of four witnesses is intended to maintain the concealment of shame.[38]

This is proof too that Sarakhsī had a sense of humour. It illustrates his general concern to embed rules in dialectical argument. The use of Companion hadith, as here, is much less a feature of the developed tradition than in Sarakhsī (though the narrative of ʿUmar reappears in Ḥaddādī's *al-Jawhara al-nayyira*). The twin processes of presentation (accompanied by rudimentary demonstrative argument), and identification of aporia (accompanied by lengthy dialectical argument) continues.

The pattern can perhaps be seen to take on an extra subtlety in the long sequence of if-clauses which terminate the chapter. Many of these are briskly embedded in dispute as in the following examples.

2. If the witnesses all recant, they are subject to the *ḥadd* of slander, and each one is required to pay one quarter of the *diya*. This according to us, but Ibn Abī Laylā and Ḥasan [Ibn Ziyād] say they are to be killed. ...[39]
3. If he fornicates with her, forcing her, he is subject to the *ḥadd* but not the *mahr*, according to us. According to Shāfiʿī, he must pay her the *mahr*. ...[40]
4. If a man fornicates with his wife's slave girl and says, 'I thought she was legitimate to me', or with his father's or mother's slave girl under the same conditions, there is no *ḥadd*, according to us. But Zufar said. ...[41]

[38] Ibid., 37–8.
[39] Ibid., 49.
[40] Ibid., 53.
[41] Ibid., 53.

The last example will perhaps forcefully make the point that is required. While that rule had to be explained by all later writers, very few indeed formulated their explanation as an argument with Zufar. Sarakhsī's preference for dialectical presentation gave way, in the later tradition, to a general preference for demonstrative presentation. But Sarakhsī (following Marwazī) found that, where dialectical argument was not available, these if-clauses offered a further analytical pleasure: that of explaining difference, as in the following examples.

5. If one witness, after stoning has taken place, says, 'I was an unbeliever or a slave on the day I testified' [there is no *ḥadd* of slander …]. But if it becomes clear [on other grounds] that he was an unbeliever or a slave [there is a *ḥadd* of slander]. …[42]
6. If witnesses testify against a man and a woman and she claims that he forced her and the witnesses do not confirm that … the two charged are subject to the *ḥadd*. But if she says, 'He married me', and the man says, 'She is lying, it was fornication', then they are not subject to the *ḥadd*. …[43]

We have already noted a tendency in *mukhtaṣars* to group certain cases so as to mark a difference and invite elucidation of the difference. This elucidation of difference becomes a systematic part of Sarakhsī's presentation, wherever he cannot establish clear dispute.

Of course, items of dispute also turn on points of difference:

7. If a sane and mature woman summons a man who is insane or a child to fornicate with her she is not subject to the *ḥadd*, according to us. But Shāfiʿī says, she is subject to the *ḥadd*; and this is a transmission from Abū Yūsuf.
8. [They argue:] Because she is a *zāniyya* and is subject to the *ḥadd* on the basis of the text. Explanation: *Zinā* means intercourse devoid of a contract, or ownership, or the appearance thereof. These factors are all present here, except that the *ḥadd* lapses in the case of one of the parties because of absence of competence. This does not prevent its imposition in the case of the other party. It is like the case of a man who fornicates with a female who is insane or a child. This is because the act of each one of them is complete, and she, by enabling it, is a *zāniyya* just like the man, by virtue of penetration. Consider, God calls her a *zāniyya*, and mentions her first [in the Qurʿan], and one who is linked to *zinā* must suffer the *ḥadd*. Further, if an act of *zinā* were inconceivable on her part, then one who

[42] Ibid., 49.
[43] Ibid., 52.

accused her would not be subject to the *ḥadd* of slander, as happens in the case of a man whose penis has been amputated [sc. if he is accused of *zinā*, there is no *ḥadd* of slander]. Also, because she, by enabling, is fulfilling her desire, just like the man, by penetration. Once the perfectedness of the act has been established on each side, the condition of each one is considered in relation to whether they are legally competent to suffer the *ḥadd*.

9. Our proof: She enabled intercourse but with a person who did not sin nor commit a crime. So she is not subject to the *ḥadd*, just as if she had enabled intercourse with her husband. The explanation is clear: for the sin and the crime depend on divine commission and the males in this case are not subject to the divine commission. The reality is that the agent of the act is the male and the woman follows, on the evidence of conceiving the act in relation to her while she is asleep. ... And, since the act itself is not *zinā*, she is not a *zāniyya*, for the establishment of a dependant act depends on the establishment of what is necessarily prior (*thubūt al-tabʿ bi-thubūt al-aṣl*). The actions of a child and one insane are *zinā* in language, but not in law, for *zinā* in law is an act which must be abstained from because of the commission of the law, hence it is associated with sin and crime, but the acts of the children and insane are not so qualified. Hence, if *zinā* is not present in law on his part, so also on her part. The *ḥadd* is a *ḥukm sharʿī* and requires to be established in law. God called her a *zāniyya* only in the sense that she was an object of *zinā*, as in *fī ʿīshatin rāḍiyyatin* – i.e., *marḍiyya* [an active participle with a passive signification] and in *min māʾ dāfiq* – i.e., *madfūq* [ditto; and accordingly the word *zāniyya*, an active participle, meaning fornicatress, should be understood as meaning object of fornication]. Further, one who slanders a woman is subject to the *ḥadd* because he attributes to her shame and merits thereby the *ḥadd*. ... This is a subtle understanding and a fine distinction (*hādhā fiqh daqīq wa-farq ḥasan*).[44]

It is indeed a subtle understanding and a fine distinction. But perhaps not particularly convincing: the Ḥanafī position on this rule was not easy to justify. Subtle understanding and fine distinctions were, precisely, here and everywhere, what Sarakhsī searched for. But these were best discovered at points of dispute or in finely distinguished rules, and it is in the accumulation and exploration of these that Sarakhsī (helped by his base text) excels.

It is worth comparing that argument by Sarakhsī with the corresponding argument by Kāsānī, for it illustrates precisely the qualities of refinement,

[44] Ibid., 54–5.

formalisation, deletion and presentational skills that Kāsānī brought to material that had been originally articulated by Sarakhsī. It is easier to grasp and follow Kāsānī's arguments than those of Sarakhsī. On the other hand, there is a kind of suggestive, exploratory richness in Sarakhsī's text which is genuinely charming. Whether correctly or not, we feel that the arguments are in the process of being discovered and articulated, almost before our eyes.

The essential characteristics of Sarakhsī's work are sufficiently indicated by noting his search for aporias, his exploration of dispute and dialectical argument, his delight in fine distinctions and subtle understanding. His text is longer than the others we have studied. Partly a result of the nature of his base text, this can be related also to his casual style and his exploratory technique; and to his willing indulgence in detail (including, for example, much use of Companion material which was mostly disregarded by the later tradition wherever Prophetic material sufficed). His unhurried style permitted also of humour and irony. His re-telling of the story of ʿUmar and the four witnesses, above, is a case in point; but I have shown elsewhere how he developed a new rule based on a witty juristic device.

That discussion related to *zakāt*. Sarakhsī noted that the muftis of Balkh required the people to pay *zakāt* a second time, after a tax of that name had been extracted by the local governors, who neither collected nor distributed the tax according to the rules of *zakāt*. Sarakhsī devised an amusing argument to demonstrate that the tyrants were in fact deeply indebted to the Muslim community, to the point where their debts considerably exceeded their assets, and so they belonged to the category of the poor. The poor were the rightful recipients of *zakāt*, and so, in paying their tax to the tyrants, the people of Balkh could formulate the intention of distributing to the poor, and if they did so, their duty would be validly fulfilled and they did not have to pay a second time.[45]

The example can probably be classified as a *ḥīla* (a juristic device, in this case deployed with irony); but it also illustrates the generation of a new rule that had not previously been articulated in the tradition. It illustrates too a feature of juristic discussion which is almost inconceivable in Mawṣilī, Marghinānī or Kāsānī: a determined turning away from the pure structure of the law as a self-contained science, and an acknowledgement of the interface with social reality. It is important to note that this kind of material has a potential place in a *mabsūṭ*, and important to note that it is rare. It is useful of course to have confirmation that social practice – that is, in this case, the tax-collecting practice of the governors – had no consonance with the rules described and preserved in the tradition

[45] Calder, 'Exploring God's Law: Muḥammad b. Abī Sahl al-Sarakhsī on *zakāt*', in Chr.Toll and J.Skøvgaard Petersen (eds.), *Law and the Islamic World, Past and Present* (Copenhagen: Det Kongelige Danske Videnskabernes Selskab, 1995), 57–73.

(though common sense would have told us this). It is unlikely that the real social governance of sexual malpractice, in his region, was covered by Sarakhsī's discussion of *ḥudūd*, but nowhere does he make a corresponding turn towards discussion of practice. Fundamentally, as with all the other texts we have studied, his book is an effort to embed inherited rules, rules given by tradition, in a pattern of justificatory argument.

Section 3. A hermeneutical tradition

1. The *mabsūts* studied in these pages span a period of approximately 200 years (from the fifth to the seventh centuries AH/eleventh to thirteenth centuries C.E., Sarakhsī to Mawṣilī). They draw, however, directly or indirectly, on an older literary tradition, a body of texts that goes back to the formative period of Ḥanafī thought, certainly the third, perhaps the second century AH/ninth century, eighth century C.E.. The continuity and development of the tradition was not merely literary, a process of reading and writing, but also practical, a process of teaching. The interplay of literary study and teaching practice, though not easily accessible to analysis, was certainly an effective factor in determining the form and the content of juristic works.

The content of these works is remarkably stable. Each of these four *mabsūṭs* demonstrates a primary concern to locate the rules of law in a network of justificatory argument. Each of them extends the rules of law beyond the provision of a *mukhtaṣar*, and relates the extended rules to the forms and structures of established rules, either within the immediate topic, or with analogical cross-reference to other topics of the law. Each of them extends the exploration of the law to points of acknowledged dispute either within the school tradition or across the school traditions (and this in turn leads to further exploration of justificatory argument). All contain the same core of rules and a broadly similar body of extended rules; they utilise the same or similar arguments and types of argument for justificatory purposes. There is very little (though some) evidence of new rules being generated. There is even less (though again some) evidence of a concern to relate the rules given by the tradition to the social reality of the day. Even the recall and expression of dispute items is not aimed at the discovery of new possibilities but at the display of arguments that justify and confirm the authoritative tradition.

Rules, justificatory argument, *ikhtilāf* items: The content of the law is relatively stable. The expression is more clearly marked by a developmental process. The strongly dialectical tendencies evident in Sarakhsī and Kāsānī are not recovered: Later texts have a broadly demonstrational approach to the law (while retaining a modest presentation of dialectical material). Already from Sarakhsī to Kāsānī, there is evidence of concern to improve structural organisation and presentational coherence. Marghinānī's *Hidāya* shows concern for the selection of material (worked out in his preliminary *Bidāya*), for refinements of classificatory terminology, and an (unfulfilled) aspiration towards logical control of disparate material. The general movement towards greater formal perfection reaches a kind of plateau in the work of Mawṣilī. Here, the balanced integration of *mukhtaṣar* and *mabsūṭ* is not only a remarkable achievement of intellectual refinement and aesthetic form, but it articulates a coherent image of the law. There is a permanent core of concepts and rules, the contents of a *mukhtaṣar*; these are justified by a reticulation of arguments (*taʿlīl*). Rules and arguments together dominate and control the centripetal deductive movement, manifested historically in *ikhtilāf* items, and currently in exploratory argument; this last, almost imperceptibly, generates new rules which are fully consistent, logically integrated and conceptually continuous with the tradition. It is an image of the law as intellectually refined, aesthetically distanced and absolutely non-contingent with social reality.

Subsequent development was not unidirectional. The various factors and tendencies that acted upon the law were differentially developed either by different jurists in different works, or by the same jurist in a single work. The conservative, preservative, non-innovatory aspect of the law was marked in the continued production of *mukhtaṣar*s which restated the core of concepts and rules; and by increasingly careful delineation in a *mabsūṭ* of the rules which, when argument and opinion proliferated, constituted the *madhhab*. The generative, progressive aspect of the law worked either (and most characteristically) by renewed exploration of the foundational texts in search of rules that offered new hermeneutical possibilities, or by logical generation of new rules which were consistent with the established core and the established patterns of justificatory argument. The interface with reality was marked in a *mabsūṭ* only where there was a problem, and that might generate, temporarily, arguments that were complex, exploratory, insecure, polemical and strongly adversarial, reflecting local and contingent issues.[46] Subsequent works, by the internal logic of the system, or by the natural caducity of academic discourse, refined and integrated the rough tones, transforming polemic into a coherent and continuous part of the traditional structure. The aesthetic aspect of the law was marked by an increasing concern with language, manifested as commentary on words, phraseology and syntax, prompted in part by the linguistic mannerism of late *mukhtaṣars*; and by a continuing concern for skilful, concise, sharply delineated presentational and organisational technique.

[46] For an example, see Ibn Nujaym's polemical material on *kharāj* in his *al-Baḥr al-rāʾiq*; Johansen, *The Islamic Law of Tax and Rent* (London: Croom Helm, 1988).

Approximately 250 years after Nasafī produced his *Kanz al-daqā'iq*, the Egyptian (Ottoman) jurist Zayn al-Dīn b. Ibrāhīm Ibn Nujaym (d. 970/1563) produced a commentary entitled *al-Baḥr al-rā'iq* (*The scintillating sea*). It is easy to detect in this work, a large *mabsūṭ*, all the tendencies I have identified above. Ibn Nujaym identifies and justifies the core rules (essentially those presented in the *Kanz*); analyses and criticises the linguistic and syntactic forms of the earlier work; explores the proliferation of new rules and relates them either to ancient tradition or to coherent and justified argument. His notion of justificatory authority reaches out beyond the textual sources of Qur'an and sunna, and beyond the foundational texts, to include the juristic productions of the later *madhhab*. He is frequently concerned with the refinement of intellectual distinctions, less frequently with the interface with reality. His presentation of the law and its justification is predominantly a neat triumph of linguistic virtuosity, more rarely, a helter-skelter profusion of imperfectly assimilated, polemically engaged arguments. His work contained and expressed all the tendencies of the law. And he was conscious that he had surpassed the major alternative commentary to the *Kanz*.

> The *Kanz al-daqā'iq* of the imam Ḥāfiẓ al-Dīn al-Nasafī is the best *mukhtaṣar* composed in the juristic tradition of the Ḥanafī imams. They have produced a number of commentaries on it and the best of these is by Zayla'ī. However, he extended himself on disputes (*khilāfiyyāt*) and did not explicate Nasafī's linguistic expression or his conceptual signification (*lam yufaṣṣiḥ 'an manṭūqi-hi wa-mafhūmi-hi*). I have devoted myself to this work since the beginning of my career, being greatly concerned with its conceptual information (*mafhūmāt*). Hence I desired to produce a commentary which would explicate the linguistic expression and the conceptual signification of the work, and would relate to these the elaborations of *fatāwā* and commentaries, while offering also many derived rules, and refined explanations (*tafāri' kathīra wa-taḥrīrāt sharīfa*).[47]

Most writers did less than this. Possibly the most significant stylistic feature of Ibn Nujaym's work is the way in which he constructed argument and exposition by the juxtaposition of citations from earlier authorities. This is certainly a reflection of a developed theory of authority, one which integrated the great masters of the *madhhab* into the constellation of relevant authorities. But it was also a literary device which made possible the expression of subtle distinctions, refined *ikhtilāf* and the prudent (and pious) avoidance of final decision. See further Section 4.3 below.

2. In spite of the occasional irruption of the local and the contingent into works of *furū'*, the essential quality of the law as a permanent system of values, not subject to change and independent of social reality, was not in doubt. Fully

[47] Ibn Nujaym, *al-Baḥr al-rā'iq* (Cairo: al-Maṭba'a al-'Ilmiyya, 1310/1892–3), I, 1–2.

backed by a theological (Islamic) and an intellectual (Aristotelian) structure, the law was presented and understood as an abstract structure, open to intellectual refinement and aesthetic exploration. The writing jurists, drawn intermittently (and unpredictably) to the interface with reality, were drawn consistently towards the analysis and exploration of concepts and arguments, towards the discovery and expression of precision, coherence, clarity and order in a permanent and unchanging system. The various conservative/preservative qualities of the law, those which ensured that it was always the same had the paradoxical effect of ensuring that it was always and necessarily different; different, that is, from any contemporary reality. The system was built on a core of fossilised terms, rules and institutional images, which, linguistically and socially, could not fail to be, at least marginally and perhaps greatly, out of line with any given contemporary social, linguistic, practical and institutional structures. The literary world of Muslim jurisprudence preserved an insistent altereity, a quality of otherness. This might be seen as a hermeneutical advantage, even a necessary condition of achieved self-understanding within a continuous tradition. Only because of its distance, its intellectual and aesthetic self-subsistence, did the juristic system permit first adventure and escape, and then appropriation and renewed self-understanding. The hermeneutical move from the self to the other is a condition of progress. While the Muslim jurists could hardly express themselves in these terms, they acted in such a way as to preserve a structural otherness in the law, while insisting on its radical relevance. That relevance could not possibly be the relevance of a template, a simple blueprint for action, it had to be the relevance of recovered meaning, recovered through exploration, understanding, interpretation and refinement of literary means; all of this being an independent activity necessarily prior to application.

Section 4. The problem of social reality

0. If it is the case that the relationship of the law to reality must, necessarily, to some degree and in some way, be oblique, it is also the case that the nature of the obliquity must vary according to the topic and expression of the law, and the nature and conditions of social reality. In the case of *ḥudūd*, as expressed in the Ḥanafī tradition, the law was so written as to give systematic priority to the principle of evasion. According to C. Imber, the Ḥanafī version of the law 'consciously and explicitly renders conviction [to a *ḥadd* penalty] impossible.'[48] That is possibly an exaggeration, but it is reasonable to assert that a certain degree of

[48] Colin Imber, 'Zinā in Ottoman Law,' in Colin Imber, *Studies in Ottoman History and Law* (Istanbul: Isis Press, 1996), 176.

hermeneutical dexterity could ensure that the *ḥadd* penalties need never take place. For all practical purposes, the management of sexual misconduct is transferred to the category of *taʿzīr*, and thereby to human discretion, and to local and contingent custom and practice. But local custom (positive law?) is not a part of divine law, and therefore (in spite of rare and tantalising glimpses) has no place in the assessment of the *sharīʿa*. The absolute independence of juristic evaluation and actual practice may be illustrated, for the topic of *ḥudūd*, on consideration of one more work of *furūʿ* and the very different concerns of the Ottoman Criminal Code of 1540.

1. The *Fatāwā* of al-Ḥasan b. Manṣūr al-Uzjandī, known as Qāḍīkhān (d. 592/1196, one year before Marghinānī) is not a *mabsūṭ* (in the terms described above), for it contains no justificatory argument for its rules, nor is it a *mukhtaṣar*, for it is not aimed at presenting the core of reliable rules that constitute the *madhhab*. It is rather an extended work of rules, without justificatory argument. In his introduction Qāḍīkhān indicates that he has mentioned in this work cases which happen frequently and for which there is a pressing need, cases that are a focus of events in the community, cases that represent the (lower) limits of the desires of the jurists and scholars (*yaqtaṣiru ʿalay-hā raghabāt al-fuqahāʿ wa-ʾl-aʿimma*). In spite of that practical sounding intention, he has derived his materials from literary sources, namely the early authorities, or the later ones. Where the later scholars have developed several opinions he has restricted himself to one or two. He has preferred to begin with what is more clear, and to open his discussions with what is more widely acknowledged, in response to the needs of students and aspirants (*ṭālibīn, rāghibīn*).[49] It is clear from all this that Qāḍīkhān intended to be, in some sense, practical. His immediate audience consisted of learners, and it is reasonable to ask what they were learning for. The first section of his work (situated immediately after these introductory remarks) relates to muftis and their task, so the answer perhaps is that he was aiming his work at students who would go on to become muftis in the community. While some muftis might be high-ranking jurists, most were not, and many would be very minor local and provincial functionaries. The tone of Qāḍīkhān's introduction suggests that he was not aiming at a sophisticated audience, nor aiming at the creation of sophistication. Here was a very basic account of the rules of the *madhhab*, where the principles of selection related to community need, and students' desires, and the highest principle of order was to bring to the fore what was clear and widely acknowledged.

In the chapter on *ḥudūd*, these general ambitions resolved themselves into the following introductory passage.

[49] Qāḍīkhān, *Fatāwā*, in margin of *al-Fatāwā al-hindiyya* (Bulaq: al-Maṭbaʿa al-Kubrā al-Amīriyya, 1310/1892–3), I, 1–2.

1. There are five *ḥudūd*: fornication, drinking, slander, theft, and highway robbery. As to fornication, it means inserting the penis in the front part of a strange woman such that it leads directly to an illegal act, and the *ḥadd* becomes mandatory. If it is possible to establish a *shubha*, it is not mandatory. There are three types of *shubha*: 1. that which prevents the *ḥadd* even if he says, 'I knew she was *ḥarām* to me'; 2. that which does not prevent the *ḥadd* even if he says, 'I thought she was permitted to me'; 3. that which prevents the *ḥadd* if he says, 'I thought she was permitted to me', but it remains mandatory if he says, 'I thought she was *ḥarām* to me.'[50]

This typology of *shubha*s serves to organise the bulk of the material for this chapter. Under type one, Qāḍīkhān identifies more than 75 categories or incidents that do not deserve the *ḥadd* even if the perpetrator admits that he knows his act is *ḥarām*. Under types two and three, he identifies less than ten categories and incidents. The chapter finishes with a discussion of *iḥṣān* and the procedure for carrying out the penalties. It is clear where the focus of interest lies: Qāḍīkhān wants to identify in detail the situations in which the *ḥadd* penalties may not be put into effect. It is impossible to avoid the conclusion that Qāḍīkhān's practical sense of what was required related directly to preventing his audience from imagining that all (or even any) acts of illicit sexual intercourse required the *ḥadd* penalty. The vast majority of identified cases were not open to the *ḥadd* penalty. They were presumably open to *taʿzīr*. Qāḍīkhān tells us very little about this phenomenon, though it is the only practical category available to the community for the control of illicit sexual acts:

2. The beating of *taʿzīr* is to be distributed across the limbs [sc. so as not to cause severe bruising or wounding such as would result from repeated beating on one limb]. It should not reach forty lashes, according to Abū Ḥanīfa. A slave-owner may not impose *taʿzīr* on his slaves, male or female, according to us.[51]

Here are some of the categories and cases, from Qāḍīkhān's first and longest list, those who, even if they know that they are committing a prohibited act are not liable to the *ḥadd*. I give the first four, a group of four from the middle, and the last four. The total of categories and cases is more than seventy-five, so this is a very small sample.

3. A man fornicates with the slave-girl of his son, or his son's son, or a descendant, he is not subject to the *ḥadd* even if he says, 'I knew she was not permitted to me.'

[50] Qāḍīkhān, *Fatāwā*, III, 467.

[51] Ibid., 474.

4. A man divorces his wife irrevocably in allusive language, then has intercourse with her during the *ʿidda*, he is not subject to the *ḥadd* even if he says, 'I knew she was prohibited to me.'
5. Likewise if he puts his wife's affair into her own hand, and she chooses freedom, and he then has intercourse with her in the *ʿidda*, the *ḥadd* is not mandatory, even if he says, 'I knew she was prohibited.'
6. Likewise if his wife becomes apostate and so becomes prohibited to him,[52] or if she becomes prohibited because he has sexual intercourse with her mother, or her daughter, or because she submits willingly to her husband's son,[53] and he then has intercourse with her, there is no *ḥadd* even if he says, 'I knew she was prohibited to me.'
7. A man says, 'I committed fornication with this woman', and the woman denies the fornication; he is not subject to the *ḥadd* according to Abū Hanīfa, but his two companions say he is.
8. A woman confesses to *zinā*, saying, 'I committed fornication with this man', and the man denies it; neither is subject to the *ḥadd* according to Abū Hanīfa, but his two companions say, the woman is subject to the *ḥadd*.
9. A man confesses, saying, 'I committed fornication with this woman', and she says, 'No, he married me'; he is not subject to the *ḥadd* and he must pay her the *mahr*.
10. Likewise if she confesses four times to fornication, on different occasions, and the man says, 'But I married her'; there is no *ḥadd* penalty, and he must pay her the *mahr*. …
11. If the witnesses testify against a man, saying that he had intercourse with this woman, or slept with her, or had relations with her [*waṭiʿa*; *jāmaʿa*; *bāḍaʿa*; the words permit of a (remote) construal of something less than sexual intercourse], failing to use the word *zinā*, their evidence is not accepted.
12. Four testify against a man, that he said, 'I do not have ownership of this slave-girl', and then he claims before the qadi that he acquired her through gift or sale, his word is accepted, and he is not subject to the *ḥadd*.
13. A group testify against a man, and then the man, after the third and the fourth have testified, confesses to his own crime; he is not subject to the

[52] Apostasy, by one or both partners, automatically entails annulment of a marriage; cf. Colin Imber, 'Involuntary Annulment of Marriage and its Solutions in Ottoman Law', in Colin Imber, *Studies*, 220–7.

[53] All of these acts are forbidden, in themselves, but they have the effect of bringing his wife into a relationship which prohibits marriage and sexual intercourse; hence this act of intercourse with his wife becomes a prohibited action.

ḥadd unless he confesses four times on four occasions according to us. If he confesses on different occasions he is subject to the *ḥadd* on the basis of his confession.

14. If four testify against a man, and they are immoral, their witness is not accepted, but they are not subject to the *ḥadd* [of slander]. If they are blind, or slaves, or have been subject to the *ḥadd* of slander, the witnesses are subject to the *ḥadd*.

Most of these have been seen before. Only numbers 6, 7, 8 and 12 are completely new. (There are a considerable number of new items in Qāḍīkhān's list, some of extreme complexity, but it would serve no purpose to itemise them all.) It is obvious that there has been a rough grouping of cases: nos. 3–6 focus on relationships between the parties; nos. 7–10 on confession; and nos. 11–14 on testimony. It is possible that there has been some attempt, within these rough groupings, to bring the most clear or the most acknowledged to the beginning but it is not obvious. It is reasonable to suppose that Qāḍīkhān derived all of his cases from the study of books; that is what he claimed and there is no counter-evidence. In fact, his note-taking and organisation can be criticised, for a number of cases are recorded twice.

15. Four testify against a man that he committed fornication with a woman they do not know, and subsequently say, 'With so-and-so'; the man is not subject to the *ḥadd*, nor the witnesses, nor the woman.[54]
16. Four testify against a man that he committed fornication with a woman, saying, 'We do not know her', and subsequently say, 'With so-and-so'; the man is not subject to the *ḥadd*, nor the witnesses.[55]
17. Four testify against a man, and the man confesses to fornication, after their testimony; he then denies it and does not confess four times; he is not subject to the *ḥadd*.[56] Cf. no. 13 above.

There is a very slight variation in the wording of 15 and 16, a slightly greater variation between 17 and 13. It is most likely that Qāḍīkhān copied these cases from different works and incorporated them at a suitable place in his list, without noticing the repetition. He may have copied them twice from the same work.

The effort behind Qāḍīkhān's text is obvious and is in line with the tendency of all the texts studied here: to evade the *ḥadd* penalty by *shubuhāt*. But, once the *ḥadd* has been evaded, there is no corresponding effort to provide guidance on what to do. Even Qāḍīkhān (who declares a practical aim and has been observed

[54] Qāḍīkhān, *Fatāwā*, III, 470, ll. 34–5.
[55] Ibid., 471, ll. 36–7.
[56] Ibid., 470, ll. 11–15.

sometimes to reflect local reality) provides no information about and no comment on local practice.

2. The Ottoman Criminal Code of ca. 1540 has been edited, translated and commented on by Uriel Heyd (ed. V. L. Ménage).[57] The section on fornication and related offences shows that the Ottoman treatment of sexual malpractice was based on a standard system of fines, conjoined with imprisonment, strokes and more serious physical penalties (including castration for abduction). Aside from refinements in the system of fines, the laws distinguish a number of offences that are not distinguished in *fiqh*: failure to guard a wife, attempted fornication, abduction, consenting to and abetting abduction, public indiscretion, sexual molestation including the infliction of indignity, procuring and a number of other offences which could hardly be absent from any moderately complex society. The requirements of evidence in the Code were a very considerable amelioration of the *shar'ī* requirements for the *ḥadd* penalties.

Both Heyd and, to a lesser degree, Imber consider that the Code is in some degree of conflict with *sharī'a*. But that need not be the case. The Code should probably be read as being effective only in cases where the statutory *ḥadd* penalties cannot be applied (indeed glosses to that effect have been incorporated into the manuscripts of the Code), and that means the vast majority, or even all possible, cases. More happily, Imber has shown that there is a consistent analogical relationship between the concepts and structures of the juristic texts and the rules of the Code. The juristic distinctions between *muḥṣan* and non-*muḥṣan*, Muslim and non-Muslim, free and non-free, for example, are analogically applied to the standard system of fines. A non-juristic, but not unreasonable, distinction between the rich, the poor and the intermediate is also present.[58] If financial exactions (fines) are admitted as a type of *ta'zīr*, then it is possible to defend the Code as fully compatible with the *sharī'a*; (just as it is possible to offer criticism and refinement of the Code in the light of the *sharī'a*; indeed a completely different system could be devised which would equally well be compatible with the *sharī'a*).[59] Imber's conclusion is that 'the

[57] Uriel Heyd (ed. V.L. Ménage), *Studies in Old Ottoman Criminal Law* (Oxford: Clarendon Press, 1973). For text and translation of the Code, see pp. 54–131.

[58] This, too, can be see as an analogical extension of a *shar'ī* rule; the payment of *jizya*, the poll tax, by non-Muslims is subject to this three-fold distinction.

[59] Article 23 of the Code states that if a person has sexual intercourse with his son's female slave or his divorced wife during her *'idda*, he shall not be subject to anything, not even *ta'zīr*. It is an odd rule, recalling some aspects of the *sharī'a*, but in an imperfect manner. The question whether it can be defended as a valid rule, not inconsistent with the *sharī'a*, depends not simply on discovering whether it is accepted within the Ḥanafī tradition, but whether there is an element of *ikhtilāf* whereby it can be justified, since, theoretically, the governor can exploit elements of *ikhtilāf* in devising a practical system.

Holy Law, modified through custom and expediency, is ... the basis of the secular law'. I would rather say that the secular law, deriving from community practice and governmental decree, has been shaped and refined (no doubt over generations) by reference to *sharīʿa*, and is open to ongoing criticism, and refinement.[60]

No Ḥanafī jurist of the sixteenth century or later, not even Ibn ʿĀbidīn, who not infrequently articulates or illustrates the interface with social reality or governmental practice, offers any (direct) comment on this or any other parallel real system of law. Only with knowledge of a real system is it possible to detect and determine *sharʿī* influence; with knowledge only of the juristic tradition, it is impossible to infer anything about the real system. (*Mutatis mutandis*, this is probably true of all topics of the law.)

3. I said above that if financial exactions are admitted as a type of *taʿzīr*, then it is possible to defend the Ottoman Code as compatible with the *sharīʿa*. Ibn Nujaym, writing in Egypt at a time when the Code was presumably still effective in Anatolia, and when some similar practice existed in Egypt, raised the issue in no more than half a dozen lines. He identified a view of Abū Yūsuf that permitted the political authority to make financial exactions a type of *taʿzīr*, then cited a couple of authorities who (possibly) strengthened and a couple who undermined that position. He was in no doubt that the *madhhab* did not permit fines, but that could not, in this case, be the end of the matter, for if the minority view of Abū Yūsuf could be clearly established, then the government, though not adhering to the *madhhab*, were working within an area of acknowledged *ikhtilāf*. Ibn ʿĀbidīn (some 250 years later) followed the same technique as Ibn Nujaym, citing and juxtaposing authorities in search of the *madhhab*.

1. [Ibn Humām] said in the *Fatḥ*: From Abū Yūsuf, *taʿzīr* by financial exaction is permitted to the sultan [political authority]; but from the other two, and from the other imams, It is not permissible.
2. Likewise in the *Miʿrāj*, where the apparent meaning is that it is a weak transmission from Abū Yūsuf.
3. In the *Shurunbulāliyya*, fatwas may not be given to this effect because it empowers the tyrants to take the property of the people and exploit it for themselves.
4. Likewise in the *Sharḥ al-wahbāniyya* from Ibn Wahbān.
5. In the *Baḥr* [of Ibn Nujaym]: i. In the *Bazzāziyya*, he states: the meaning of *taʿzīr* by financial exaction, conceding the view that it is permitted, is that the ruler seizes a portion of [the criminal's] property temporarily, in

[60] Imber comes much closer to the view expressed here in his later assessment of the relationship between *sharīʿa* and *qānūn*; Imber, *Ebuʿs- Suʿud*, 24–62.

order to deter, and then returns it to him. It does not mean that the ruler takes it for himself or for the treasury, as is imagined by tyrannous rulers (*ka-mā yatawahhamu-hu al-ẓalama*), for it is not permitted to a Muslim to take the property of another without a *sharʿī* cause. ii. In the *Mujtabā*, he did not mention the manner of taking; in my view he should take it, and hold it, and when he despairs of the repentance of the criminal, he should spend it as he sees fit. iii. In the *Sharḥ al-āthār*, *taʿzīr* by financial exaction existed in the beginning of Islam, but was abrogated. In sum, the *madhab* is that there is no *taʿzīr* by financial exaction.[61]

Formally, that is a characteristic piece of late Ḥanafī juristic discourse that relates to an uncertain item of the law. It is built up entirely out of citations. These are not random; both selection and organisation suggest a position, and articulate a commitment to the law as tradition and continuity. Ibn ʿĀbidīn has chosen his first citation to make the point that there exists a transmission from Abū Yūsuf which clearly states the case for financial exactions as a potential resource for the government in *taʿzīr*. It is, however, a view opposed by the other two Ḥanafī and all the other major authority figures. The existence of Abū Yūsuf's view is confirmed in the *Miʿrāj*, the *Shurunbulāliyya* and the *Sharḥ al-wahbāniyya*, though characterised as weak (at 2) and removed from the area of fatwa (at 3).[62] The citation from Ibn Nujaym omits the marginally more positive citations which Ibn Nujaym had given from the *Ẓahīriyya* and the *Khulāṣa*.[63] The citations demonstrate the gradual emergence of efforts at *taʿlīl*, the discovery and expression of reasons for the law. Juxtaposed thus, they are a prompt to reflection, a balanced assessment of tradition, and, perhaps, a principled evasion of final decision. The whole passage represents juristic discussion of a view that emerged in the earliest texts, and is consistent with the general principle that the law is a self-subsistent, non-contingent system, growing through and out of tradition and without explicit reference to contemporary reality. It is extremely negative in respect of governmental use of fines, though whether it has absolutely made these a matter

[61] Ibn ʿĀbidīn, *Radd al-muḥtār* (Beirut: Dār al-Fikr, 1979), IV, 61.

[62] Ibn ʿĀbidīn is citing a series of works in the Ḥanafī canon: Ibn Humām (d. 861/1457), *Fatḥ al-qadīr*, a commentary on the *Hidāya* of al-Marghinānī; Qiwām al-Dīn al-Kākī (d. 749/1348), *Miʿrāj al-dirāya*, a commentary on the *Hidāya*; al-Shurunbulālī (d. 1069/1658), *Ghunya dhawi al-ahkām fī bughya durar al-aḥkām*, a commentary on the *Durar al-aḥkām* of Molla Khosraw; Ibn Wahbān (d. 768/1306), *ʿIqd al-qalāʾid*, a commentary on *Qayd al-sharāʾid* by the same author; Ibn Nujaym (d. 970/1563), *al-Baḥr al-rāʾiq*; Ibn Bazzāz (d. 817/1414), *al-Fatāwā al-bazzāziyya*; Mukhtār al-Zāhidī (d. 658/1260), *Mujtabā*, a commentary on *al-Matn* of al-Qudūrī; al-Ṭaḥāwī (d. 321/933), *Sharḥ maʿānī al-āthār*.

[63] The references are to Ẓahīr al-Dīn AbūBakr (d. 619/1222), *al-Fatāwā al-ẓahīriyya*, and Iftikhār al-Dīn al-Bukhārī (d. 542/1147), *Khulāsat al-fatāwā*.

of tyranny (which was clearly the aim of the *Bazzāziyya*), or left them a highly disliked but potential area of *ikhtilāf* is a matter of debate. Certainly, there has been no attempt to register or comment on the actual practice of government in this area of secular law.

Section 5. Conclusions

In Sections 1 and 2 of this chapter, I have offered a preliminary assessment of the forms and characteristics of *mukhtaṣars* and *mabsūṭ*s, together with an indication of how they developed through time. In making that assessment, I have stressed that these literary types draw on and constitute an independent and self-referential literary tradition: it is, not exclusively or absolutely but primarily and fundamentally, a representation of permanent and unchanging terms, norms and arguments. It is in the selection and omission of details, the management and manipulation of linguistic means, and in the conscious adoption of a style (or styles) that particular jurists make their particular and unique contribution to the tradition. The passage of time brought increased awareness of this essentially conservative task, with the result that the most characteristic features of development through time are those that reflect, not an interest in new rules, but a self-reflective interest in the tradition itself and in the modes of expressing inherited rules. In the *mukhtaṣar* tradition, one can point to mannerism, the self-conscious foregrounding of linguistic technique as the means to hold and express the ever-weightier burden of reflections on the *madhhab*. In the *mabsūṭ* tradition, one notes the use of citations and their juxtaposition, as a means to discover and express the *madhhab*, but also as a means to refrain from final decision, to express the difficulty of or failure to discover final decisions, or to acknowledge the subtle indeterminacies of juristic exploration. One notes also an increasing concern with the mechanics of language, so that discourse is proportionately less and less about the law, more and more about the expression of the law and the adequacy of particular linguistic forms to articulate what can be or has been discovered in the *madhhab*. It is necessary to stress that I make these observations not with the intention of suggesting that this literature was utterly disengaged from social reality. That is not the case: The contents of the law were always potentially a judgement of reality and the contents of a *mabsūṭ* at least could include direct expression of the struggle to accommodate the tradition to particular realities. But the fundamental trajectory of the literary tradition seems best expressed in terms of the type that I have chosen. Section 3.1 offers further reflections on this theme, and 3.2 suggests one (amongst several) possible ways of expressing the hermeneutical significance of the tradition, based on the idea that an understanding of something radically other is a necessary prelude to the development of self-understanding.

That Islamic law-books had an impractical or idealistic bias was noticed, usually with distaste, by Western scholars up to and including Joseph Schacht. A more recent scholarly approach, notably associated with Wael B. Hallaq, has tried to defend Islamic law by presenting it as practical and efficient.[64] Characteristic of this tendency, and chosen more or less at random, is the following.

> A legal system is not a rigid entity, but rather fluctuates and evolves with changing circumstances and times. One may say that to the extent that law influences and shapes reality, it is itself influenced by and adapts to social practice. This understanding of the nature and function of the law was common among Muslim jurists. …[65]

This is not untrue and may be merely common sense. But, as a way of characterising the complex and varied particularities of 'Islamic law', it lacks discrimination. What, in an Islamic context, could be the referent of 'a legal system' or even 'law'? It does not seem possible to make that kind of assertion either of *sharīʿa* or *fiqh*; but nor can the writer be assumed to be talking merely about the actual practice of this or that Muslim community at a particular place and time. In Section 4 of this chapter I have approached this problem by noting that neither, on the one hand, does a practical-seeming work of *fiqh* tell us about practice (4.1), nor does an authoritative government codification of practice tell us about God's law (4.2). That, I think, is an essential conclusion: The relationship between the law (as expressed in works of *fiqh*) and reality is always oblique and unpredictable, and it varies across the different topics of the law. (See also Chapter 3, Section 3.)

In Section 4.1, the work known as the *Fatāwā* of Qāḍīkhān was found to resist easy assimilation to the literary types of *mukhtaṣar* and *mabsūṭ*. It is tempting to think that its characteristic feature is its 'practical' aspect and that this is reflected in the use of the word *fatāwā* to describe its contents. In fact, in the next chapter, we shall discover that this literary type is not restricted to the Ḥanafī tradition: there are works with the same formal features which occur also in the Shāfiʿī (and presumably in other) traditions, and they are, without doubt, works of *furūʿ al-fiqh*, to be assimilated to the literary type of the *mabsūṭ*. The use of the term *fatāwā* in the titles of a lengthy sequence of works within the Ḥanafī tradition should not delude us into thinking that this type of literature is closer

[64] Wael B. Hallaq, 'From *Fatwās* to *Furūʿ*: Growth and change in Islamic substantive law', *Islamic Law and Society*, 4;2 (1997): 131–55.

[65] Gideon Libson, 'On the development of custom as a source of law in Islamic law', *Islamic Law and Society*, 1;1 (1994): 131.

to the literary form of the fatwa, or the collection of fatwas. This is not the case. They are works of *furūʿ al-fiqh*, and the later works of the type – for example, the *Fatāwā Hindiyya* – have the literary characteristics of late *mabsuṭ*s (e.g., composition by juxtaposition of citations from earlier authorities) while lacking any noticeably 'practical' aspect.

The general tendency of these conclusions will be tested and elaborated in the following chapter, which offers a different sondage, in a different juristic school.

2

Nawawī and the Typologies of *Fiqh* Writing

Introduction

For the history of Shāfiʿī *fiqh*, the works of Yaḥyā b. Sharaf *Muḥyī* al-Dīn al-Nawawī (631–76/1233–77) offer a unique point of convergence, for he analysed and summarised all that came before, and his work was the starting point for all that came after. He was a contemporary of Mawṣilī, the most formal and classical of the Ḥanafī authors studied in the previous chapter. His academic career was spent in Damascus, during the early Mamluk period. He was trained at various madrasas, and became a teacher, associated in particular with the Dār al-Ḥadīth al-Ashrafiyya in Damascus. He died at the age of 44, having produced a large corpus of academic works of which the most important for the history of *fiqh* are the *Majmūʿ* (a commentary on the *Muhadhdhab* of Abū Is*ḥ*āq Ibrāhīm b. ʿAlī al-Shīrāzī, d. 476/1083), the *Rawḍa* (a summary, with additions, of the *Sharḥ al-Wajīz* of Abūʾl-Qāsim ʿAbd al-Karīm b. Muḥammad al-Rāfiʿī, d. 623/1227?), the *Minhāj al-Ṭālibīn* (a *mukhtaṣar*, based on an earlier *mukhtaṣar* by al-Rāfiʿī), and the commentary on the *Saḥīḥ* of Muslim. Each of these will be discussed in this chapter, in Sections 1, 2, 3 and 4, respectively. His scholarship, conforming to the patterns of the time, had a broader range than just *fiqh*: Subkī said that he was skilled in a variety of sciences, including *fiqh*, hadith, biographies, language and *taṣawwuf*.[1] The accounts of his life stress his asceticism, his association with miracles and his confrontations with the Mamluk Sultan al-Malik al-Ẓāhir Baybars.[2]

[1] Subkī, *Ṭabaqāt* (Cairo: ʿĪsā al-Bābī al-Ḥalabī, 1971), VIII, 395.

[2] For more on Nawawī's biography, see the French edition of the *Arbaʿīn*. Nawawī (edited and annotated by Mohammed Tahar), *Les Quarante Hadiths* (Paris: Deux Océans, 1980).

Section 1. The *Majmūʿ Sharḥ* al-Muhadhdhab

1. In the introduction to the *Majmūʿ*, Nawawī gave a brief history of *fiqh*. Mankind had been created for worship (*ʿibāda*), for the work of the next world and for renunciation of this world (*al-iʿrāḍ ʿan al-dunyā bi-ʾl-zahada*). The highest of tasks available to the righteous (after knowledge of God and performance of prescribed duties) was the clarification of valid forms of acts of worship (or ritual, *tabyīn mā kāna musaḥḥaḥan min al-ʿibādāt*). This task had been carried out for centuries in books of *fiqh*. The *ʿulamāʾ* had multiplied the composition of such works, in the forms of *mukhtaṣar* and *mabsūṭ*, and had stored in them their studies, investigations and precious conceits (*al-mabāḥith wa-ʾl-tahqīqāt wa-ʾl-nafāʾis al-jalīlāt*), thereby leaving succeeding generations with clear and precise information. Within the Shāfiʿī *madhhab*, the most famous and the most studied of earlier works were the *Muhadhdhab* of al-Shīrāzī and the *Wasīṭ* of Ghazālī, works which had become the focus of study and teaching in all regions and cities. Therefore, there was a pressing need for commentaries on these works. For they contained, amongst all their benefits, many topics that had been denied and rejected by the learned, for which, in some cases, there were clear replies, in other cases not; and they contained hadith, words, named transmitters, distinctions, problems, ambiguities and principles that required investigation and explanation. Hence Nawawī had decided to write a commentary on both works, and offered here his commentary on the *Muhadhdhab* of Shīrāzī.[3]

In fact, Nawawī did not complete the *Majmūʿ*, and left only fragments of his commentary on the *Wasīṭ*. The composition of books of this kind depended on the long-term accumulation of notes, was probably associated with teaching, and required constant revision and editorial effort. Even while writing the introduction to the *Majmūʿ*, Nawawī referred to another of his major works of *fiqh*, the *Rawḍa*. But the latter was not then a completed work, for it was eventually to contain summarised versions of material that appeared in the *Majmūʿ*. These references across the two works indicate that both works were works-in-progress; though the *Majmūʿ* was the primary and the more ambitious work. But the ambition had to be curbed. Nawawī records that he had adopted for the earliest chapters such an expansive style that he had filled three fat volumes when he reached the end of the chapter on menstruation (i.e., still within the topic of purity, the *kitāb al-ṭahāra*, which is the first in a work of *fiqh*). Thereafter he adopted an intermediate style, avoiding excessive length and extreme brevity. Nevertheless, it was an immense work, and he claimed for it a proportionate stature: It was not merely a commentary on the *Muhadhdhab* but a commentary

[3] Nawawī, *Majmūʿ* (Cairo: Maṭbaʿa al-ʿĀṣima, 1966), I, 5–7.

on the *madhhab*, in fact a commentary on all *madhhabs*, on hadith, language, history and biographies.[4]

2. The *Muhadhdhab* was written by Shīrāzī, who died in 476/1083. He was a contemporary (probably slightly older) of Sarakhsī (who worked mostly in Transoxania), and an older contemporary and colleague of Ghazālī. The two Shāfiʿī scholars flourished under the Saljuqs, and benefited from the patronage of the Saljuq minister Niẓām al-Mulk.[5] Their works demonstrate a degree of formal development, a commitment to structure and organisation, that marks an advance on Ḥanafī works of the same period. The formal qualities of Shīrāzī's work (much more akin to the formality of Marghinānī or even of Mawṣilī – respectively one and two centuries later – than to the rambling, if penetrating, genius of Sarakhsī) are marked in the following passage. This is taken from the *kitāb al-zakāt*. It is a complete chapter devoted to the question of how to distribute *zakāt* (or *ṣadaqāt*, the terms are synonymous in works of *fiqh*).

Chapter: On the distribution of alms (*ṣadaqāt*).

1. i. It is permissible for the owner of wealth to distribute *zakāt* on 'hidden' goods by himself. Hidden goods are gold, silver, trade goods and treasure trove. This is based on the hadith from ʿUthmān, that he said in the month of Muḥarram, 'This is the month of your *zakāt*, so he who has a debt, let him pay his debt, then let him pay *zakāt* on the remainder of his wealth.'
   ii. It is permissible for him to appoint an agent to distribute on his behalf. This is because *zakāt* is a claim on wealth, and it is permissible to appoint an agent to execute it, as with debts between men.
   iii. It is permissible that he pay his *zakāt* to the Imam. This is because the Imam is the representative of the poor. His status is like that of a guardian to an orphan.
2. On the question which is the best mode of conduct, there are three views:
   i. The best mode of conduct is that the owner should distribute his *zakāt* by himself. This is the apparent meaning of the text [*naṣṣ*, a reference to Shāfiʿī's words as preserved in the *Mukhtaṣar* of Muzanī[6]]; and he is secure in respect of his own paying, but not secure in respect of anyone else paying.

[4] Ibid., I, 12.

[5] For a general history of the Shāfiʿī and Ḥanafī *madhhabs* in Iran and Transoxania, see Wilferd Madelung, *Religious Trends in Early Islam* (Albany, NY: Bibliotheca Persica, 1988), 26–38.

[6] I would be inclined to read the word *naṣṣ* here as referring to the hadith from ʿUthmān, given at para. 1(i), which does indeed point in the direction required. I have given the alternative because it is preferred by Nawawī, who presumably knew better how to read and understand this terminology.

ii. The best mode of conduct is that he should pay the Imam, whether the Imam is just or unjust. This is because of what is related concerning Mughīra b. Sha'ba. He said to a client of his, who had the stewardship of his property in Ṭā'if, 'What do you do about alms (*ṣadaqa*) on my property?' The client replied, 'Some of it I distribute directly as alms, and some of it I give to the authorities (*sulṭān*).' Mughīra asked what he knew about the latter portion. The client explained: 'They buy land and marry women with it'. Mughīra said, 'Pay it to them; for the Prophet of God commanded us to pay them.' Also because the Imam is more knowledgeable about the poor and the extent of their need.

iii. Amongst our companions there are some who say that if the Imam is just, payment to him is the best mode of conduct; but if he his unjust, then distribution by the owner of wealth is best. This is because of the Prophet's words, 'He who asks for it as it should be, let him be given it; he who demands more than he should, let him not be given it.' Also because the donor is secure in paying it to a just Imam, but is not secure in paying it to an unjust Imam, for the latter may spend it on his own desires.

3. As for 'manifest' goods [as opposed to 'hidden' goods], these are animals, cereals, fruits, minerals etc. There are two views on the distribution of *zakāt* on these goods:

i. Shāfi'ī said in his old view, 'It is obligatory to pay it to the Imam; and if the owner distributes it himself, he is subject to liability.' This is based on the Quranic verse, 'Take from their wealth *ṣadaqa* that you might purify and cleanse them' [Q9.103]. Also because this is property in which the Imam has the right of demand, with the consequence that payment to him is obligatory, as with *kharāj* and *jizya*.

ii. In his new view, Shāfi'ī said, 'It is permissible for the owner to distribute the *zakāt* on manifest goods himself. This is because it is *zakāt* and the owner of wealth may distribute it himself, as with "hidden" goods.'[7]

This is organised very neatly into three paragraphs, the first two dealing with hidden goods, the third with manifest goods. Para. 1 offers three permitted modes of distribution, para. 2 three preferred modes and para. 3 two views on manifest goods. Each of my numbered items (1.i, 1.ii, 2.i, 2.ii, etc.) consists of a rule and a reason or reasons for the rule. There is obviously a *mukhtaṣar* tradition behind this (giving order and structure to the rules), but the technique

7 Shīrāzī, *Muhadhdhab*, Beirut: Dār al-Ma'rifa (1959), I, 175; also in Nawawī, *Majmū* (Cairo: Maṭba'a al-Imām, 1969), VI, 161.

corresponds precisely to that identified in the previous chapter as characteristic of the genre of *mabsūṭs*. The most important elements of the technique are the provision of justificatory argument and the exploration of dispute. Both of paras. 2 and 3 are built on an exploration of dispute.

The passage is built on distinctions. Fundamental is the primary distinction between two types of wealth. Manifest goods are those that are open to inspection (and possibly in need of protection) by the governor. Hidden goods are those that are (at least theoretically) not so accessible. The first paragraph (dealing with hidden goods only) identifies and distinguishes four principals: the owner, the owner's agent, the recipient, the governor (who is conceived of as representative of the recipients/the poor). This paragraph relates to what is permitted, and contrasts with para. 2, which is concerned with what is best. Exploration of what is permitted is fully and logically worked out: Distribution can be from the owner to the recipient (1.i), from the owner to his agent (1.ii), and from the owner to the governor (1.iii). These are all permitted and there is no other logical possibility, though the analysis leaves one obvious logical space (noted and filled by Nawawī in his commentary), namely the question of distribution from the agent (either directly to the recipient or to the governor). Para. 2 asks what is the best mode of conduct, and identifies three possibilities: The owner pays the recipient directly, he pays the governor whether just or unjust, he pays the governor only if just. They cannot of course all be best. Shīrāzī is here reporting what has emerged in the tradition. The result is still an exploration of logical space and, within the limitations of the question, it is a complete exploration. There is, again, an obvious logical gap: Is it better to pay by oneself or through an agent? The gap was noted and the answer articulated later by Nawawī.

The three 'best' modes of conduct can be interpreted as representing differential stress on different aspects of the ritual of *zakāt*. Mode i stresses the right of the donor to carry out his own ritual duty; mode ii stresses the right of the governor to mediate this duty (irrespective of his justice); and mode iii stresses the right of the recipients, which is only fully acknowledged when there is a just imam. The passage, in fact, has an exploratory, philosophical, quality: It identifies and acknowledges the various tensions that emerge when the concept of *zakāt* is analysed intellectually. There is, of course, as a result of this analysis, a consequence for practice, though a complex one. Any consideration of how to distribute *zakāt* at a particular time and place must (one assumes) take into account the qualities implied here: It is not merely a personal ritual, nor merely a governor's task, nor merely aimed at the social end of ameliorating the condition of the poor. It is at least all of these things. Shīrāzī does not express a preference relative to his own time, nor does he translate this intellectual model into a terminology appropriate to his time: His discourse is precisely not related to a particular time and place.

This is an intellectual task, which relates to a model of religious and social life, explored in this context in complete abstraction from social reality.

The intellectual task, however, is completed by arguments which justify the model. As we have already seen in the Ḥanafī *mabsūṭs*, these arguments are characteristically based on hadith, both Companion (at 1.i) and Prophetic (at 2.ii and 2.iii). These are accompanied by rational arguments, and arguments of analogy (at 1.ii, 1.iii and 3.i), which give to the immediate topic rational justification, as well as coherence and integration within the larger structure of the law.

Para. 3 identifies an obligation as the old view of Shāfiʿī and a permission as the new view. As in the case of the three best views, these cannot be combined. There is a general Shāfiʿī presumption that the new view prevails, and this may have been Shīrāzī's intention, though he does not make it clear (just as he does not identify which of the 'best' views is best); but Nawawī's commentary was to identify this as one of the rare cases where the old view of Shāfiʿī was accepted as the *madhhab*. The expression of the new view leaves considerable unexplored logical space. The fact that it may be permissible to distribute by oneself does not fully clarify the question whether, in these circumstances, it is permissible to pay the governor, and whether there are restrictions on such a permission – for example, a requirement that he be just. It is possible that Shīrāzī interpreted Shāfiʿī's new view as meaning that manifest goods were to be assimilated totally to hidden goods, but it was an unexplored item that remained for later analysis and commentary.

This analysis of Shīrāzī's passage is intended to stress that the discourse type is fully independent of social reality, fully committed to the idea of continuity and loyalty within a school tradition, and fully acknowledges the need for relating law to justificatory argument. It is not obviously exemplary in the sense of providing a decision on what to do. (Even if these generalities were translated into particulars – this time, this place, this governor, these goods – it would not be easy to isolate simply one preferred mode of conduct.) We are faced here with an intellectual exploration of inherited concepts, norms and structures. These constitute a model (in some respects an imitation of reality) which is independently existent and autonomous, largely self-referring, potentially coherent. The only external reference is to the structures of hadith (and Qurʾan, etc.). This particular passage gives sharp expression to a problem which recurs throughout the discussion of *zakāt*: the tension between *zakāt* as a ritual duty (stressing the donor), a social mechanism (stressing the recipient) and a political and administrative process (stressing the governor). At a normative level, the problems that the passage leaves are those that arise out of logical spaces (and we will see that these are taken up and moved forward by Nawawī). At a justificatory level, the problems that are left are problems of value and judgement related to the hadith, and, possibly, to the arguments of rationality, coherence and analogy; these too will be taken up by Nawawī.

3. The commentary on this by Nawawī has two major phases. In phase one, he deals with the hadith contained in the passage; in phase two with the rules.

The passage contains three hadith: one from ʿUthmān, at 1.i, and two from the Prophet, at 2.ii and 2.iii. Here is Nawawī on the first of these hadith:

> The report from ʿUthmān is *ṣaḥīḥ*. It is transmitted in Bayhaqī in his *Sunan al-kabīr* in the *kitāb al- zakāt* in the *bāb al-dayn maʿa al-ṣadaqa*, with a valid *isnād* from Zuhrī from Ṣāʾib b. Yazīd the Companion, that he heard ʿUthmān, while preaching from the minbar say, 'This is the month of your *zakāt*, so if any of you has a debt, let him pay it ... and then pay his *zakāt* on the remaining wealth.' Bayhaqī said, 'Bukhārī transmits it in his *Ṣaḥīḥ* from Abūʾl-Yamān from Shuʿayb.' But this is to be rejected because Bukhārī does not give it thus in the *Ṣaḥīḥ*; he gives it from Ṣāʾib b. Yazīd that he heard ʿUthmān [preaching] from the minbar of the Prophet. No more than that.[8] He mentions it in the *kitāb al-iʿtiṣām* in relation to the minbar. Likewise al-Ḥumaydī mentions it in his *al-Jamʿ bayn al-saḥīḥayn*, from Bukhārī, in the form I have given. Bukhārī's aim was simply to establish [the use of] the minbar. It seems that Bayhaqī meant that Bukhārī had transmitted its root (*aṣl*), not all of it. God knows best.[9]

Nawawī here, for Shīrāzī's hadith, identifies an established canonical source, namely Bayhaqī, and indicates its location within that work. He recalls the immediate transmitters, and assigns the hadith to an established classification, here *ṣaḥīḥ*. Led by Bayhaqī's (erroneous) comment, he identifies also a truncated version of the same hadith in Bukhārī, and indicates its situation in that work. The version in Bukhārī does not contain any reference to *zakāt*; it merely refers to ʿUthmān on the minbar, preaching and is intended to establish the use of the minbar for that purpose. This takes us some way from the juristic question at issue, namely the personal distribution of *zakāt*. But that reflects the principled separation, by Nawawī, of the hadith from their context. For the purpose of this phase of commentary, he looks at the hadith, for their own sake, and offers a brief synopsis of their *isnād*s, their validity, their place in established collections, variant versions, etc., and deals with any further problems that arise. It is hadith as revelation, objectively considered, that concerns this part of his commentary. He deals with the next two hadith more briefly: the first is found also in Bayhaqī, unproblematically, and the second in Bukhārī.

But that does not finish Nawawī's analysis of hadith. There are other reports from the Prophet and from Companions that deal with the same issue. Nawawī identifies five which favour distribution to the governor, just or unjust, three

[8] The hadith appears in this truncated form in Bukhārī, *K. al-iʿtiṣām*, *Bāb ma dhakara al-nabī*, hadith 18. ʿAsqalānī, *Fatḥ al-bārī* (Beirut: Dār al-Maʿrifa, 1975), XVII, 73.

[9] Nawawī, *Majmū*, vol.6, 162.

Prophetic and two from Companions. He gives each one in full, with sources. Here are the first three:

1. From Jarīr b. ʿAbdallāh: A group of Bedouin came to the Prophet of God and said, 'Some of the tax-collectors come to us and cheat us.' The Prophet said, 'Be content with your tax-collectors.' Transmitted by Muslim in his *Saḥīḥ*.
2. From Anas: A man said to the Prophet, 'If I pay my *zakāt* to your messenger, have I fulfilled my duty to God and to his Prophet?' 'Yes, if you pay it to my messenger, you have fulfilled your duty to God and his Prophet; the reward is yours, and any sin belongs to him who takes your place.' Aḥmad in his *Musnad*.
3. Suhayl b. Abī Ṣāliḥ from his father: 'I accumulated wealth subject to *ṣadaqa*' – he meant it had reached the *niṣāb* – 'so I asked Saʿd b. Abī Waqqāṣ [and other Companions ...] whether I should distribute it myself or pay it to the *sulṭān*. They commanded me, all of them, without exception, to pay it to the *sulṭān*.' In one version, Suhayl said to them, 'But this *sulṭān* acts as you see, and shall I pay my *zakāt* to them?' They all replied, 'Yes, pay it.' Saʿīd b. Manṣūr gives both versions in his *Musnad*.[10]

The discovery and presentation of these hadith represents a scholarly activity of research, pure and unbiased research, not apparently constrained by mere concern for the rule of law that might or might not emerge. Nawawī goes on to identify only one report, from ʿUmar, which advocates distribution directly by the donor, found in Bayhaqī.

At this phase in his commentary, Nawawī is identifying and categorising revelation (or, if Companion reports are not recognised as revelation, then quasi-revelation[11]). Neither here nor later does he attempt, himself, to draw rules out of sources. He merely identifies relevant sources, all those that relate to the issue in question. Effectively he is repeating the task of the early great collectors whom he uses as his sources: Having established an issue of law, he draws under it all the relevant material of revelation, thereby creating a body of sources which is much broader than that made available in any single one of the standard collections. His definition of sources includes not only the standard collections[12] that had emerged as the central canon, but also such other collections as Aḥmad's *Musnad*, Bayhaqī's *Sunan*, and more peripheral, minor collections like the *Musnad* of Saʿīd b. Manṣūr.

[10] Ibid., VI, 162–3.

[11] Functionally, of course, all the reports cited here, Companion and Prophetic, represent revelation: They are materials adduced as potential justification of legal norms.

[12] He identified five collections as containing the fundamentals of the Islamic faith, the five *uṣūl al-islām*: Bukhārī, Muslim, Tirmidhī, Abū Dawūd, Nasāʾī. See below, Section 1.4.

Nawawī's achievement here has gone beyond justification of a rule. That required less material, less detail, less digression. By lifting the justificatory hadith out of their immediate context, and by dealing with them, as ends in themselves, in relation to *isnāds*, place in canonical collections, variants, and so on, he has focused the reader's attention on revelation, its nature, its extent and its complexity. This focus reflects developments in the understanding and assessment of revelation since the time of Shīrāzī. For it was in the intervening period that the community had firmly established the study, analysis and categorisation of hadith, and the identification of canonical collections. This task was a sacred activity and a pure science, also of course a central activity within the schools (indeed within the school where Nawawī taught); it had not been carried out always or merely with a view to the law. To define the limits and extent of revelation, like so many other aspects of ritual discourse (scholastic discourse), was an independent and autonomous task, generating its own parameters of interest and endeavour. By juxtaposing, even in summary form, the results of that endeavour with the juristic rules that had been expressed by Shīrāzī, Nawawī was effectively affirming the community's commitment to the whole corpus of revelation (even with its uncertain boundaries) and the consequent difficulty of understanding of the law – its *fiqh*. Nawawī's transfer of interest, in this phase of his work, from the rules to the sources was no longer merely a means to justify the rules, but an affirmation of the formidable task that the community was faced with, first in identifying and holding what was so large, so complex, so ambiguous of boundaries, and second in moving from this so complex body of revelation to a pattern of rules. It was not the particularity of the rules that was justified, it was the nature and complexity of the law, not the law of or on this or that, but the law as a system, with its *ikhtilāf*.

Phase two of Nawawī's commentary focused on the pattern of rules. Here too he was concerned with the academic study of texts, the texts of the Shāfiʿī *madhhab*, and he carried out his task with a similar concern for precision, detail, clarity and truth – truth not about the individual rules, for that remained unavailable, but truth about the difficulty of discovering them. Nawawī's analysis uses a special terminology of *ikhtilāf*, which had developed in the Shāfiʿī tradition (given its final refinements by Nawawī himself): the word *qawl* indicates an opinion of Shāfiʿī, the word *wajh* a dispute amongst scholars of the immediately succeeding generations, and the word *ṭarīq* a dispute of still later generations. The literal meaning of these words is irrelevant: They are code words for dispute. Here is the first part of Nawawī's discussion of the rules.

1. Shāfiʿī and his companions said that the donor has the right to distribute *zakāt* on hidden goods by himself. There is no dispute on this, and our companions transmit consensus of all Muslims on this matter.

2. Hidden goods are gold, silver, treasure trove, trade goods and *zakāt al-fiṭr*.[13]
   i. There is a divergent *wajh* on the last of these, namely that it belongs to the category of manifest goods. This is recorded by the author of the *Bayān* and others. The author of the *Ḥāwī* transmits it from the companions [sc. of Shāfiʿī], but he chose for himself that *zakāt al-fiṭr* was a hidden good. The latter view is the *madhhab*, decisively chosen by the majority, including the Qāḍī Abū al-Ṭayyib, Muḥāmilī in his two books, the author of the *Shāmil*, Baghawī and others. It is also the apparent meaning of Shāfiʿī's text. It is the well-known view (*mashhūr*) and the majority have declared it decisively, most of them mentioning it in the *bāb zakāt al-fiṭr*.
   ii. Our companions say that trade goods belong to the category of hidden goods, though they are in fact manifest [i.e., open to investigation] because it is impossible to know whether they are intended for trade or not; for goods do not become trade goods except subject to conditions which have been discussed earlier.
3. As to apparent goods, namely grains, livestock, fruit, and minerals:
   i. There are two well-known *qawl*s on the permissibility of the donor's distributing by himself, both mentioned by the author [Shīrāzī] with their proofs. The more valid (*asaḥḥu-humā*) is the new view, that it is permissible. The old view is that it is prohibited, and payment to the imam or his representative is mandatory. It is mandatory whether the imam is just or unjust, because, in spite of his injustice, he is executive of the law (*nāfidh al-ḥukm*). This is the *madhhab*, and has been declared decisively by the majority.
   ii. Baghawī and others relate a *wajh* that it is not necessary to pay him if he is unjust, but permissible. Ḥannāṭī and Rāfiʿī relate a *wajh* that it is absolutely not permissible to pay the unjust ruler; and Māwardī expressed this view towards the end of his *bāb niyyat al-zakāt*. … But this *wajh* is extremely weak, indeed an error; it is opposed by the hadith and reports cited above. Likewise the *wajh* of Baghawī is weak.
   iii. Our companions say, According to this old view, if he distributes by himself it does not provide reward, and he must pay it a second time to the imam or his representative. He must wait for the agent, and delay his *zakāt* as long as he has hope of the agent's arriving, but when he despairs, he should distribute by himself and it will provide reward because it is a locus of necessity (*mawḍiʿ ḍarūra*).[14]

[13] *Zakāt al-fiṭr* is the payment to the poor required of individuals at the end of Ramadan.
[14] Nawawī, *Majmūʿ*, VI, 163–4.

It will be recalled that Shīrāzī's text began with the assertion that it was permissible to distribute *zakāt* either by oneself, or through an agent, or to the governor. This is Nawawī's commentary on the first of these. His next two paragraphs (*masāʾil*) deal with the other two. The analysis has a natural focus on dispute and on problems. Where there is dispute, Nawawī provides considerable detail including specific named references to Shāfiʿī scholars and their works. But dispute, though fully acknowledged, does not preclude decision, and decision depends, not on argument, but on authority, the authority of the *madhhab*, and that is really a matter of discovering the majority. That is obvious at 2.i (where no argument is adduced except that of identifying the majority), and clarified by 2.ii which shows the essentially arbitrary nature of the classification. The distinction between Shāfiʿī's two *qawls* (3.i) is particularly interesting, for it shows that a view acknowledged to be more valid (*asaḥḥ*) is in fact not preferred by the majority and is therefore not the *madhhab*. The preference of the *madhhab* is of course defensible, as is evident from the dismissal of the variant views offered under 3.ii, but it is not because of superior argument that a particular view is adopted, it is because of loyalty to an established tradition of juristic thought (albeit a tradition buttressed by argument). The passage as a whole exemplifies the central paradox of juristic thinking – namely that the processes of juristic thought do not offer single, secure, and final answers (consider the *ikhtilāf* amongst the great scholars), but there is a need for a single, secure and final answer (hence the search for a majority view within the *madhhab*).

That passage dealt with what was permitted. When Nawawī turned to consider what was (amongst the permitted possibilities) the best mode of conduct, he clarified first the question whether it was better to pay directly or through an agent, and then whether it was best to pay directly or to the governor. In the latter context, he dealt first with hidden, then with manifest goods. He was able to be brief about the latter since the rules (and the disputes) had already been clarified in his earlier discussion. Here is the passage as it deals with first the agent (para. 1), then hidden goods (para. 2).

On clarification of the best mode of conduct.

1. Our companions say that distribution by himself is better than appointing an agent, with no dispute, because he is secure of himself, but not of his agent. On the hypothesis of the agent's betrayal of trust, the donor's duty is not fulfilled. … This is different from payment to the imam, for, simply by his receipt of the goods the donor's duty is fulfilled. … Māwardī and others have said, Payment to the imam is likewise better than appointment of an agent, for the reasons given.

2. As to the issue of distribution by himself or payment to the imam, on the question of which is best there is a distinction (*tafṣīl*).
   i. Our companions say, If the goods are hidden goods and the imam is just, there are two *wajhs*. The most valid, according to the majority, is that payment to the imam is best because of the hadith cited above; and because he is certain of the fulfilment of his duty, which is not the case if he does it himself; and because the imam is more knowledgeable of the recipients, the general welfare, the extent of the need, who has already received from others etc. This *wajh* is the view of Ibn Surayj and Abū Isḥāq al-Shīrāzī. Muḥamilī said, in his *Majmū'* and his *Tajrīd*, 'This is the view of the generality, and it is the *madhhab*.' Others said the same. Rāfi'ī said, 'This is the more valid according to the majority of the Iraqis and others.' Ṣaydalānī and others declared it decisively. The alternative *wajh* is that distribution by oneself is better. This is the view decisively chosen by Baghawī. The author [Shīrāzī] said, 'This is the apparent meaning of the text.' He meant the text of Shāfi'ī in the *Mukhtaṣar*: 'I prefer that the donor should undertake distribution by himself so as to be certain of its distribution.' This is Shāfi'ī's text, and the apparent meaning is as the author claims. But the majority have interpreted it (*ta'awwala-hu*), saying that the aim here was to prefer distribution by the donor over delegation to an agent. The justification given by Shāfi'ī confirms this because certainty as to fulfilment of the duty is achieved only by payment to the imam, even if he is unjust, and not to an agent.
   ii. If the imam is unjust, there are two *wajhs*, as reported by the author [Shīrāzī] and other companions. First, the best conduct is to pay the imam, for the reasons given above. But the more valid is that distribution by himself is best in order to achieve the end of *zakāt*. This is the position declared valid by Rāfi'ī and others.[15]

Para. 2 of that passage illustrates again that the discovery of a single preferred view within the *madhhab* depends not only on fine distinctions (hidden versus manifest goods, just versus unjust imams) but on acknowledgement of dispute, dispute which only just permits, after much study, the emergence of a preferred view. In this case, the preferred view of the majority has amongst the arguments arrayed against it the text of Shāfi'ī, which therefore required special analysis (*ta'awwala-hu*, 2.i). When Nawawī summarised, he found that there were six views within the *madhhab* on the best mode of conduct.

[15] Ibid., VI, 165–6.

Payment to the imam is best, in manifest goods absolutely, in hidden goods only if he is just;

distribution by the donor is best absolutely;

payment to the imam is best absolutely;

payment to the imam is best if he is just, distribution by the donor if he is unjust;

payment to the imam is best in manifest goods, distribution by the owner in hidden goods;

it is not permissible to pay an unjust imam.[16]

How the distinctions – and the conjunctions – multiply! The most valid, however, representing the preference of the Shāfiʿī scholars, was the first.

If we ask how Nawawī had developed or changed the law that he found articulated in Shīrāzī's text, the answer lies in part in the discovery of distinctions and the filling of logical gaps. Broadly accepting the structure that he inherited, he offered a still closer and more detailed analysis, one that brought out previously unarticulated refinements. This was not an addition of something new to the law, but an articulation of details already implicit in the structure. The law was preserved, repeated, refined, but not changed. This, however, is an imperfect answer, for the two phases of Nawawī's commentary, effectively repeated throughout the whole of the work, for every topic and for every item of the law, represent precisely his sense of what could be added to the earlier achievement of his companions: a fuller and more detailed confrontation with revelation, and a clear, detailed, unambiguous acknowledgement of uncertainty and dispute within the *madhhab*. That is the insistent message of his work: to remember revelation, its extent, its quality and its ambiguity; and to remember juristic dispute. But, in spite of this, for all questions, a decision may be discovered: It is found in and through the *madhhab*. The refinement of distinctions, the confrontation with revelation, the acknowledgement of dispute and the discovery of one answer: The processes were all embedded in the language and structure of Shīrāzī's text. Nawawī pushed them further, deeper, with an apparently infinite capacity for exhilaration and delight in his task.

4. The study of the law was a joy and a delight. Nawawī had said it several times in the introduction to the *Majmūʿ*, where he set out, programmatically, an account of his aims. While these include a suggestion of rather more than we have discovered in this analysis, the two phases that have been described above coincide broadly with his own sense of what he was to achieve. He promised in the introduction to give an account of hadith, including an assessment of their categories (*ṣaḥīḥ*, *ḥasan*, *ḍaʿīf*, *marfūʿ*, etc.). He would analyse difficult words,

[16] Ibid., VI, 166.

give an account of transmitters and locate the hadith in the standard collections of Bukhārī, Muslim, Abū Dawūd, Tirmidhī and Nasā'ī (he calls these the five *uṣūl* of Islam), or elsewhere if necessary. He would supplement established hadith with extra ones or with arguments of analogy where necessary.[17] As to rules of law, since these were the aim of the book, he would explain them with the greatest clarity and precision, adding details that would delight the attentive reader. Since the books and writers of the Shāfi'ī *madhhab* contained severe *ikhtilāf*, he would leave nothing unexplained, no *qawl*, no *wajh*, but would follow up the details and the arguments, from the time of Shāfi'ī and through the writings of his successors, in order to establish the preponderant view. God had multiplied the books of the Shāfi'ī *madhhab*, in the form of *mabsūṭ* and *mukhtaṣar*, both rare and famous, and Nawawī's readers would find in his book such an account of those as would give delight and increase the student's desire to work and study. Nawawī would also mention the positions adopted and the arguments used by the Companions, the Successors and the jurists of the cities and he would respond to these with fairness, briefly or at length, according to need. Knowledge and understanding of the proofs used by the forefathers was the most important of needful things, for their dispute (*ikhtilāf*) in *furū'* is a mercy. By appreciating their arguments and their evidence the competent scholar would develop an ability to distinguish the preponderant and the weak and he would become aware of the difficulties of argument: he would gain experience in question and answer, his mind would be sharpened, and he would gain distinction amongst the wise and the learned. ...[18]

The whole of this passage, though it acknowledges amongst its aims the search for a preponderant view, emphasises *ikhtilāf* and argument. And that indeed is what emerged when he put his programme into practice. The account of the law is embedded in an exploration of *ikhtilāf*. The *ikhtilāf* in turn is related to the nature of revelation which is a vast body of materials, demanding classification and analysis, and open to just those arguments which, once mastered, give distinction amongst the wise and the learned. Distinction apparently lies in knowing (but knowing fully and in precise detail) how little we know, and yet working through that un-knowing towards satisfaction in a final submission to authority, represented by the majority in the *madhhab*.

Section 2. The K. Rawḍat al-ṭālibīn wa-'umdat al-muftīn

1. Nawawī's *Rawḍa* is a lesser work than the *Majmu'*, lesser in the simple sense that it contains less. It omits the sources, giving simply an account of the law

[17] Nawawī, *Majmū*, I, 7–8.

[18] Ibid., 8–11.

and its *ikhtilāf*. In this respect, like the *Fatāwā* of Qāḍīkhān, it seems to be a *mabsūṭ*, but lacking one characteristic of that form, namely *ta'līl*. Provisionally at least, and with reference only to this quality of being clearly large explorations of the law while containing no arguments based on sources, I would recognise both works as belonging to the same broad type. However, they are quite remarkably different in tone. There is clearly a need for a more discriminating classificatory terminology to identify the qualities and to classify the types of works of *furū'*. For the present, I offer only rough refinements of the general types of *mukhtaṣar* and *mabsūṭ*.

The *Rawḍa* is based on (it is a replication, a re-enactment of) a work by Abū'l-Qāsim 'Abd al-Karīm b. Muḥammad al-Rāfi'ī (d. 623/1226). Rāfi'ī lived and taught in the city of Qazwin, apparently far from the great centres of academic life, but, within the Shāfi'ī *madhhab*, achieved recognition as one of the most wondrous of scholars. It was as if, according to the biography by Subkī, he had found the science of *fiqh* dead and brought it back to life. He was, in *fiqh*, a full moon from whom the real moon and the sun hid themselves, shamed by his brilliance. He was a race-horse not to be caught by other horses when he galloped along the paths where he transmitted *qawl*s and discovered *wajh*s.[19] Though he also had his miracles (*karāmāt*), it was his discovery of the multiplicity of the paths of the law that prompted his biographers to metaphor. It was the same quality that led Nawawī to choose Rāfi'ī's work as the basis for his own. This was the scholar who had brought together the diverse paths of the tradition and had refined the definition of the *madhhab* (*jama'a 'l-ṭuruq al-mukhtalafāt wa-naqqaḥa 'l-madhhab aḥsana tanqīḥin*): again, that two-fold achievement of acknowledged multiplicity and discovered unity. Rāfi'ī had produced a commentary on the *Wajīz* of Ghazālī, a work that combined comprehensive coverage with concision and clarity of expression. But it was excessively large, and Nawawī was inspired by God to produce a summary, in which he would follow a middle path, neither too long nor too short. In particular he would omit proofs, but would include all of the *fiqh* of Rāfi'ī's work, even the rarest and most outlandish views. He would restrict himself to rules, omitting discussion of lexis and language, but including, from time to time, some criticism and refinement of the positions adopted by Rāfi'ī.[20] Whereas the *Majmū'* had attempted to cover all of the discourse types relevant to an understanding of the law (analysis of revelation, of lexis and language, and of law), this work was to offer only rules.

A work that is only rules, but is unsparing in its assessment of their variation, has a tone quite different from a work that intercuts the rules and revelation. There

[19] Subkī, *Ṭabaqāt*, VIII, 282.

[20] Nawawī, *Rawḍa al-ṭālibīn* (Beirut: al-Kitāb al-Islāmī, n.d.), I, 4–5.

is nothing new, of course, in this work. Though Nawawī derived his structure, his order, his rules, even his words and phrases from the earlier work by Rāfiʿī, they echo the structure, order, words and phrases of his *Majmūʿ*. The depiction of the law was a matter of roughly parallel paths in search of a path: There was no surprise and no embarrassment in the way that scholars borrowed from each other and from their own works. For the law, the knowledge of the law, was a ritual, a function primarily of repetition and renewal, not discovery.

> Devotion to knowledge is the most noble approach to God, the highest act of obedience, the most pressing category of the good, the most secure act of worship, and the most worthy thing to which to devote one's most precious hours. ... And the highest type of knowledge in these times is knowledge of juristic details (*al-furūʿ al-fiqhiyyāt*) because all of the people have need of them under all circumstances. ...[21]

The need was not merely practical, since Nawawī promised, only a paragraph later, that he would present in this book even the most outlandish and rejected of views. The need can only have been the need to know the nature of the law, to take delight in its paths (so many, so various), while finding security in its path (the one *madhhab*). The full title of Nawawī's book (*Rawḍat al-ṭālibīn wa ʿumdat al-muftīn*) reflects its contents: *A garden for seekers, a pillar for muftis*. (All were seekers, even the most high-ranking of scholars.) The nature of society's need for a garden (a place of repose and re-creation, a delight for the eyes) was quite different from the nature of its need for a pillar. But this book promised both.

2. Here, for a renewal of what we already know, is, in full, that patch of the garden we have already visited.

Chapter on payment of *zakāt*.

- 0. It is *wājib* immediately, as soon as it becomes possible. Payment requires an act and an intention.
- 1. As to the act, it is of three types.
  - 1.1. The owner distributes by himself.
    - 1.1.i. This is permissible in hidden goods, namely gold, silver, trade goods, buried treasure, and *zakāt al-fiṭr*. **I say**[22]: On *zakāt al-fiṭr* there is a *wajh*, namely that it is a part of manifest goods. This is related in the *Bayān*, and transmitted in the *Ḥāwī* from the companions absolutely. But he [al-Rāfiʿī] chose to consider it as hidden; and this is the manifest meaning of Shāfiʿī's text. It is the *madhhab*. **God knows best**.

[21] Ibid., I, 4.

[22] The bulk of the contents of the *Rawḍa* is understood to be derived, through summary, from Rāfiʿī's commentary on the *Wajīz*. Where Nawawī introduces his own material, he introduces it with the words 'I say' and marks its conclusion with 'God knows best.'

1.1.ii. As to manifest goods, namely animals, crops subject to the tithe, and minerals, there are two *qawls* on the question whether they may be distributed by the owner himself. The most manifest (*aẓhar*), which is the new opinion, is that it is permissible. The old opinion is that it is not permissible; rather, they must be paid to the imam if he is just. And if he is unjust, there are two *wajh*s first, it is permissible but not necessary, but the more valid view is that it is necessary to pay it to the imam because of the prevailing of his authority and because he is not deposed [sc. for his injustice]. On this basis, if he distributes by himself it is not counted in his favour. Further, he must delay payment for as long as he hopes for the arrival of the tax collector. Only when he despairs, he may distribute by himself.

1.2. He distributes to the imam; this is permissible.

1.3. He appoints an agent to deliver to the imam, or to distribute to the recipients where distribution by himself is permitted.

2. As to the best of these types: distribution by himself is better than the appointment of an agent, with no dispute; this is because an agent may betray his trust and the duty of the donor may not be fulfilled.

3. As to the best of the other two.

3.1. If the goods are hidden goods, two *wajh*s: i. The most valid according to the majority of the Iraqi companions and others, and the one decisively chosen by al-Ṣaydalānī, is that payment to the imam is better because one becomes certain of the fulfilment of the duty thereby, which is not the case if one distributes by oneself, for one may pay to one who is not a rightful recipient. ii. The second *wajh* states that to distribute by oneself is best, because it is more sure, in order to participate directly in the ritual, and in order to favour relatives, neighbours, and the more deserving.

3.2. If the goods are manifest goods, payment to the imam is best absolutely. This is the *madhhab*, and is decisively preferred by the majority; Ghazālī rejected any dispute on this matter.

4. Thereafter, if we say that payment to the imam is best, that is if he is just; but if he is unjust, two *wajh*s: i. He is like the just imam. ii. The more valid *wajh* states that distribution by oneself is better. We have a third *wajh*, namely that it is not permissible to pay an unjust imam. But this is eccentric, weak and rejected.

5. **I say**: payment to the imam is best, on the part of an agent, absolutely. This was stated clearly in the *Ḥāwī*, and he provided it with *wajh*s as above (*wajjaha-hu. …)*.

6.1. If the imam demands the *zakāt* on manifest goods, it is mandatory to submit it to him – there is no dispute on this – as an acknowledgement of obedience. If they refuse, the imam may fight them, even if they respond by distributing the goods themselves. If the imam does not demand them, and the tax-collector does not come, the owner should delay paying for as long as he hopes for the arrival of the collector. When he despairs, he should distribute by himself. Shāfiʿī left texts to that effect. Some of the companions have said, This is a detail based on the permissibility of distributing by himself; others have said, this is permissible according to both opinions, as a protection of the right of the recipient against delay. Thereafter, if he distributes by himself, and the tax collector comes demanding it, the owner is believed with an oath. Is the oath mandatory or preferred? Two *wajh*s. If we say it is mandatory, and he refuses, the *zakāt* is taken from him, not because of the refusal but because it was a duty, and there is a presumption of it remaining so. **I say**: the more valid view is that the oath is preferred [not mandatory]. **God knows best**.

6.2. As to hidden goods. Māwardī said, 'The governors (*wulāt*) have no supervision over *zakāt* of this type; the owners have more right to distribute it. But if they pay it to him voluntarily, the governor should accept it.' If the imam knows that a man does not pay by himself, may he say, 'Either you pay by yourself or you pay me so that I can distribute it'? Two *wajh*s: following the pattern of a demand in oaths and atonements. **I say**: The more valid view is that this is mandatory, in order to remove what is prohibited. If the tax-collector demands more than is mandatory, the surplus is not binding. May one refuse to pay the mandatory element in view of the collector's transgression; or is it not permissible, out of fear of opposition to the governors? Two *wajh*s: the most valid, the second. **God knows best**.

7. As to the intention. …[23]

To read this requires both intellectual commitment, and an ability to hold on to hypothetical cases, fine distinctions and multiple rulings. If we are dealing with hidden goods, and the imam is just, then there are two views (3.1); but, if the imam is unjust, there are three views (4). If we are dealing with hidden goods, and the imam is just, it is best for the donor, by virtue of the *madhhab*, to pay the imam (3.1). But the imam has no right to demand hidden goods, and the donor (in spite of what is, by virtue of the *madhhab*, and in defiance of dispute,

[23] Nawawī, *Rawḍa*, II, 204–6.

best, namely to pay the imam) has no duty to obey should the imam demand such goods (6.2). The passage, however, is orderly and its principles of organisation familiar. Para. 1 focuses on what is permissible: distribution by oneself, to the recipient, or to the imam. Paras. 2–5 focus on what is the best mode of conduct. And all of this material can be seen as a logical development of what we saw in Shīrāzī. Except that Shīrāzī's text is not in the direct line of transmission here, since Rāfiʿī's base text was the *Wajīz* of Ghazālī; the paths, however, ran closely parallel to one another. Para. 6 deals with an issue I have not introduced before but it can be followed securely back through the Saljuq scholars to the texts of Shāfiʿī himself. This text, then, articulates the same concern for repetition, renewal and refinement, within a highly stable and non-developing model, that we have already recognised as essential to the discipline of *fiqh*.

To approach this text with the question, 'What shall I do?' or 'How shall I act?' is a possible, but not the most obvious way of reading and appreciating it. *Fiqh* is a science, and we shall see in Chapter 3 that it was perceived by some of its practitioners in precisely those terms: The elder Subkī was to characterise the law as a matter of universals, and the task of the mufti (not to be confused with the academic jurist) as the application of the universals in the light of particulars (*tanzīl al-kulliyyāt ʿalā ʿ l-juzʾiyyāt*). The universals of the law were derived from revelation, and explored through tradition;[24] they were multiplied through argument and uncertainty, and resolved into a decisive singularity through the authority of the *madhhab*. This process of discovering the generalities of the law, the law as a science, at least conceptually, was quite distinct from the process of applying the law. The latter task, the mufti's task, involved consideration of particulars (this governor, these goods). We shall see later that it was classified as an inferior task; certainly there was no need for it to take place in a work of *fiqh*. We have seen some instances of the specific mention of particulars, within a work of *fiqh*, in works of the Ḥanafī tradition. There are no such instances in the *furūʿ* works of Nawawī: He obviously had a very pure concept of what was the function and the permissible contents of a work of *furūʿ*.

The metaphors that the jurists found for their existential predicament (which was simply that the divine law had come to them in precisely this form – as generalities derived from revelation, mediated through the *madhhab*) related to the sea, to treasure, to gardens and pillars. If one turns to the passage quoted above with the pressing question, 'What shall I do?' or, worse, 'What shall I do now, in present circumstances?' the result seems likely to be confusion and despair.

[24] I am not of course talking about the real history, the historian's history, of Islamic law (which I have tried to describe, in part, in my *Studies in Early Muslim Jurisprudence*, Oxford: Clarendon Press, 1993) but the theological buttress to Islamic law, Islamic law as it was perceived by those who participated in it.

So many distinctions, views, uncertainties are there, already articulated, in the model, that they can only be compounded (and must compound our confusion) if we add to them the uncertainties of particulars (*this* governor, *these* goods, *my* situation). But that is not how Islamic culture chose to approach books of this kind, or rather, that is one of the most trivial approaches to such books. For, the jurists who wrote the books and those who studied with them, and in them, found in the multiple uncertainties of the law, in its distinctions and hypothetical cases, in its complex and unendingly argued relationship to a complex and unendingly analysed revelation, delight: a scintillating sea, a treasury of subtleties, a garden; the most noble approach to God, the highest act of obedience, the most pressing category of the good, the most secure act of worship and the most worthy thing to which to devote one's most precious hours. It was the thing in itself, the closed structure of movement between revelation and law, that gave delight and offered repose. The application of the law, the mufti's task, had no doubt its rewards, but was a lesser and a messier business.[25]

3. Within a single topic of the law (like the topic of *zakāt*), discussion of different issues (like the issue of how best to distribute one's goods) necessarily generated a distinctive local tone, with a local decorum sanctified by tradition. A different issue might generate quite a different tone, and a different set of linguistic and (perhaps) emotional responses. Consider the issue of assessing the *zakāt* on camels. As with all goods, there was, for camels, a *niṣāb*, a specified quantity under which no *zakāt* was required to be paid. For the Shāfiʿīs, the *niṣāb* on camels was five.

There is no *zakāt* on camels until they reach five. At that point they are subject to one sheep, and that does not increase until the camels reach ten. They are then subject to two sheep. On fifteen, three sheep. On twenty, four sheep. On twenty-five, a *bint makhāḍ*. On thirty-six, a *bint labūn*. On forty-six, a *ḥiqqa*. On sixty-one, a *jadhʿa*. On seventy-six, two *bint labūn*. On ninety-one, two *ḥiqqa*. Thereafter, there is no increase until the camels reach more than one hundred and twenty. At one hundred and twenty-one, three *bint labūn*. ... After one hundred and twenty-one, the matter becomes orderly: on every forty, a *bint labūn*, and on every fifty, a *ḥiqqa*. The duty changes with every increase of ten. For example, on one hundred and thirty, two *bint labūn* and a *ḥiqqa*; on one hundred and forty, two *ḥiqqa* and a *bint labūn*; on one hundred and fifty, three *ḥiqqa*; on one hundred and sixty, four *bint labūn*; on one hundred and seventy, three *bint labūn* and a *ḥiqqa*; on one hundred and eighty, two *bint labūn* and a *ḥiqqa*. And so on.[26]

A *bint makhāḍ* is a two-year old female, a *bint labūn* a three-year old female, a *ḥiqqa* a four-year old female and a *jadhʿa* a five-year old. The terminology is fossilised, archaic, timeless (like nearly everything else in a work of *fiqh*). The focus of interest is taxonomic and classificatory. Experience of camels is immaterial.

[25] Below, Chapters 3 and 4.

[26] Nawawī, *Rawḍa*, II, 151.

The words create a model of a pastoral economy, evoking in an Islamic context a reminder of the Bedouin background to revelation (an equivocal reminder, for while the Bedouin were the bearers of a linguistic and poetical heritage that was important to Islam, they were also notoriously uncertain in their allegiance). Questions naturally emerge: about the quality of the animals to be paid, the nature, type, age, of the sheep that are required for the first fifteen camels, the possibilities of substitution, of alternative animals, of cash values, and so on. Then there is the question of flocks owned in common, or of flocks that pasture in common, a fine distinction. The discourse necessarily refers to the tax-collector (the *sāʿī*) and his conduct, just or unjust. The issues of quantity and of quality have to be balanced against the ritual requirement of right timing (*al-ḥawl*), the nature and persistence of ownership (*baqāʾ al-milk*), the distinction between grazing and working animals, the relevance of a requirement for fodder. The types and qualifications of ownership have to be defined and analysed, including consideration of debt, absent owners, transfers of ownership, and increases and decreases in numbers due to birth, inheritance, sale, and so on. There are possibilities and conditions for advance payment, and for deferred payment. There are problems that relate to the governor, his justice and injustice, his duty to send out collectors, the preferred time and place of their activity, the owner's obligation (or otherwise) to gather his flocks at a waterhole for the convenience of the collectors. Endlessly, infinitely, on; with *ikhtilāf* all along the way.

The whole is an exploration of a purely notional world: a complete model of a pastoral economy, exquisitely detailed and absolutely autonomous, expressed in a terminology that is fossilised, and in normative sentences that express layers of hypothetical possibilities. The focus is always on precise distinctions (of types of animal, types of ownership), on meticulous measurement of values, of timing, of qualities, of rights, duties, permissions. This unsparing, obdurate, concern for detail is ritualistic, not practical, and, though realistic, not real. The tone might be characterised as nostalgic, but that misses the mood. A brilliant imitation of reality, sharply characterised, precisely delineated, charmingly evocative, the whole is literature and displacement, not reality, and not simply a manual of right conduct. This is art, and it reminds this reader of nothing so much as a medieval miniature. But it is art to work with, for, though the figures and topoi (the rules and concepts) of this pastoral economy remained broadly the same as they were passed on from generation to generation, each generation had opportunities to re-new the image, to re-write the law. Like a garden, it suffered from neglect. (Rāfiʿī, we have seen, brought *fiqh* back to life after it had been dead, killed off by ignorance and buried in its grave.[27])

[27] Subkī, *Ṭabaqāt*, VIII, 282.

A complete account of the law of *zakāt* would move from camels to sheep, to cows, to crops, to trade goods, to minerals, to the qualities and conditions of the recipients, to the rights and duties of the donor and the governor in distribution and in collection, and so on; as in the *kitāb al-zakāt* of any work of Islamic law. The governing image of the topic is that of a society organised (through governor, tax-collector, donor and recipient) for ritual, precision and obedience, and it has, of course, as all law must have, and this law more than most, qualities of unreality and idealism. Reality, in fact, is not the orientation of the law. The law, derived from revelation, preserved in the *madhhab*, would be precisely thus, even if there were no camels, and no tax-collectors, and no individual ownership. The difference between model and reality is constantly signalled, partly by the sporadic references to injustice (and these, for the system as a whole, relate to and include the injustice of the Prophet's tax-collectors: not even his government achieved the ideal form) which, by evoking reality, mark the ideal nature of the thing shown; and partly by the inexpungable reference to juristic dispute which signals the disparity between juristic articulation and the thing it falls short of articulating. This is not God's law made articulate, but man's effort at defining God's law, inevitably imperfect. By its own testimony, this is the portrayal of an ideal that is only aimed at, and an exercise in the making of images. The images are built out of sacred sources – but the images, though securely present, finely detailed, neatly organised, precisely distinguished, are only images, the effort of one tradition (here the Shāfiʿīs) to build out of revelation a normative mimesis of a distant structure: an image of an image. The reality of the law lies with God, who sent it in the form of revelation, which is the immediate (but only mediate) source for *fiqh*. The law, as described in a work of *fiqh*, is neither the real thing – the law of God which is contained within revelation (witness *ikhtilāf*), nor the real thing – the hard facts of contemporary life. But it is, by virtue of the *madhhab*, which is a temporary stasis within an endless process, a real thing of a kind.

4. Just what kind of thing the law is can perhaps be more easily experienced than described. By the seventh/fourteenth century, what the jurists (and through the jurists – who controlled public education, Muslim culture in general) experienced was a garden, or a treasure trove, or a scintillating sea. I would say a ritual, transformed into art; a cultural artefact to share and to discuss, a sublimation of reality, an escape, a discovery and exploration of otherness.

Amongst the fixtures of the garden (the subtleties in the treasure chest) were hermaphrodites, humans who had the sexual and excretory organs of both the male and the female.

To resolve ambiguity in hermaphrodites there are tests.

1. Amongst them, the passage of urine. If he urinates with the male organ alone, he is a male; if with the female organ, a female. If he urinates with

both, there are two *wajhs*: (i) There is no indication. (ii) The more valid is this: the first to flow is indicative, if they stop at the same time; the last, if they start at the same time; if one organ is first to flow and the other the last to flow, the first is indicative. If they are precisely equal but one gives more than the other, or if both flow, or both spray, then according to one *wajh* there is no evidence. According to the other, quantity is indicative, or a flow indicates a male, or a spray a female. But if they are equal in quantity, or one organ flows and the other sprays, there is no evidence.

2. Also, the emission of sperm or of menstrual fluid. …
3. Also, the production of a child. …
4. Also, the growth of a beard, or development of breasts, or differential development of two sides of the chest. The valid view is that these do not constitute evidence. The other view is that a beard is indicative, failure to develop the right side of the chest is a male, and development of breasts or equal development of the two sides indicates a female.
5. Also, sexual inclination. If he says, 'I prefer women', he is a male; or if he prefers men, he is a female; but only on condition of the failure of all the previous signs, for they are prior to inclination …[28]

The presence of hermaphrodites in the structure of the law is not an intrusive element of unreality in an otherwise real structure. They have exactly the same degree of reality as everything else in the structure of the law. What is real is the model and its autonomous, self-referring, self-generating qualities. An ambiguous hermaphrodite exists in the same way as a *bint labūn*. An ambiguous hermaphrodite, in fact, is considerably more versatile than a *bint labūn*, for the latter functions nowhere outside the topic of *zakāt*, and there only for the assessment of *zakāt* on camels.[29] The ambiguous hermaphrodite brings his peculiar local flavour to all kinds of issues (to discussions of marriage, fornication and retaliation for example) though he has his most proper place in the topic of purity. There, his activities might shock a sensitive morality.

1. If a hermaphrodite penetrates the female organ or the backside of another hermaphrodite, or each one penetrates the other, either in the female organ or the backside, there is no requirement for major or minor ritual ablution. Except in the case of the emergence of a penis from the backside: then there is a requirement of minor ablutions because of the emergence of something from the backside. …

[28] Nawawī, *Rawḍa*, I, 78.

[29] [The jurists also use camels as units of assessment in valuing human life and limb in cases where *diya* is payable. Ed.]

2. If a hermaphrodite penetrates an animal, or a woman, or a man's backside, there is no requirement of major ablutions for anyone, but the woman is subject to minor ablutions because of something emerging; likewise a man or a hermaphrodite penetrated from behind is subject to minor ablutions.
3. If a man penetrates the female organ of a hermaphrodite, there is no requirement of major ablutions, nor minor ablutions for either of them, because of the possibility that the hermaphrodite is a man.
4. If a man penetrates the female organ of a hermaphrodite, while the hermaphrodite penetrates a woman [with his male organ], the hermaphrodite incurs major impurity, but not the man or the woman. The woman must perform minor ablutions.[30]

A central theme of twentieth century anthropology has been the significance of boundaries, both real and conceptual. Mary Douglas's *Purity and Danger* has notably crystallised some of the familiar ideas that underlie or are associated with systems of purity: a concern with classification, order, hierarchy and boundaries. The boundary of ownership (*milk*) is one of the most pervasive throughout the many topics of a work of *fiqh*, and it has one of its most complex manifestations in relation to *zakāt*. There, the transfer of ownership, which is elsewhere for the most part unambiguously either unilateral or bilateral, by virtue of declaration or of contract, and enacted by the owner, is peculiarly ambiguous. The source of the complication lies in the suspicion that the transfer of ownership is not fully under the control of the owner himself. The normal assumption lying behind the idea of ownership is precisely that it excludes control by the non-owner except in circumstances envisaged and dealt with by the law (as for example the appointment of an agent). In the case of *zakāt* the ontological power of God's command is such that a charge is established on property without any overt action by the owner. In real life, someone who cheats on his *zakāt* may use the goods concerned (which, at a level different from that of social practice, are no longer his in ownership) for normal purposes, but *sub specie aeternitatis*, they had ceased to be his to use, and the debt against him accumulates. In this case, as so often, the reality of the law and of society diverged. The intervention of the governor (who, as agent to the poor, may acquire possession and control not ownership), and the rights of the recipients (who become owners, but with considerable uncertainty as to how and when) serve to multiply the complexities. For these and related reasons, the issue accumulates a charge of tensions which make it peculiarly and sharply a focus of dispute and distinctions. The

[30] Ibid., I, 82–3.

taxonomy of camels did not generate problems to the same degree. The immediate interest was, however, still in the marking of boundaries and types, and in the establishment and preservation of a nomenclature. The development and extension of the topic was ultimately again about ownership and the methods of defining, assessing and transferring it.

The boundary between males and females is even more fundamental than the boundaries of property, and the determination to overcome ambiguity (disorder) in this sphere, in favour of order and classification, is nowhere more marked than in the effort we have seen above to disambiguate the hermaphrodite. The fully ambiguous hermaphrodite is the final residue of inescapable disorder: Both male and female, he is obdurately resistant to category. He is a symbol of boundaries confounded, of liminality, of danger and excitement. The transgression of boundaries is an element of human experience which anthropologists have found, in many societies, to be expressed in modes of ritual and ceremony, often permitting obscenity, parody and the temporary breakdown of hierarchy and rules.

Nawawī's discussion, in the passage cited above, of the hermaphrodite's susceptibility to impurity in relation to the sexual act is formally related to the application of certain principles for the discovery of rules. The principle which governs his discussion states that an instance of what is certain and sure is not cancelled by an instance of what is doubtful. The hermaphrodite, prior to the sexual act, was pure. In so far as he carried out a (parody of) the sexual act, using an organ which could not be firmly established as being his sexual organ, and since only one organ could be the real organ (for it was not finally allowed that the ambiguous hermaphrodite was both male and female, only that a disambiguating factor had not been discovered), there was always only doubt as to whether a real sexual act had taken place. Since doubt does not overcome a prior certainty, the hermaphrodite remains in a state of purity – except in the case where both his organs are simultaneously brought into play, as in para. 4 above. It is not reality that generated the cases that Nawawī presented here, but logical finesse within an established structure.

The various categories of logical play that are brought into existence on the surface of Nawawī's text should not obscure the fact that this issue permits an experience of disorder and liminality which reaches deeper than logic: There is a moment of shock and the release of shock, of lawlessness articulated (which contrasts with and affirms the law), and of humour. The reappearance of the ambiguous hermaphrodite in various other contexts of the law allows repetition and recall of these moods. This example must suffice for the present to establish the fact that different topics of the law, and, within a topic, different aspects, generate quite different moods and concerns. A taxonomy of sexual positions open to hermaphrodites does not evoke the same reactions as a taxonomy of camels – though both might be equally alien to the real experience of individual jurists. A law book like the *Rawḍa*, one which has no passages of justificatory argument or reference to Qurʿan or hadith, but which is unsparing in exploration of detail, offers, most vividly and intensely, a model of a social reality which is precise, realistic, captivating and engaging. By virtue of explored and acknowledged *ikhtilāf*, it draws its reader into layers of meaning and significance which seduce and entangle (though I think they might also, and did sometimes, appal). A work of law offers its readers a literary experience – diverse, various, profound. It is not like a manual of instruction.

Section 3. The *Minhāj al-ṭālibīn*

1. The *Minhāj al-ṭālibīn* is Nawawī's *mukhtaṣar*. It represents the end of a logical progression: from the *Majmūʿ*, which focused equally on revelation, dispute and the *madhhab* (together with a considerable if unsystematic concern for language), through the *Rawḍa*, which eliminated revelation while retaining a complete account of dispute and of the *madhhab*, to this work which eliminates both revelation and (on the surface) dispute, offering only a statement of the *madhhab*. It is logically the last of his works, since its conclusions follow from the studies and the surveys of the preceding two. In practice, as we have seen, it is not necessary to think that he wrote and completed any one of these works prior to starting the next. Rather he developed them in parallel. Their relationship is essentially logical. Nonetheless, such evidence as can be thought relevant suggests that he did in fact complete this work after he had completed the bulk of the other two. His introduction initially echoes the introductions to his other works:

> Devotion to knowledge is amongst the most noble acts of obedience. … Our companions have multiplied compositions in the form of *mukhtaṣars* and *mabsūṭs*. …[31]

The finest of *mukhtaṣars*, Nawawī went on, was the *Muḥarrar* of Rāfiʿī. It was a pillar in defining the *madhhab* (*ʿumda fi tahqīq al-madhhab*), a support for the mufti. Its author had undertaken to declare what was valid according to the majority of the companions (i.e., Shāfiʿī jurists), and he had fulfilled his undertaking. It was, however, a little large, too much so for the majority of the people of this age, and so Nawawī had decided to abbreviate it, to about half its original size, in order to facilitate memorisation. He had also added something to the original. This included: for some rules, notice of qualifications omitted in the original; identification of a small number of issues where Rāfiʿī had

[31] Nawawī, *Minhāj al-ṭālibīn* (Cairo: Mustafā al-Bābī al-Ḥalabī, 1338/1919–20), I, 2.

misidentified what was the *madhhab*; some change of wording where Rāfiʿī had used unusual or incorrect forms; a number of recondite problems (*masāʾil nafīsa*) which Nawawī had marked with *qultu* at the beginning and *wa-ʾllāhu aʿlam* at the end; and, finally, a clarification of *qawl*, *wajh*, *ṭarīq*, *naṣṣ* and the layers of dispute (*marātib al-khilāf*). The terms *qawl*, *wajh* and *ṭarīq*, as pointed out above, refer to dispute at the levels, respectively, of Shāfiʿī, his companions and their successors. The word *naṣṣ* represents an allusion to a text of Shāfiʿī. Nawawī would represent these layers of dispute by a code:

Wherever I use the terms *al-aẓhar* (the more manifest) or *al-mashhūr* (the well-known), it is a reference to [the existence of] two or more *qawls*. If the dispute is strong, I say *al- aẓhar*, otherwise *al- mashhūr*. Wherever I use the terms *al-asaḥḥ* (the more valid) or *al-saḥīḥ* (the valid), it is a reference to two or more *wajhs*. If the dispute is strong, I say *al-asaḥḥ*, otherwise *al-saḥīḥ*. Wherever I say the *madhhab*, it indicates two or more *ṭarīqs*. Wherever I say the *naṣṣ* it refers to a text of Shafiʿi and signifies the existence of a weak *wajh*, or a derived *qawl*. Wherever I refer to the new view, the old view is its opposite; and if I refer to the old view, then the new view is its opposite. If I say *wa-qīla* (it is said), this indicates a weak *wajh* and the valid or the more valid view is its opposite. Wherever I say, according to a *qawl*, then the preponderant one is its opposite.[32]

There were a few other conventions and achievements to which Nawawī wished to alert his reader, but that set of verbal clues was the essential key to reading this book. Not only does it mean that the book is strictly untranslatable, because the words do not carry their normal etymological meaning. But also, the whole paraphernalia of dispute, though eliminated in its details, is brought back into play by this encoding of dispute in single words.

2. Nawawi's aim was to achieve the utmost concision, while maintaining detail and precision, and signalling the presence of *ikhtilāf*. His success was variable (and nothing like that achieved a generation or so later, under roughly similar conditions, by the Mālikī scholar Khalīl b. Ishāq [d. 776/1374]). One of his less successful moments was his summary of that passage of the law that we have become familiar with. Here is the whole of his material on distribution of *zakāt*. (I leave the coded symbols of *ikhtilāf* in Arabic.)

He may distribute by himself *zakāt* on hidden goods. Likewise on manifest goods, *ʿalā ʾl-jadīd*. Also, he may appoint an agent, or pay the governor. *Al-aẓhar*: that payment to the governor is best, unless he is unjust.[33]

This is a remarkable reduction, but not perhaps a fully correct one. The second sentence tells us that the donor may distribute *zakāt* by himself on manifest goods, according to the new view, and thereby indicates an old view that is the

[32] Ibid., 2.

[33] Ibid., 34, ll. 6–8.

opposite: That is, he may not distribute by himself. It is clear, however, from the presentation of the *Majmūʿ* and the *Rawḍa* that the old view is the *madhhab*, and its meaning is that it is mandatory to pay *zakāt* on manifest goods to the imam, whether the imam is just or not. And this is not made clear in the present text. The final sentence, beginning with the words *al-aẓhar* indicates that this is the best of two or more *qawl*s, and that the dispute in question is strong. (Had the dispute been weak, implying a greater degree of certainty that the declared view was the correct one, Nawawī would have said *al-mashhūr*.) But, the discussion of what was best was carried out in the *Majmūʿ* and the *Rawḍa* not in terms of *qawl*s but in terms of *wajh*s. It may be that Nawawī intended here to indicate that the *wajh*s themselves can be traced back to the previously established *qawl*s, but that is not clear. In any case, the final sentence as to what is best had been stated by Nawawī in the *Majmūʿ* as follows: 'Payment to the imam is best, in manifest goods absolutely, in hidden goods only if he is just.' This is confirmed in the *Rawḍa*. In the present text, a subtlety has got lost, and can only be recovered by a pre-determined reading – that is, by assuming that the last sentence refers to hidden goods only, though that is not apparent from the text.

(It will be noticed that this commentary of mine on the text of Nawawī's *Minhāj* takes the form of a syntactical assessment of whether Nawawī has in fact achieved what he set out to achieve, namely a concise but exact depiction of the *madhhab*. This is a natural and logical result of developments within the literature of the law, and it is a major feature of later commentaries on the *Minhāj*: they analyse the text of the *Minhāj* and comment on whether it has successfully achieved, in linguistic terms, a summary of the *madhhab*. To a considerable degree, in the later tradition, the focus of hermeneutical activity is transferred from the texts of revelation to the texts of the *madhhab*.[34])

The following passage may give a better indication of how Nawawī's summarising and encoding activities work. I give only the first few lines from a chapter. Grammatical ellipsis and semantic density are so great that I have adopted the format of a running commentary as most likely to sustain the interest and provoke the precise and pointed reading that is required to appreciate this material.

1. Chapter: On those subject to *zakāt* and what it is incumbent on them (*Bāb man talzimu-hu ʿl-zakāt wa-mā tajib fi-hi*).

This chapter heading distinguishes two tasks, that of identifying persons subject to *zakāt* and that of identifying goods subject to *zakāt*. The verbs used (*lazima* for persons, *wajaba* for things) are exploited in what follows in order to facilitate ellipsis.

[34] We have already noted a similar process in Ḥanafī law. See Chapter 1, Section 3.

2. The conditions for the incumbency of *zakāt* on wealth are Islam and freedom. It is binding on the apostate, if we consider that his ownership of goods continues; but not on the *mukātab*.

The reference to the apostate's ownership of goods is a cross-reference to the topic of apostasy where this is an item of *ikhtilāf*. The *mukātab* is a slave who has a contract with his master whereby he buys his freedom in installments. The point of the reference is that an apostate might seem to lack the condition of Islam, but is nonetheless subject to *zakāt*; and a *mukātab* might seem to be partially and increasingly free, but is nonetheless not subject to *zakāt*.

3. It is incumbent on the property of a child and one insane. Likewise [on the property of] one who owns a *niṣāb*, by his free part, *ʿalā ʾl-aṣaḥḥ*.

I have expanded an ellipsis here for ease of reading. The term *niṣāb* refers to the specified minimum after which goods become subject to *zakāt*. The reference to a person who is partially free means a slave (not a *mukātab*, as explained above) who has acquired partial freedom – for example, because he was owned by two masters, one of whom set him free while the other did not. In these circumstances, he becomes half free, and can own goods in his own right by virtue of that half which is free, not by virtue of that half which is unfree. The property of a slave is owned by his master. The phrase *ʿalā ʾl-aṣaḥḥ* indicates that there is a strong dispute at the level of *wajh*s on this issue, the alternative view being that someone who is only partially free does not pay *zakāt*.

4. Also [it is incumbent on wealth] that has been usurped, lost, or challenged *ʿalā ʾl-aẓhar*; but payment is not required until it returns [to the owner].

Again I have filled in ellipses. The terms 'usurped' (*maghṣūb*), 'lost' (*ḍāll*) and 'challenged' (*majḥūd*) are all technical terms explored elsewhere in a work of *fiqh*. The reference here is perhaps formal, in the sense that the claim that goods have been usurped or lost should be placed before a judge. Goods challenged (*jaḥada*) are those where ownership has been challenged or denied, again probably before a judge. The situation is that usurped goods (etc.) are subject to *zakāt*, in the sense that *zakāt* must be computed annually as if they were ordinary goods in ownership and possession, but payment is not required until the goods come back into the donor's possession. Effectively the computed *zakāt* remains a debt against the donor until he gets access to his goods. The phrase *ʿalā ʾl-aẓhar* means that there is strong dispute at the level of *qawl*s on this matter, the alternative *qawl* being that such goods are not subject to *zakāt*.

5. And [it is incumbent on the property of] the buyer prior to receipt. It is said (*qīla*), there are two *qawl*s.

This means that if someone completes a transaction of sale, and becomes the owner of goods, they (the goods) are subject to *zakāt* from the moment he becomes the owner, even if receipt of goods is delayed. The phrase *wa-qīla fī-hi al-qawlān* is a very subtle statement about *ikhtilāf.* It does not mean simply that there are two *qawl*s on this matter, but there is *wajh* (i.e., a report from one of the companions or immediate successors of Shāfiʿī) stating that there are two *qawls*.

6. It is incumbent immediately on absent goods if one can manage it; otherwise they are like usurped goods.
7. As to debt, if it is animals or non-binding, like the contract of *kitāba*, there is no *zakāt.* If trade goods or cash, likewise, in the old view. In the new view, if due immediately and difficult to secure because of hardship etc, then like usurped goods; if easy, then incumbent immediately; or [if due] at a specified future date, then the *madhhab* is that debt is like usurped goods. It is said (*qīla*), payment is incumbent before receipt.[35]

Para. 6 is self-explanatory, para. 7 more complex. The reference is to debts owed to the donor. He is the real owner of such goods, though he does not have them in possession or under his control. If the goods owed to the donor are in the form of animals they are not subject to *zakāt.* Likewise if the debt is non-binding. A slave who is buying his own freedom (a *mukātab*) has a contract with his master (a contract of *kitāba*) to pay him regular installments. This debt is non-binding, meaning that the master cannot sue his slave for failure of payments, and it is not subject to *zakāt.* With regard to trade goods and cash, there are two views. The old view (*qawl*) is that these too are not subject to *zakāt.* The new view is that debts of this kind are subject to *zakāt.* If the debt is due immediately, then either it is hard to get it, in which case the situation is like that prevailing for usurped goods, or it is easy to get it, in which case the *zakāt* is due immediately. If the debt is due for repayment at a specified future date, then the *madhhab* is that it is like usurped goods. The final phrase (*wa-qīla*) indicates the existence of a weak *wajh*, which states that *zakāt* must be paid on debts of this type prior to receipt. This means that the strong view is that payment is due only after receipt.

The passage continues with the question whether debt that is owed by the donor can be counted against his *zakāt*: There are three *qawls*. Enough, however, has been cited to demonstrate the mood and the concerns of the passage (and of the book as a whole). The passage is concerned with distinction and discrimination at two different levels. The first level discriminates and explores marginality

[35] Ibid., 33.

in relation to persons and goods. Para. 2 is concerned with the person subject to *zakāt* and discriminates the general conditions (Islam and freedom) from marginal cases (the apostate and the *mukātab*, the first marginally a Muslim, the second marginally a slave). Subsequent paragraphs can be interpreted as focusing on other cases of ambiguity and marginality. Para. 3 specifies the goods of children and the insane, partly because they are a focus of dispute with the Ḥanafīs (unarticulated), partly because they are, in themselves, marginal cases. The person who is partly free and partly unfree is to be distinguished from either the free, or the slave, or the *mukātab*. Goods that have been usurped, lost, or challenged remain in ownership of the donor but he has lost full control over them. Absent goods are the same. With regard to debts, ownership is vested in the creditor, but he has again no direct control. The passage is about and continues to be about the ownership of goods, and it focuses on ambiguous and marginal cases. The next issue, after debts, is undistributed booty held for more than a year and subject to *zakāt*, in a context where the soldiers have opted to acquire ownership of the booty … The refinement of interest throughout all this focuses on the need to make a decision about the boundaries of ownership, the duties and responsibilities that therefore accrue and the conditions and qualifications that govern those duties and responsibilities.

At a different level the passage is concerned with distinction and discrimination in the nature of *ikhtilāf*. Directly or indirectly, every numbered paragraph in the above passage (except the title) contains a reference to *ikhtilāf*. The apparent exceptions are para. 2, which contains a cross-reference to *ikhtilāf* in the law of apostasy, and para. 6, which contains a reference to usurped goods, themselves a focus of dispute. Every other paragraph contains at least one of Nawawī's coded references to dispute, locating the dispute in the work of Shāfiʿī, in that of his companions and immediate successors, or in that of later scholars. It is clear that Nawawī's intention to create a *mukhtaṣar*, a work which would articulate in the briefest possible compass the *madhhab*, did not free him from the duty to indicate and record *ikhtilāf*. The message that there is a *madhhab*, that the Shāfiʿī tradition has for all problematic and ambiguous cases come down on one side or the other, is inextricably enmeshed with the message that the *madhhab* emerges in a context of uncertainty and dispute. Nawawī did not acknowledge a duty, nor enact a desire, to state the *madhhab* in a way that would free it from the nexus of dispute.

3. The works of Nawawī were recognised later as the definitive articulation of the Shāfiʿī *madhhab*. The *Minhāj* in particular became a focus of commentary. The nature of that commentary, at least in part, was dictated by the literary and historical situation of the law. My own efforts at commentary, illustrated above, since they too are controlled by the literary form of the text and its relationship

to a long tradition of juristic thought, mirror those of commentators within the tradition. In explaining the *Minhāj*, there is an initial need to clarify lexical items and to signal technical terms. There is then a need to clarify syntax, usually by recovery of ellipsis since that is the most striking feature of the prose style of this *mukhtaṣar*. The expansion of syntax must be related to the re-discovery and the re-expression of the *madhhab* by substituting for the semantic compression of the original a more relaxed and accessible account. The *ikhtilāf* that has been signalled must be explicated. Details that have been omitted may be recovered to whatever degree seems appropriate. These tasks are the inevitable minimal requirements of a teacher's approach to the *Minhāj*. They can be carried out of course with style, or without it. With the passage of time and the measured if rare emergence of great scholars who participated significantly in the assessment of *ikhtilāf*, or advocated a different assessment of what was the *madhhab*, or re-created or re-assessed the arguments of the law, these too were recalled in the body of a commentary. The recognition of a good commentary depended partly on style, but more on a secure mastery of the details of the law and the history of the *madhhab*, its scholars and its rules. The two great commentaries on the *Minhāj* are the *Tuḥfat al-muḥtāj* of Ibn Ḥajar al-Haythamī (909/1504–974/1567) and *Nihāyat al-muhtāj* of Shams al-Dīn Ramlī (917/1511–1004/1595).

The commentarial tradition was frequently accompanied by a spirit of collegial criticism and competition, leading, characteristically, to criticism of Nawawī's linguistic capture of the law, and the proposal of a better, more stringent, more subtle, linguistic form; one that more securely caught the idiosyncracies of the *madhhab*, or more finely exploited the capacities of the Arabic language. Much of the material content of a late commentary consists of efforts to emulate and surpass the linguistic achievement of the original author. This in turn was the first step towards the composition of a new *mukhtaṣar*. All subsequent Shāfiʿī efforts at the production of a *mukhtaṣar* started from and were in competition with the *Minhāj* of Nawawī. The aim was to achieve a virtuoso performance: a formal, linguistic structure that outclassed that of Nawawī. Such books are necessarily repetitions, and, at first glance may seem to deviate little from Nawawī. The Yemeni Shāfiʿī scholar Ibn al-Muqriʿ (838/1434) produced a *mukhtaṣar* known as the *Irshād*. 'It is a precious book on Shāfiʿī *furūʿ*, elegant in expression and sweet in diction, extremely concise and dense with meaning. He himself wrote a commentary on it, in which he flew to the circumambient horizons.' So the nineteenth century scholar Muḥammad b. ʿAlī al-Shawkānī (1250/1834)[36] characterised Ibn al-Muqriʿ's achievement. It is the elegance and sweetness, concision and density of the *mukhtaṣar* that deserves praise – that is, its language and its structure.

[36] Shawkānī, *al-Badr al-ṭāliʿ* (Cairo: Maṭbaʿa al-Saʿāda, 1348/ 1929–30), I, 143.

The circumambient horizons that characterised the corresponding *mabsūṭ* meant the elucidation of language, the elaboration of dispute, the recovery of sources and the demonstration of familiarity with the juristic heroes of the *madhhab*.

Section 4. The commentary on Muslim

1. In all three of the works considered so far Nawawī's starting point and his finishing point are the same: the *madhhab*. The *madhhab* was the beginning in the sense that it existed prior to the experience of Nawawī, as of every other jurist (after Shāfiʿī), and was the focus of his loyalty. It was what he already, by virtue of history and community, possessed. Nawawī begins with the *madhhab* in the sense also that he chooses a prior articulation of the law within the Shāfiʿī *madhhab* as the basis for his own work. He then re-enacts, with a greater or lesser degree of detail, the processes of exploration and argument, whereby the *madhhab* can be grounded in the body of revelation, the studies of Shāfiʿī, and the disputes and explorations of his companions and followers. And he concludes with a renewed (and not very different) statement of what is the *madhhab*. The historical experience of earlier jurists, their experience specifically as scholars, is the criterion which permitted all articulations of the law (perhaps that of Shāfiʿī himself, and certainly that of jurists like Shīrāzī, Ghazālī, Rāfiʿī and Nawawī). The end of all the explorations was to arrive with renewed understanding at the beginning, that is, at a statement of the *madhhab*. The renewed understanding, in Nawawī's works, was much less a renewed understanding of individual rules, than of the nature of the law as a structure and a process of understanding ('understanding' being precisely the literal meaning of *fiqh*). The nature of the law and its infinitely disputed relationship to revelation is a fundamental part of the message articulated even in the slimmest and most pared of Nawawī's works.

But the independence and self-sufficiency of the Shāfiʿī tradition is also enacted in these works, for they notably have no space for reference to the other *madhhab*s. The Muslim community, or more specifically the Sunni community, as a whole, shares in the possession of revelation (and of that extended revelation which is the words and deeds of the Companions and Successors), but the Shāfiʿī community alone figures in the re-enactments of interpretative understanding that constitute a normal work of *fiqh*. Unity and difference are thus enacted and affirmed in the process of discovering and articulating the rules of the *madhhab*. There is a kind of unspoken acknowledgement of the other *madhhab*s in the very fact of foregrounding only the Shāfiʿī tradition; and there is a more clearly articulated assertion of Sunni unity in the re-discovery and foregrounding of revelation which is essential to the profoundest articulation of the *madhhab*, represented, in

Nawawī's works, by the *Majmūʿ*. That work aspires at least, for every item of the law, to identify and classify the range of relevant revelation – and falls short, as Nawawī confesses in his introduction. The horizons of understanding lie beyond the capacities of an individual jurist. They are more adequately explored in the total history of a juristic school, and reach their furthest bounds only in the conjoined histories of all the major *madhhab*s. The homogeneity of the literary enterprise ensured that a full understanding or exploration of the law was not required of, or achieved by, one scholar, but was worked out by many, over generations.

It was possible to conceive of a different beginning, a beginning in revelation. This is what we find in Nawawī's commentary on the hadith collection of Muslim. In his introduction, Nawawī explained what prompted him to this work. (In fact, it was a necessary part of his function as a teacher in the Dār al-Ḥadīth al-Ashrafiyya.). He began with a familiar and conventional statement about knowledge as worship: Devotion to knowledge is the highest approach to God, the noblest act of obedience, etc. Amongst the most important categories of knowledge were those concerned with the science of hadith. This meant the classification of hadith (*ṣaḥīḥ*, *ḥasan*, *ḍaʿīf* and so on), study of their *isnād*s, knowledge of their transmitters, analysis of variants, and so on. The proof that the science of hadith was of the highest degree of importance lay in the fact that the law (*sharʿu-nā*) was based on the Book and on transmitted *sunna*, and the vast bulk of *fiqhī* rulings (*al-ahkām al-fiqhiyya*) were dependent on *sunna*. The most reliable of books on hadith were the two *Ṣaḥīḥ*s of Bukhạrị and Muslim. Nawawī had gathered material for a commentary on the former, but, seeking guidance from God, had embarked on a complete commentary on the latter. This commentary would be of intermediate size avoiding excessive concision and excessive expansion (neither *mukhtaṣar* nor *mabsūṭ*). Had it not been for the weakness of aspirations, the paucity of seekers, and fear that such a book would have no market, students being little inclined towards long books, he would have written an expansive work, a work stretching to more than a hundred volumes, without repetition or pointless expansion. The *Ṣaḥīḥ* is worth such a commentary, since it contains the words of the most eloquent of mankind, the Prophet of God.[37]

Now, hadith collections contain more than merely juristic hadith. But the bulk of the major collections, including that of Muslim, relates to the law. This commentary then provides yet another opportunity to re-state the law, to re-enact the movement from revelation to *madhhab* that we have seen enacted in works of *fiqh* of the *mabsūṭ* type, and notably in the *Majmūʿ* of Nawawī.

2. The discrepancy between potential and reality marked by Nawawī's acknowledgement that his work falls short of what it might have been in a longer

[37] Nawawī, *Sharḥ Muslim* (Cairo: al-Maṭbaʿa al-Misriyya, 1349/1929–30), I, 3–5.

and more perfect version means also, and perhaps necessarily, that there was considerable variation in realised achievement. The diverse subject matter occasioned by the organisational framework of Muslim, or by the disparate implications of a particular hadith or group of hadith, ensured that Nawawī had constantly to make choices as to what to omit. For the juristic material, it is nonetheless possible to detect a kind of schematic framework which catches most of the possibilities of commentary, though these are often fragmented, and subject to an apparently arbitrary process of ellipsis, expansion and interpolation in particular instances.

A fairly clear version of the basic scheme can be found in the commentary on Muslim's material relating to a dog's lapping at water.[38] Muslim offered amongst the numerous hadith of his *K. al-ṭahāra* a group of six hadith relating to a dog's lapping at water in a bowl. These specified that the water should be thrown away (mentioned only once), the bowl washed seven times (mentioned in all hadith), the first washing carried out with dust (once), or an eighth washing with dust (once). The last of the six hadith distinguishes hunting and herding dogs from others.

Nawawī isolates this group of hadith and makes his discussion of them a single chapter (*Bāb ḥukm wulūgh al-kalb*). His commentary has five components:

1. Textual variants in the transmission of Muslim.
2. Consideration of *isnād*s and lexical items.
3. Derivation of juristic rules.
4. Problems of harmonisation of hadith (includes reference to variants from other collections).
5. Extended analysis of juristic rules.

The first of these is very brief and simply records minor textual variants discovered by Nawawī in the different transmissions of Muslim's text, as available to him. The second is also relatively brief and involves picking up named transmitters in an *isnād*, or lexical items in a *matn*, which might cause problems. Nawawī goes through the material, schematically, in order: the first *isnād*, the first *matn*, the second *isnād*, the second *matn* and so on. The problems here, again, are relatively few and this section too is brief. Slightly longer is section three which begins with the words *ammā aḥkām al-bāb*. Nawawī identifies four rules which can be drawn directly from these hadith: the impurity of dogs, the impurity of that which they lap at, the command to pour away what they lap at, and the necessity of a seven-fold washing of the vessel involved. For each of these, Nawawī gives an outline of the rule and an indication of *ikhtilāf*. Unlike works of *fiqh*, the commentary here goes beyond the Shāfiʿī *madhhab* and includes

[38] Ibid., II, 182–6. Cf. for an analysis of early discussions of this problem, Calder, *Studies*, 78–82.

reference to the view or the views of Mālik, Abū Ḥanīfa and Ahmad, with a very brief suggestion of how arguments were deployed by the various schools. That Nawawī favours the Shāfiʿī school is not hidden in any way; he refers to the Shāfiʿīs as *madhhabu-nā*. The fourth section is introduced with the words *ammā ʿl-jamʿ bayn al-riwāyāt*. Here Nawawī identifies an apparent discrepancy in the various versions of this hadith, not only as transmitted in Muslim, but in other versions found in other collections, namely that they differentially identify, or fail to identify, a requirement for the first or the last or the eighth washing to be in dust. Nawawī records the ruling of the *madhhab* (*madhhabu-nā wa-madhhab al-jamāhir*), which is that there should be one washing with dust either first or last or whatever.

The last component is perhaps the most interesting and the most revealing, for here Nawawī turns to the law as an independent structure and introduces details from that structure into his commentarial discourse, though there are, in fact, no pegs in the base text for him to hang his discourse on.

1. Know that there is no difference, in our view (*ʿinda-nā* – i.e., in the Shāfiʿī school) between a dog's lapping [with his tongue] and other parts of the dog's body. If a dog touches, with its urine, or excrement, or blood, or sweat, or hair, or spittle, or any of its limbs, anything that is pure, in a situation where either one of the two elements involved is wet, a seven-fold washing becomes mandatory, one of which is to be with dust.
2. If two dogs lap [successively], or one dog several times, at a vessel, our companions have three *wajh*s …
3. An eighth washing in water alone does not take the place of the washing in dust, nor does plunging the vessel into plentiful water and leaving it there. This is the more valid view (*al-aṣaḥḥ*). It is said (*qīla*), these actions do [take the place of the washing in dust].

Para. 1 there is a statement of something that is true for the Shāfiʿīs but not for the Hanafīs. Paras. 2 and 3 show Nawawī slipping into juristic terminology and simply using the hadith as a motive for exploring the *madhhab*. The characteristic phraseology of *wajh*, *al-aṣaḥḥ*, *qīla* are sufficiently revelatory of his intention.

There are significant similarities and differences between the task accomplished by Nawawī in his *Majmūʿ* and in the *Sharḥ Muslim*. In the former work, he started with an exposition of the *madhhab* which already contained at least some reference to hadith (and Qurʾan of course, but necessarily much less). His commentary aimed to identify and expand the revealed material but went on from here to an expanded exploration of the details of the law and its *ikhtilāf*, culminating (where it began) with an assessment of the *madhhab*. The *Sharḥ*

Muslim begins with a pre-existing collection of hadith and aims first to comment on the hadith for their own sake (*isnāds* and lexical items), and then moves on to the law. That move towards the law opens up a degree of exploration which was not possible in his other works, namely an exploration of inter-school *ikhtilāf* (not just Shāfiʿī *ikhtilāf*). However, reasons of space, the imperatives of selection and omission, make it quite impossible for a full account of the law and its *ikhtilāf*. Even in respect of the issue of *wulūgh al-kalb*, the *Rawḍa* contains a much larger body of juristic material than is incorporated into the *Sharḥ Muslim*. There is something essentially arbitrary about the selections Nawawī makes, as he himself perhaps implies by hinting at the size and scope of a real commentary which would be more than a hundred volumes in length. What is achieved in the *Sharḥ Muslim* is an indication, but only an indication, of the broad range of *ikhtilāf* experienced by the community in its interpretation of revelation. In addition to reference to the Shāfiʿīs and to the other major *madhhabs*, there is also much scattered reference to Companions, Successors and other great juristic heroes, which implicitly creates and defines the limits of Sunni orthodoxy.

The *Sharḥ Muslim* then aims first to fix and analyse the details of the hadith that are contained in the *Saḥīḥ Muslim*, including some cross-reference to other collections where Nawawī is conscious of a need. Beyond that (for juristic hadith) he aims to suggest, to allude to, to call to mind, the processes of moving from hadith to the law. There is no real effort to be comprehensive, and even the neatly distinguished schema of approaches that I have identified above may disappear in favour of a running commentary which takes up whatever names, words, phrases, or juristic items seem to Nawawī worthy of remark. For the *K. al-zakāt*, Muslim's introductory hadith relate to the establishment of *niṣābs* in a number of different types of property. Nawawī gives the juristic background to this in the form of an introduction, and then moves into a consideration of the lexical items that are problematic, and the juristic rules they imply. Although he is able in context to establish the basic *niṣāb* on camels, he does not see this as an opportunity to give a precise, overall assessment of the type we saw above in the *Rawḍa*, nor does he find any further opportunity to explore this material. The first heading within the *K. al-zakāt*, in Nawawī's work, is devoted to *zakāt al-fiṭr*. The commentary moves rapidly from concern with lexis to concern with juristic exposition. The juristic material alludes to all of the major schools, to Companions and Successors and to scholars and jurists through the ages whose opinions seemed worth preserving. As in the case of the dogs, the material is both broader than the *Rawḍa* (because it alludes to other *madhhabs*) and narrower (because it does not offer a full exploration of detail even within the Shāfiʿī school).

Here are the first sentences of the chapter on *zakāt al-fiṭr*.

Chapter on *zakāt al-fiṭr.*

1. [Muslim's] words: That the Prophet of God imposed *zakāt al-fiṭr* in the month of Ramadan as a duty upon the people. … The people have disputed on the meaning of the verb 'to impose a duty' (*faraḍa*) here. The majority of early and later scholars say it means to make binding or mandatory. Hence *zakāt al-fiṭr* is a mandatory duty (*farḍ wājib*) in their view; because it comes under the general provision of God's words, 'Give *zakāt*' [Q2.43] and because of the Prophet's use here of the word *faraḍa* … Ishāq b. Rāḥawayh said that the incumbency of *zakāt al-fiṭr* is like [the incumbency established by] consensus. One/some of the people of Iraq, one/some of the companions of Mālik, one/some of the companions of Shāfiʿī, and Dawūd in his final view declared that it was *sunna*, not *wājib*. They say that the meaning of *faraḍa* here is construed as equivalent to *nadaba* (recommended). Abū Ḥanīfa said it was *wājib*, not *farḍ*, in conformity with his practice of distinguishing *wājib* and *farḍ*. According to the Qadi (ʿIyāḍ), some have claimed that *zakāt al-fiṭr* has been abrogated by *zakāt*. This is a clear error. The truth (*al-ṣawāb*) is that it is a mandatory duty (*farḍ wājib*).
2. His words: In the month of Ramadan. [This is] an indication of the time of its incumbency. There is dispute amongst the scholars. The valid view of Shāfiʿī (*al-ṣaḥīḥ min qawl al-Shāfiʿī*) is that it becomes mandatory at sunset, with the onset of the first part of the night of the festival. The other view is that it becomes mandatory at dawn following the night of the festival. Our companions say that it is mandatory only with both sunset and dawn, such that if a child is born after sunset, or if a person dies before dawn, it is not binding. There are two transmissions from Mālik corresponding to the two views of Shāfiʿī. According to Abū Ḥanīfa, it is mandatory at dawn. Al-Marīzī said: 'It is said that this dispute is based on the words "*al-fiṭr* in the month of Ramadan"', the question being whether *fiṭr* here has the meaning it normally has for the rest of the month of Ramadan, in which case the reference is to sunset, or whether it has a special meaning and refers to dawn …

Para. 1 here relates a dispute about the word *faraḍa* to a minority opinion held by some of the followers of Abū Hanīfa, Mālik, and Shāfiʿī, as well as Dawūd al-Ẓāhirī. Ishāq b. Rāḥawayh is a famous traditionist whose view strengthens the majority position. The reference to Abū Hanīfa establishes a difference in terminological use across the schools. The Qadi ʿIyāḍ had previously commented on the *Saḥīḥ Muslim*. Though a Mālikī, he is frequently quoted by Nawawī as a reliable authority. The paragraph as a whole both establishes the majority view and its grounds, while recognising the minority view and its adherents. Para. 2

identifies a basic dispute within the Shāfiʿī school which has ramifications across the other schools. The citation from al-Marīzī attempts to account for this basic dispute. This material is characteristic of the tone of the *Sharḥ* as a whole. It is about the enactment of dispute, the identification of participants in dispute, the discovery of authority (through argument and through the *madhhab*) and the citation of other scholars who had, wisely, well, or otherwise interestingly, commented on the process of dispute and discovery that lies between revelation and the law. This exploration of dispute is in part an acknowledgement of the mystery of the law; but it is also a drawing of lines since it distinguishes both what lies broadly inside the Sunni tradition, and, within that tradition, what distinguishes the various *madhhabs*. It is also an exploration of the passage of time and continuity within the tradition: The reference to scholars like the Qadi ʿIyāḍ and al-Marīzī acknowledges their place in this ongoing conversation about the nature and limits of the law.

It is unnecessary here to explore further the characteristics of the *Sharḥ Muslim*. It is necessary, however, to insist that this exegetical genre, though it must, by virtue of the content of the *Saḥīḥ*, go beyond juristic discourse to theological, ethical, narrative and other material, consists predominantly of juristic discourse. Though it has some different stresses and some different orientations, it shows a primary concern for the same kind of thing as is evident in the law books proper: an exploration of the space between revelation and law, an acknowledgement of *ikhtilāf*, an acknowledgement of loyalty to *madhhab* and the need to identify for those that belong to a particular *madhhab* a final answer to legal questions. In responding to hadith, Nawawī does not meditate directly on the significance they have or might have for him, he demonstrates what significance they actually had for the historical community. His commentary consists broadly of reports of what other scholars derived from the hadith together with indications of their arguments and the place of these arguments in relation to his own and other established schools of law.

Section 5. Conclusions

1. *Mukhtaṣars*. The form and content of Nawawī's *mukhtaṣar* confirms the general conclusions about works of this type reached in Chapter 1. They are brief summaries of the *madhhab*, couched in a highly refined and formally structured style. Nawawī's *Minhāj* represents the transition to what I have called the mannerist style. In this case, it is not simply that his syntax is precise, careful and deployed towards a startling concision; he has enhanced his capacity for expressing much in little by adopting a linguistic code for *ikhtilāf* which distances the text from literal meaning and makes it a technical tour de force,

barely accessible to the untrained. That it was possible to refine that style still further, towards something even more mannered, exquisite, recondite and linguistically dazzling might seem surprising, but that was the achievement, a generation or so later, of the Mālikī scholar Khalīl b. Ishāq (d. 776/1374). He too adopted a linguistic code for the expression of *ikhtilāf*, and achieved a refined density of language that transformed the law (the *madhhab*) into a precious and multi-faceted jewel: a puzzle, a delight, a tortuous path, a vision of dispute and a resolution of dispute, couched in language dizzily elliptical, dazzlingly correct. Works aspiring to these characteristics became fairly standard in all later depictions of the law, across the *madhhabs*, without necessarily displacing earlier, easier, more classical works which retained their place in the curriculum. Khalīl's *Mukhtaṣar* did not eliminate the famous early Mālikī *mukhtaṣar* by Ibn Abī Zayd al-Qayrawānī (d. ?386/996) which continued to attract commentaries through the centuries. The classical and the mannerist styles had each their part to play in the learning and in the memorisation of the law.

2. *Mabsūṭs*. In the same general way, the formal components of Nawawī's *mabsūṭs* conform to the characteristics of the Ḥanafī *mabsūṭs* described in Chapter 1. Formally, and in spite of a marked difference in tone, the *Rawḍa* of Nawawī corresponds to the *Fatāwā* of Qāḍīkhān, the *Majmu*ʿ to the general run of *mabsūṭs* that contain justificatory argument. Nawawī's works, naturally, are marked by processes of selection, argument and presentation that make them distinctively his own. In the case of the *Majmū*ʿ, the separation of the two tasks of exploring, on the one hand, revelation, and, on the other, the *madhhab* is remarkable. The result is to move the stress from justification of rules to justification of the system. Because revelation has its peculiar nature (immense in scope, uncertain of content and of boundary, insecure of meaning), the law necessarily has its features (an endless process of argument, a pattern of *ikhtilāf*). Resolution of *ikhtilāf* is found in and through the *madhhab* which offers authority – much less, however, through formal assessment of argument than through discovery of the majority view. The *Majmū*ʿ binds together a number of allied sciences: the science of biography in relation to *isnāds*, the science of language in relation to lexis and syntax, the science of hadith in identifying authoritative collections and variants, the various sciences of juristic argument, *ikhtilāf* and assessment of *madhhab*. The whole is a dense reticulation of knowledge and meaning that justifies and creates the religious history of the community – the Shāfiʿī community within the Sunni community.

The *Rawḍa* has a different tone and a different intention. It sets out the *madhhab* in all its detail, but without reference to justificatory argument or revelation. Here the law is an autonomous, self-subsistent structure, a complex model of a social reality, uniquely Shāfiʿī, because uniquely derived from the great juristic works of the Shāfiʿī school.

Both in his *mukhtaṣar* and in his *mabsūṭ*s, Nawawī demonstrates a very pure sense of the jurist's task: He never moves from the assessment of juristic generalities to the identification of contemporary particulars. That move, from the universal structures of the law to the local and the contingent, we discovered to be less rare in the Ḥanafī tradition. Sarakhsī and Ibn Nujaym have been recognised as making the move on occasion, and it is a marked feature of the *Radd al-muḥtār* of Muḥammad b. 'Umar Ibn 'Ābidīn (1252/1836). It can be classified as a move from the jurist's task to the mufti's, and while it clearly has a potential place in the literature of *furū' al-fiqh*, it can be, and frequently was, eliminated. The terminology of 'general' or 'universal' contrasted with 'particular' was to be developed and exploited to characterise the different tasks of the (teaching or writing) jurist and the mufti in the writings of the Shāfi'ī scholar – and mufti – 'Alī b. 'Abd al-Kāfī al-Subkī (756/1355).[39]

3. It is tempting to characterise the tradition of juristic exploration in Islam as constituted by first a stable body of revelation and then a more free and productive body of derived rules. That seems to me, at a certain level, not absolutely wrong, but it does miss some essential qualities of the system. It would be more accurate to say that the juristic tradition consists of i. a relatively stable body of revelation, ii. a set of normative structures (the four *madhhab*s) only marginally less stable than the body of revelation and iii. a set of arguments that link the one and the other. This is essentially a timeless and non-developing system. The body of revelation consists primarily of Qur'an and hadith. But the latter in particular is an unwieldy bundle of disparate texts about which there was constant dispute, both in respect of individual items (the classification of hadith as *ṣaḥīḥ*, *ḥasan*, etc.) and in respect of relevant collections (not only the five or six 'valid' collections, but a very considerable bundle of potentially relevant ancillary literature). In stressing the essentially stable nature of the *madhhab*s, I have not wished to deny that there might be some changes in the preferred norms of a particular school over time, or that there was accommodation to this or that particular social reality. In spite of these, the fundamental character of school literature was conservative, fossilised, stable, a matter much more of restating traditional and established norms than of changing them or accommodating them to particular realities. The process of justifying the (given) normative structures by showing how they might be derived from the (given) body of revelation was an essential part of juristic literature and might be enacted either at the level of individual norm, or, as we have detected in Nawawī, at the level of system – the general nature of the law, with its variety and recorded dispute, is a result of the general nature of revelation.

[39] See Chapter 3, Section 2.

Nawawī's commentary on the *Ṣaḥīḥ* of Muslim, his *Sharḥ Muslim*, is yet another effort at juxtaposing revelation, *madhhab* and justificatory argument. In this work he is to a considerable extent freed from the particularities of the Shāfiʿī *madhhab*. Making one standard work of revelation his starting point, he relates it to all the major *madhhab*s, with varied reference to justificatory argument, named authorities and minority views. Like the *Majmūʿ*, it is a work that binds all the major sciences of revelation and the law: *isnād* criticism, lexicography and syntax, exploration of hadith collections and variants, assessment of *ikhtilāf* across the *madhhab*s, exploration of juristic literature, and so on. His work, by his own account, falls short of all that might be said and so has a suggestive, allusive, partial, highly selective nature – qualities that he had also acknowledged in his *Majmūʿ*. The assessment of revelation, law and justificatory argument was so large and complex an ambition that it could not effectively be achieved for even one *madhhab*, never mind the larger ambition of charting the almost infinite ramifications of thought and opinion that characterised the total history of the Sunni community. The ambition, however, even or perhaps precisely because of its (inevitably) imperfect achievement, was of immense importance. The *Sharḥ Muslim* speaks of the fundamental nature of revelation and the historical experience of the Sunni community in translating revelation into law. Imperfect and abbreviated though it must be, it reveals, in an endless pattern of authoritative comment, the difficulty, the intricacy, the mystery, the polyvalency and the endless delight of the law. This was not the first such work but it was a major stage in the development of a genre. The genre reached its highest point in the *Fatḥ al-bārī sharḥ al-Bukhārī*, by Ibn Ḥajar al-ʿAsqalānī[40] (d. 852/1448–8), a work of dazzling scholarship and the most magnificent achievement of exegetical discourse in the whole of Islamic history. It is a work almost totally unappreciated by Western scholarship.

[40] See n. 18.

3

Scholars, Muftis, Judges and Secular Power

The Need for Distinctions

Introduction

1. A mufti is a scholar who responds to specific questions about the law, different therefore from the writing jurist who gives a general and structured assessment of the law. The mufti's response is a fatwa, the questioner or petitioner, a *mustaftī*. The task, or process, of giving a fatwa is *iftā'*. A fatwa can be sought and given orally, but, more typically, the question is given in written form and a written reply is elicited. The two components of a written fatwa are the *mas'ala* or question and the *jawāb* or answer. As a written item, the combination of *mas'ala* and *jawāb* is called a fatwa, though the term might more strictly be applied only to the *jawāb*. In some contexts, it was necessary to distinguish the ideal fatwa – which could be issued only by the highest ranking jurists – from the actual practice. In this case normal linguistic usage was deemed to describe an imperfect realisation of the ideal.[1] The processes of *iftā'*, when analysed, were always found to depend on hierarchy, a grading of scholars according to their knowledge, the lower grades dependent on the higher grades. The highest grades were invariably located in the persons of the founding Imams and their companions.

Joseph Schacht, in so far as he recognised an adaptive and developmental quality in Islamic law, located it (primarily) in the activities of the mufti.

> New sets of facts constantly arose in life, and they had to be mastered and moulded with the traditional tools provided by legal science. This activity was carried out by the muftis.[2]

[1] Ibn 'Ābidīn, *Radd al-Muḥtār* (Beirut: Dār al-Fikr, 1979), I, 69, for an expression of the ideal. 'The writers of *uṣūl* have established that the mufti is a mujtahid. A non-mujtahid who has learned the opinions of a mujtahid is not a mufti. ... Hence it is known that the fatwas of our time, given by those who exist now, are not fatwas, but transmission of the words of the [real] mufti.'

[2] Schacht, *An Introduction to Islamic Law* (Oxford: Clarendon Press, 1964), 73.

This intuition (for it was not demonstrated) was perhaps uncertain, for, two paragraphs later, he rephrased it slightly: 'the doctrinal development of Islamic law owes much to the activity of muftis'. Much, but not all. More recent scholarship has not deviated from the general, if insecure, tenor of Schacht's opinion. Change and development in Islamic law is generally perceived as intimately related to *iftāʿ*, the mufti's task.[3]

The management of the law as a total system depended in fact upon three major functionaries, the teaching/writing jurist, the mufti and the qadi. The proposal that one was, more than the others, responsible for development and change must depend on distinguishing and characterising these functions. This has been attempted, either directly or indirectly, by modern scholarship,[4] but the practitioners themselves, in the pre-modern period, were acutely aware of the boundaries they honoured (or transgressed) as they participated in the various activities of the law. When a powerful scholar who was also a judge and mufti felt moved to observe himself his observations have, necessarily, a psychological intimacy, a dynamic immediacy, and, at their best, a niceness of expression denied to the mere observer and late-comer. Such at least is the case for ʿAlī b. ʿAbd al-Kāfī al-Subkī, known as Taqī al-Dīn, Chief Judge (qāḍī al-quḍāt) of Damascus for 17 years in the eighth/thirteenth century, subject and citizen of the Mamluk sultans and their governors. A persistent, almost a compulsive, writer, he copied, stored and preserved many of his own fatwas, together with other juristic studies, until, after his death, his papers were collected and organised by his son, in a work known as the Fatāwā of Subkī. Born out of the particularities of a busy life, and expressive of a dutiful and pious concern for the law and his own salvation, they have remarkable revelatory power.

2. Subkī was born in 683/1284–5, in Mamluk Egypt.[5] He had a conventional jurist's training in the madrasas of Cairo, where he covered the usual spectrum of academic studies, and sat with all the major teachers of that time and region. He travelled, of course, in search of hadith, but not beyond the narrow boundaries

[3] The view is widespread, but particularly associated with the writings of Wael B. Hallaq; see especially his 'From *fatwās* to *furūʿ*: Growth and change in Islamic substantive law', *Islamic Law and Society*, 1;1 (1994): 29–65; also Muhammad Khalid Masud, Brinkley Messick, and David S.Powers, 'Muftis, fatwas, and Islamic legal interpretation' in Masud, Messick, Powers (eds.), *Islamic Legal Interpretation: Muftis and their Fatwas* (Cambridge, Mass. and London: Harvard University Press, 1996), 3–32.

[4] Again by Hallaq, in 'From *Fatwās* to *Furūʿ*'; also A. Kevin Reinhart, 'Transcendence and Social Practice: *Muftis* and *Qadis* as Religious Interpreters', *Annales Islamologiques*, 27 (1993 [1994]): 5–28; Masud, Messick, Powers, 'Muftis, fatwas, and Islamic legal interpretation'. All of these are directed primarily at the distinction between the qadi and the mufti, apparently little concerned with the role of the scholar jurist.

[5] For the following information, unless otherwise signalled, Ibn Ḥajar al-ʿAsqalānī, *al-Durar al-kāmina*, (Dār al-Kutub al-Ḥadītha, 1966), III, 134–42.

of Mamluk power: The biographers mention Syria, Alexandria and the Hijaz. As a bright young scholar he naturally moved into teaching posts, at the madrasas of the Manṣūriyya, the mosque of al-Ḥākim, the Ḥakāriyya and others. The trajectory of a scholar's career in those days owed much to the proliferation of teaching establishments, funded by waqf endowments, which was a feature of Ayyubid and Mamluk Egypt and Syria.[6] The supervision of waqf endowments was to constitute a major part of Subkī's duties as a qadi in Damascus, and his constant participation in their financial nexus, which was rarely unsullied, was remembered towards the end of his life in a sorrowful lamentation at the imperfections of worldly activity.[7]

His early career took shape under the modest political stability offered by the long (if interrupted) reign of al-Malik al-Nāṣir Muḥammad (693/1293–741/1341). Ibn Ḥajar (d. 852/1448–9), in his biography of Subkī, relates that the great ministers of state noticed and esteemed him; and when the Shāfiʿī *qāḍī al-quḍāt* of Damascus, Jalāl al-Dīn al-Qazwīnī, died in 739/1338–9, al-Nāṣir himself participated in the choice of his successor, Subkī. Already in his mid-fifties, Subkī was perhaps not an obvious choice; he had not previously held a judicial post (though his father had been a provincial judge). Convention and piety required some signs of regret from a scholar who had been elected to the invidious and dangerous post of qadi. These are obvious enough in the writings of Subkī (an example, below, Section 1.3), but combine there with a sense, possibly a sad sense, of efficient mastery of a necessary duty. He flourished, expanded his authority by taking up extra posts (teaching posts at the Dār al-Ḥadīth al-Ashrafiyya and the Madrasa al-Shāmiyya al-Barrāniyya), made an unavailing attempt to gain the post of *qāḍī al-quḍāt* in Cairo in 746/1345–6, lived through the Black Death of 749/1348–9 (and incurred no criticism, it is said, for the numerous problems of inheritance that came before him in that period), and remained thereafter an efficient, ascetic, pious, effective and strong-willed qadi. He relinquished his judicial post when he fell ill towards the end of his life, passing it to his son, and died shortly afterwards, in Cairo, in 756/1355. (Dynasties of qadis were a feature of the age; it reflects the importance of this office as a focus of social stability in a period when the governing elite were obsessed by the inner workings of factional rivalry and the surface trappings of power.)

Subkī never stopped writing. Ibn Ḥajar remarks, on the evidence of his works, that he never came across a strange or difficult problem without writing something on it, long or short, in which he gathered together its diverse aspects. The point is

[6] Ira M.Lapidus, *Muslim Cities in the Later Middle Ages* (Cambridge, MA: Harvard University Press, 1967). See especially Appendix A.

[7] Below, Chapter 4.

obvious from any reading of the *Fatāwā* and was obvious to Subkī himself. In an isolated passage found amongst his papers when he died, he commented

It is necessary to adopt the writing of knowledge as an act of worship (*'ibāda*), whether you expect benefit to follow from it or not. I, in what I write, have this intention.[8]

In his old age he wrote because he had developed the habit of writing, and, for some of his works, could do no more than hope that somebody might read them, perhaps benefit from them[9] – even if that was not a necessary condition of his activity as a writer. More formally, he wrote for his public, decisive replies to the questions of his judicial deputies, interventions in public debates, responses to petitioners, statements of opinion, numerous and varied responsa directed at the masses or at the elite, covering a multitude of topics, but having a central focus in the judicial affairs of Damascus.

He was devoted to hadith [said Abū al-Maḥāsin al-Ḥusaynī[10]] and he wrote in his own fine, clear, skilful hand much on all the other Islamic sciences. He was one whose fame reached all kingdoms, whose conduct was familiar to anybody who knew the affairs of men. Horsemen carried his writings and his fatwas to all corners of the land. He was one who combined all types of knowledge with frugality and piety, much worship, recitation of the Qur'an, courage and severity in religion. …

The horsemen, whether privately commissioned or a part of the Mamluk postal system, were certainly kept busy by this indefatigable qadi.

Section 1. Generalities and particulars: scholars, muftis and judges

1. In the year 749/1348–9, Subkī produced an important assessment of the three functionaries of Islamic law. The context was a fatwa which offered a number of expository rulings related to the document which had created a waqf in favour of the mosque known as al-Madrasa al-Shāmiyya al-Juwāniyya[11] in Damascus. Subkī first cited, in his own summary, those parts of the foundation document he wanted to discuss. He then proceeded to distinguish and comment on twenty problems. The tone is academic and scholarly, the structure loose and open to digression; the results, however, are practical, and probably related to discussions with the supervisor (*nāẓir*) of the waqf (whose discretionary powers are maintained

[8] Subkī, *Fatāwā* (Beirut: Dār al-Ma'rifa, n.d.), II, 369.

[9] Ibid., II, 102, ll. 12–13, cited below, Chapter 4.

[10] Subkī, *Fatāwā*, introduction, 3, citing Abū al-Maḥāsin al-Ḥusaynī's *Dhayl tadhkirat al-ḥuffāẓ*.

[11] Subkī, *Fatāwā*, II, 52–9. Like much of the rest of this poorly edited work the text is full of errors. Where they can be overcome, I have not drawn attention to these, but tacitly emended them. Where my emendations are more than merely standard, I draw attention to them in a footnote.

or expanded throughout). One important issue relates to a clause in the foundation document which specified that the jurists and trainee jurists (*al-fuqahāʾ wa-ʾl-mutafaqqiha*) who worked in the madrasa and benefited from the waqf should not exceed twenty in number. Subkī, taking advantage of a clause which permitted variation should the waqf increase in value, declared that the numbers of the jurists could increase, and their payments vary, as the supervisor saw fit.[12]

Some time later he had to take up the problem again, clearly because there had been objections to his first ruling. It was not the supervisor who objected; in fact, again, there is evidence that he had prompted or at least abetted Subkī's intervention.[13] It could have been the *fuqahāʾ*, for their income was at issue and had been left by Subkī almost entirely subject to the discretion of the supervisor. As before, Subkī quotes relevant items from the foundation document, then starts abruptly his own argument which relates now to two major issues. One was the question whether the words of the founder could be so construed as to permit an increase in the number of recipients beyond twenty, and the other whether, that conceded, there were any limitations on the supervisor's discretion, either as to numbers, or as to the sums to be paid to individual jurists. On both points a limitation had been previously imposed, namely that sixty jurists should be graded in three ranks, each of which would receive a specified sum of, respectively, sixty, forty and twenty dinars per year. This ruling had emerged in a judicial (possibly governmental) review which had taken place in 727/1326–7, during the governorship of Tengiz. Subkī declined to see that review as binding and reaffirmed the wide discretionary powers of the supervisor.[14]

These details have their own interest, but are offered here only as background. My immediate intention is to isolate a fragment of Subkī's argument. For, in this second fatwa, he followed up his statement of his own views with a set of arguments, conventionally arranged under a stylised Q[uestion] and A[nswer] format (*in qulta* … *qultu* … – possibly recalling a real debate). One of these questions prompted his analysis of the three functionaries of the law:

0. Q. A group of *ʿulamāʾ* from the Egyptian lands have issued a fatwa stating that [rulings like yours in this case] are forbidden.
1. A. May God be pleased with the *ʿulamāʾ*; they are rewarded for their *ijtihād* and for their aiming at the truth. Know, O my brother, that the outstanding and perfect *ʿulamāʾ* are, in relation to *fiqh*, in three ranks.

[12] Ibid., see *masʾala*s 9,10,11,13, 17, 18, 19.

[13] Ibid. The whole fatwa is found at II, 118–25; at 120, l.27, we learn that Subkī has been given, by the supervisor, a general financial overview which helps his argument.

[14] Ibid., 120–1, for Subkī's general position; 122, l.11 for the earlier judicial review, which took place in the time of Tengiz.

i. Knowledge of *fiqh* for itself. This is a matter of universals (*huwa amr kullī*). For the master of *fiqh* in this sense considers universal matters and the rules pertaining to them, as is the habit of writers, teachers and students. This rank is the root of the others.

ii. The rank of the mufti. This relates to the forms of the particular (*ṣūra juzʾiyya*), and to the application (*tanzīl*) of what has been established in the first rank. It is the mufti's duty to consider what he has been asked about, and the conditions of the event (*aḥwāl tilka ʾl-wāqiʿa*). His answer should be related to these conditions. He informs the petitioner that God's ruling (*ḥukm Allāh*) on this event is such-and-such. This is different from the absolute *faqīh*, the writing and teaching *faqīh*, who does not pronounce on 'this event', but rather on 'such-and-such an event'. There may well be a difference between the latter and that [particular] event. For this reason, we find that many *fuqahāʾ* do not know how to give fatwas, do not know that the special function of the mufti is the application of the universal law to the particular situation (*tanzīl al-fiqh al-kullī ʿalā ʾl-mawḍiʿ al-juzʾī*). This task requires insight over and above the memorising of *fiqh* and its proofs. It is also for this reason that we find in the fatwas of some early scholars some factor that requires restraint in accepting them into *fiqh*. This does not arise from any inadequacy in the mufti – Heaven forbid! – but because there may well be in the event he was asked about something that required that special answer. So it is not dismissed in all its aspects. This may happen in some cases; we have found it, through trial and experience, in some cases but not many, the majority being such that they can be accepted. So be aware of this possibility, for necessity may require it in certain situations, and we will be unable to admit a fatwa of this kind to the *madhhab* without much consideration.

iii. The rank of the qadi. This is more specialised than the rank of the mufti. For the judge considers precisely the particular matters that the mufti considers, plus the establishment of their causes, the rejection of opposition, and so on. Matters become evident to the qadi which are not evident to the mufti. Hence the consideration of the qadi is wider than that of the mufti, and that of the mufti is wider than that of the *faqīh*. But the *faqīh*'s consideration is the most noble and of most general benefit (*aʿammu nafʿan*).

2. Once you know this, [you will recognise] that *fiqh* is general, noble, and offers a benefit that is universal (*nāfiʿ nafʿan kulliyyan*). It is the foundation of religion and the world (*qiwām al-dīn wa-ʾl-dunyā*). Giving fatwas is a speciality; it comprises all that and also the application of the universal

to the particular (*tanzīl al-kullī ʿalā ʾl-juzʾī*), in a non-binding manner. Judicial activity is a speciality within a speciality; it comprises all that and more. One of its extra aspects is proofs (*ḥujaj*); the other is the quality of being binding.

3. In whichever of the three ranks you act, your intention is solely for the sake of God. If there is someone who differs from you, consider his words and try to find a reason for them. If you find a reason that is more correct than yours, then revert to his view. But if you find the situation otherwise, then pray for mercy upon him, and recognise the extent of God's bounty who has led you where he did not lead the other. Give thanks to your Lord, and do not demean your brother.[15]

2. In this passage we learn that *fiqh* in the pure sense is an activity characteristic of writers, teachers and students, an essentially academic activity. It deals in universals (*kulliyyāt*) (para. 1). By contrast, the functions of the mufti and the qadi require the consideration of particulars (*juzʾiyyāt*). This means events (*wāqiʿa*), their forms (*ṣūra*) and their qualities (*ḥāl*). The task of the mufti is to bring the universals of *fiqh* to bear upon the particulars of daily life, to apply them – *tanzīl al-kulliyyāt ʿalā ʾl-juzʾiyyāt*. The terminology recurs frequently in Subkī's *Fatāwā*, and may (as in the present instance) constitute a significant component in a longer argument. A further example may be found in a small independent treatise, written in 748/1347–8, relating to the use of astronomical calculation to establish the end of Ramadan. In the course of a many-faceted argument, Subkī refers to a youth who was under the impression that if a qadi issued a judicial declaration (*ḥukm*) that Ramadan had ended, it became prohibited for individuals to continue their fast.

> [This youth] has not distinguished between the particular and the universal, nor between the words of a mufti and those of the *ʿulamāʾ* in books. For the task of the *ʿulamāʾ* in their books is to deal with universal problems (*al-masāʾil al-kulliyya*), while the task of the mufti is to apply those universals to particular events (*tanzīl tilka ʾl-kulliyyāt ʿalā ʾl-waqāʾiʿ al-juzʾiyya*). If the mufti knows that such and such a particular can be brought under (*indaraja*) such-and-such a universal, he should give a response that accords with the ruling mentioned in the books.[16]

The task of the mufti is to apply to particulars the universals of the law, to bring particulars under universals. The terminology is not quite original, but it has a compelling and a revealing quality.[17]

[15] Ibid., II, 122–3.

[16] Ibid., I, 213, l.12ff.

[17] Nawawī had already used the term *indirāj*, and 'linking' (*ilḥāq*). See Norman Calder, 'Al-Nawawī's Typology of Muftis and its Significance for a General Theory of Islamic Law', *Islamic Law and*

Subkī's conception of a fatwa includes the expectation that it will coincide with the *madhhab*. But it will also be entangled with particulars and that may well make it, in appearance, out of line with the *madhhab*. A fatwa has to be considered in the light of the *madhhab*. In a bundle of repetitive, apologetic clauses, Subkī makes it clear that a fatwa may have to be dismissed (not because of the mufti, Heaven forbid), at least in some of its aspects, if it cannot be accommodated to the *madhhab*. Its inextricable entanglement with particulars makes it unsuitable as a direct expression of the law, that is, of the *madhhab*. The process of consideration and accommodation, represents, of course, the task of the academic jurist and this prompts an initial qualification of the proposal that the mufti is the prime or the only agent of change in Islamic law. The mufti is an inferior rank, his task an inferior task and his statements require 'restraint' and may have to be 'dismissed' after due consideration of *fiqh* and the *madhhab*. It is the academic jurist who passes judgement on fatwas by acknowledging that they do or do not represent the *madhhab*.

The hierarchical ranking of the functionaries is not in doubt (para. 2). The writing and teaching *faqīh* had the noblest task, the one of most general benefit. Its usefulness, like its subject matter, was a universal (*kullī*). It was the foundation of religion and the world. The mufti informed of God's ruling (*ḥukm Allāh*) – but that was a derivative task, dependent on a prior knowledge of *fiqh*. The mufti in relation to the *faqīh* was a specialist, and the judge in relation to the mufti a still narrower specialist.

There is perhaps a paradox here in that the ideal judge had all the qualities of the mufti and more, and the ideal mufti had all the qualities of the *faqīh* and more. On that basis surely the judge is the highest rank? That is not the case. The ideal judge derived his competence as a judge from his prior competence as a mufti, and the ideal mufti derived his competence from his prior competence as a *faqīh*. The universals of *fiqh* were the base (Subkī says the root, *aṣl* – para. 11) of the lower (derived) functions. The paradox arises out of the schematic and idealised presentation: Subkī admits that what he is presenting here is 'the outstanding and perfect *'ulamā'*'. A real qadi might not be an ideal qadi, and an ideal jurist might avoid the task of being a qadi. Indeed, more frequently than not, that was the situation. The functions of the jurist, mufti and qadi were often separate. An adequate functioning qadi might not have a very good knowledge of the law, he might be a very inferior scholar, in which case he would be almost totally dependent on more learned muftis and jurists to establish the law that

Society, 3;2 (1996): 155. Both of these terms, and *kulliyāt* and *juz'iyyāt*, are used (much later) by Ibn Khaldūn, whose works perhaps reflect an established analytic terminology. *Muqaddima* (Cairo: Maṭba'a Muṣṭafā Muḥammad, n.d.), Ch. 6, Sec. 4, 435; cf. Ch. 6, Sec. 34, 542.

he must apply. A low-ranking mufti likewise might be dependent, at least for difficult and unusual cases, on higher ranking muftis – those who had more of the quality of *ijtihād*. Any abstract consideration of the tasks and qualities of a mufti requires some acknowledgement of hierarchy. The need is pressing and its fulfilment obvious in the many accounts of *iftāʿ* which offer some representation of the hierarchy of muftis.[18]

Clearly the functioning mufti, because he will be frequently under pressure from events (particulars), may be involved in processes of change and adaptation. But the management, acceptance and justification of change, the accommodation of change to the *madhhab* must be a function of the jurist. When a high-ranking jurist is also an active and busy mufti, in a time of change, as is the case with Subkī, then we may expect a steady and intense confrontation with change. But there is no reason in principle why a mufti should not stand against change; and no reason in principle why a jurist, while avoiding the tasks of *iftāʿ*, should not manage and accommodate change through his professional tasks of teaching, expounding and writing. The dominant (if qualified) view of modern scholarship that the mufti is the obvious or the primary agent of change in Islamic Law may be a distraction. *Iftāʿ* after all is a process in which the universals of the law are brought to bear upon the particularities of a problem: It is a matter of negotiating the space between the jurist *qua* jurist and the jurist *qua* mufti. But the space is controlled by the jurist (not least if he is also a mufti).

3. Subkī's *obiter dicta* permit a number of other observations about the distinction between the writing jurist, the mufti and the qadi. Writing in the year 754/1353–4 a small treatise, apparently private, about the special and superior authority of the Shāfiʿī judge in Damascus in relation to the supervision of waqfs, he made the following remarks.

I dislike discoursing on this matter, and had intended not to write this, for I am a Shāfiʿī qadi and it may well be believed that what prompted me to this task was my desire to [preserve and increase my supervision of waqfs]. So I reflected on this and found opposing arguments in my love for knowledge and its clarification, and in the task imposed by God upon the *ʿulamāʿ* to inform the people and not to conceal knowledge, and also in the hope that it might benefit those after me, when I shall have no personal interest in the matter. I found the latter arguments more weighty and wrote what I have written. May God forgive both me and those who think ill of me. I am a warning to those who have a capacity for knowledge, that they should not take up a judicial post, for the words of the *ʿulamāʿ* are accepted, but the words of the qadis are contaminated by suspicion. Though there is a reward attendant on qadis in respect of particular events, there are great rewards for knowledge, the knowledge that we write down; these rewards are dedicated to

[18] For example, Nawawī; see Calder, 'Al-Nawawī's Typology'.

universal matters which will last till the day of resurrection, while particulars are subject to the vicissitudes of time (*li-anna-hā umūr kulliyya tabqā ilā yawm al-qiyāma walākinna 'l-juzʾī maʿa 'l-maqādir*).[19]

Again the terminology of 'universal' and 'particular' is pressed into the cause of making distinctions. Here the distinction is between the qadi on the one hand and the jurist (or mufti?) on the other. Subkī characterises his present task as a response to the general duty of the *ʿālim* to inform the people and disseminate knowledge. Though he is dealing with particulars (the real situation of judges in his time), he clearly feels that he is relating them to the universals of the law. If he is indeed acting as a mufti, he is working at the highest level of *iftāʾ*, negotiating the space between universals and particulars. And the focus of his interest is upwards, towards the expression of universals. It is that focus of interest that distinguishes his present task from that of the qadi (who is devoted to particulars) and gives his arguments enduring value (and, as he claims here, secures for him greater heavenly reward). Behind the mufti there must be a jurist from whom the mufti derives his (inferior) competence. Many of the items preserved in the *Fatāwā* of Subkī, including this one, even when they deal with particulars, have a predominantly juristic quality. They survive, not because they are fatwas, but because they reveal the jurist behind the mufti. At least, in the present instance, that is what Subkī claims (or aspires to), though conscious that, by virtue of his other function, as qadi, he might be (perceived as) entangled with particulars to the point of bias. Therefore it is better for the *ʿālim* to avoid the post of a qadi. It was an ideal that Subkī had been unable to achieve.

4. The writing jurist and the mufti had by virtue of their different tasks different audiences and this too implied distinction. In an undated treatise on the rights of Christians to repair their churches, Subkī adopted a rather stringent view. Many jurists had issued fatwas declaring it permissible, and government decrees (*marāsim*) to that effect had been issued by kings and qadis,[20] but this was wrong, for the building and the repair of churches were equally *ḥarām*, by consensus. So the jurists affirmed. Or Subkī said they did, though it involved an obvious contradiction, since they had also issued fatwas declaring it permissible. Subkī explained the discrepancy by reference to language.

The jurists are in dispute only on the question whether they [the Christians] are to be prevented from repair and renewal or not to be prevented. Those who say they are not to be prevented do not say that it is permitted to them, nor that it is a legal and permissible act. If such words occur in the discourse of some writers they are to be read as an

[19] Subkī, *Fatāwā*, II, 24, l.19ff.
[20] Read *bi'l-idhn* for *bi-lā idhn* at 369, l.19.

unqualified expression and a linguistic transformation suited to the understanding of jurists (*iṭlāq al-ʿibāra wa-ʾl-iḥāla ʿalā fahm al-faqīh*) since they know the foundations of *fiqh*. Those who are ignorant should not be deceived by such expressions. The writing jurist may use words in a metaphorical fashion because he knows that the jurists will be familiar with his intention, and he is addressing jurists. As to the mufti, for the most part he is addressing the masses, so he has no excuse for such a practice. It is his duty to avoid metaphorical speech, and all speech that might be understood differently from its surface meaning.[21]

Though the reference to universals and particulars is missing here, the necessity to distinguish between muftis and writing jurists is maintained. They had different audiences, the jurist addressing himself to an educated elite, the mufti addressing, predominantly, the masses. This had consequences for how to read their works, and generated, for the mufti, a duty, namely to speak clearly and to avoid metaphor.

5. So far, the distinction that has most drawn our attention is that between the writing/teaching jurist on the one hand and the mufti and qadi on the other. But the last two had also to be distinguished. The extra aspects that Subkī noted above (Section 1.1; para. 2) as representing the speciality of the judge related to proofs (*ḥujaj*), and to the quality of being binding (*ilzām*). He had occasion to expand on these distinctions.

0. *Masʾala*: On one who says, 'The mufti rambles, the qadi rules' (*al-qāḍī yuftī wa-ʾl-muftī yahdhī*).
1. *Jawāb*: This is a serious saying; it is to be feared that the utterer becomes a *kāfir*. This is because a fatwa has the qualities of God's ruling (*sunan ḥukm Allāh*). The root of a fatwa lies in the clarification of what is difficult, hence the mufti clarifies God's ruling; he is the inheritor of prophecy. This [at least] is the situation of the mufti if he responds rightly (*idhā aftā bi-haqq*). God says, 'Say, "God gives you a fatwa"' [Q4:176]. The qadi is one who gives a decision (*yafṣilu*), and makes binding the requirements of a fatwa. Judicial authority comprises the quality of bindingness, and the rendering of a decision (*al-ilzām wa-ʾl-faṣl*). God says, 'God judges rightly' [Q40:20]. Hence the mufti, if he responds rightly, and the judge, if he judges rightly, is each rewarded with a great reward. The mufti is higher, and the qadi is subordinate to him.
2. If a difference of opinion should emerge between them, it arises out of *ijtihād* in the matter of the fatwa; for the qadi must be always subordinate to the fatwa of his Imam if he is *mujtahid*, or to the fatwa of

[21] Ibid., II, 370, ll.14ff.

another[22] if he is *muqallid*. The function of judicial authority is only the rendering of a decision and the quality of bindingness.

If anyone says that the mufti rambles, while believing that his fatwa is correct in a context where he speaks on God's behalf, then he is a *kāfir*. Hence it behoves a man to think carefully before uttering this phrase; for many a one utters it without realising what lies behind it, as we have explained. What they mean is merely that a judicial decision is binding and a fatwa is not, and neither the petitioner nor the qadi is required to listen to it. This too is an error. For each is required to listen unless he has some knowledge which outweighs the fatwa. If this is not the case, it is not permissible to evade the ruling of the fatwa, for it is an utterance on God's behalf (*ikhbār ʿan Allāh*).

3. It is conceivable that a difference of opinion between a qadi and a mufti might arise in relation to the interpretation of the form of an event, or in relation to the emergence of its causes. For the qadi investigates and uncovers the causes of a judicial decision that are not uncovered by the mufti. This however is not a real difference and does not imply any contradiction between the fatwa and the judicial decision in respect of a particular event. But God knows best.
4. Supposing that the mufti is ignorant or in error or such like, then of course these considerations do not apply, for the qadi too might be in a like situation, and the present discussion relates only to a judge who is right. But God knows best.[23]

This fatwa confirms much that we already know. The mufti's task is to explain and clarify God's ruling (*ḥukm Allāh*); he is, in this respect, heir to the prophet (here, *wārith al-nubuwwa*), a well-established and familiar attribute of the mufti's task. A fatwa is an utterance on God's behalf (*ikhbār ʿan Allāh*). The qadi's task is to provide a decision, a discrimination, which is binding – binding, that is, for the litigants. The qadi is subordinate to the mufti.

The rulings of a qadi and a mufti may differ. This possibility is central to the present context because it is the factor identified by Subkī as most likely to have generated the saying that he disapproves of. The implication of the saying is that, in case of difference, the mufti's view is irrelevant, because not binding. Subkī recognises three categories of difference, corresponding to paras. 2, 3 and 4 of the passage above. Difference may arise out of *ijtihād*, that is established

[22] The text is a little odd, but the meaning is clear. A qadi who is *mujtahid* (this means *mujtahid fī ʿl-madhhab*) must make his judgement based on the established opinion of the founder of his school. A qadi who is *muqallid* will seek a fatwa from a high-ranking mufti. See further below.

[23] Ibid., II, 543–4.

ijtihād, because of dispute within the *madhhab*. Difference cannot arise out of personal and fully creative thought by the qadi because the qadi, even if he is *mujtahid* (capable of reasoned preference for one view over another) is bound to follow the fatwa of his Imam (here the founder of a *madhhab* – e.g., Shāfiʿī) when he is making a judicial declaration. If a qadi is *muqallid*, he will fall back on another mufti, who will in turn be *muqallid* to the Imam. (A qadi and a mufti are both, for Subkī, in their official capacity, bound by the *madhhab*; see Section 2, below.) Subkī also insists that a fatwa must be followed, whether by the judge or by the petitioner, unless there is reason based in knowledge for rejecting it. Only a jurist of some ability could discover a reason, based in knowledge, for rejecting a fatwa. The full significance of this is not discussed here (perhaps because this is a fatwa directed at the masses), but will be found elsewhere (below, Section 2.3).

A second reason for difference between the mufti and the qadi is that they might have a different assessment of reality, that is of particulars, the form of an event and its causes (*ṣūrat al-masʾala, asbābu-hā*, para. 3). This does not reflect on the law but on the qadi's greater concern with particulars. And finally, a difference may arise out of ignorance on the part of either, but this is not at issue here; para. 4.

6. These rather theoretical considerations of the three functionaries have carried us some way. They betray the direct and persistent concern of Subkī for establishing and thinking about these differences. Subkī's assessment has a practical clarity and a revealing precision, which makes it superior, I think, to, say, the study by Reinhart.[24] That study, and I think also much of Hallaq's discussion in 'From from *fatwā*s to *furūʿ*', focuses primarily on the distinction between qadi and mufti, while largely disregarding the distinction between mufti and teaching/writing jurist.

Omitted, however, by Subkī is any mention of what might appear to an observer to be the decisive criterion that separates a judge from the other two. A judge becomes a judge only as a result of appointment by secular authority. After training, development of skills and participation in the educational process, a student might gradually and through consensual recognition by his peers be recognised and established as a teaching/writing jurist. By making himself available to, and acquiring a following amongst, the people at large, he might be recognised as a mufti. Though both functions might be marked by the acquisition of posts (a teaching post in a madrasa, the mufti-ship of a particular community), they were essentially informal. They permitted, but they did not require,

[24] Reinhart, 'Transcendence and Social Practice'.

institutional realisation. A qadi, by contrast, became a qadi only if appointed by a governor, and remained a valid qadi even if deficient in character or knowledge.[25] The point is of some importance because the institutional framework of the qadi is such that it is always possible, by reference to the framework, to distinguish that function from any other that the qadi might also fulfill. It is not so easy to distinguish the functions of mufti and jurist. Subkī was certainly all three. His achievement as a judge is a matter of interest to historians and sociologists, but is unlikely to be sufficiently well-documented to be assessed in detail. His achievement as a jurist/mufti is of vital importance to the development and continuity of the Shāfiʿī *madhhab* and is massively documented in those of his works that have been preserved. It seems important, however, to reiterate that it is not their quality as fatwas that make his fatwas worth remembering, it is their juristic quality that makes them important. Juristic discourse, as Subkī himself said, relates to universals and has enduring value. A qadi's judgements have importance only within the framework of historical and social particulars, which can, from a juristic viewpoint, be safely forgotten. (Muslim societies in the pre-modern period have shown little interest in the long-term preserving of judicial documents; even when preserved they have no status in the interpretation of the law.[26]) A mufti's opinions have an intermediate status, and acquire enduring importance only as they take on the forms and the substance of juristic discourse.

Section 2. Judicial rulings and fatwas: The qadi and the mufti

1. The generic term preferred by Subkī to indicate the ruling of a qadi is *ḥukm*. (Another term with the same meaning is *qaḍāʾ*.) It is a term with a wide range of technical usage since it is also used to refer to the legal categories or rulings that classify human acts: *ḥarām*, *ḥalāl*, *mubāḥ*, and so on. Hence, God's rulings, *aḥkām Allāh*. In the following passages, which are all concerned with judicial cases and the interaction of judicial decisions and fatwas, the word *ḥukm* is normally translated as 'judicial decision' or 'judgement'. Subkī – it will be already evident – moves rapidly from a concern with particulars (events, their forms and their causes) to generalised and generalising remarks about universals. He is actively engaged in the process of negotiating between universals and

[25] It seems that the post of mufti became more formal with the passage of time; under the Ottoman Empire, a mufti as much as a qadi depended on official appointment; cf. Masud et al., 'Muftis, Fatwas and Islamic Legal Interpretation'.

[26] We shall see in Section 3 that custom, welfare, and governmental decrees affect local legal practice. To establish local practice, it might be useful or necessary to preserve judicial documents; but local practice is not a part of the subject matter of a work of *fiqh*.

particulars. Though my intention in what follows is to establish the general (or universal) relationships that subsist between fatwas and judicial decisions, it will be illuminating to embed the present search (for Subkī's generalisations) in the particulars which generated them.

2. The first fatwa to be considered relates to a waqf created by a certain Badr al-Dīn Ibn ʿAsākir. The *masʾala* consists of two elements, first a citation of the relevant parts of the foundation document, and then a summary of the situation that brought about a judicial dispute. Clearly a subordinate qadi prepared the citation and the summary and sent it to Subkī for his opinion.

1. *Masʾala*: A waqf in favour of Badr al-Dīn ibn ʿAsākir, based on his own affirmation, the property being in his possession. Then to his children and his descendants. If one of the children or the descendants dies leaving descendants, his share goes to his descendants in order, to males twice the share of females. If one of his children, or his children's children, or their descendants, dies leaving no issue, his share goes to those in his own generation (*darajati-hi*), giving preference to the nearest to him and then the next nearest, siblings by two parents sharing with siblings by the father only (*yashtariku fi-hi al-ikhwā min al-abawayn wa-min al-ab*).
2. Badr al-Din subsequently died leaving four children, Aḥmad, Ibrāhīm, Sitt al-ʿArab and Zaynab. Zaynab died without issue; then Sitt al-ʿArab died, leaving two daughters by one husband, Zaynab and Malika, and two daughters by another, Dunyā and Alatī. Dunyā died without issue, leaving as sole participants in the waqf, Aḥmad, Ibrāhīm, Alatī, Zaynab and Malika. Zaynab died leaving four children, and Malika died leaving two daughters. After the death of these two, a Ḥanbalī judge gave a judicial decision (*ḥakama*), confirming the transfer of the share of the three sisters, the two who had died and the one still living, to their children, in accord with the condition laid down by the founder. The judge specified that he knew of the difference of opinion, and that the words of the founder 'siblings by two parents sharing with siblings by the father only' were explicit here. Subsequently Alatī and the children of her sisters appeared [before a judge] in dispute. The share of Dunyā remains up to the present in the possession of Alatī, and she says that neither she nor her agent was present when the aforementioned judge gave his judgement. …[27]

That is, at first sight, rather a dense mass of particulars, but it is not too complicated. A diagram may help.

[27] Subkī, *Fatāwā*, II, 10–11

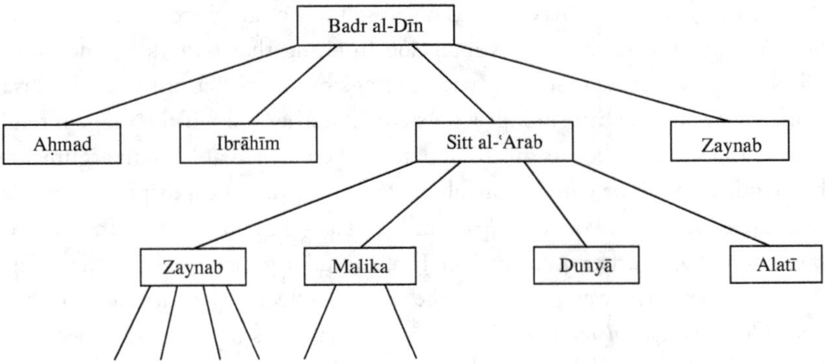

On the death of Badr al-Dīn the proceeds from the waqf were first distributed amongst the four children. When Zaynab died childless, her share was re-distributed to her three siblings (those in her degree or generation, as specified by the founder). When Sitt al-ʿArab died, her share was distributed to her four daughters, equally.

Subsequent events are less clear. First, Dunyā died and her share was appropriated by Alatī, presumably on the grounds that she was the 'nearest' relative to Dunyā, as specified by the founder. Subsequently, Zaynab and Malika died, and at this point a Ḥanbalī judge was invoked. The children of Zaynab and Malika must have gone before the Ḥanbalī judge (in person or through an agent) claiming that they had a right also in the share of Dunyā. Their argument was (presumably) that the four daughters of Sitt al-ʿArab were equally 'near' to one another, and therefore Alatī should not have acquired the whole of Dunyā's share: it should have been re-distributed at that time to the three remaining sisters, thereby augmenting the share that passed now to the children, and diminishing Alatī's share. The Ḥanbalī judge found in their favour, and some of his reasoning is cited.

His judgement necessarily implies that siblings who share two parents are not 'nearer' to one another than siblings who share only one parent, in this case the mother. That is a crux and it is the pivot of Subkī's response. But the Ḥanbalī judge's words, as reported in this summary, do not fully clarify the grounds of his decision. He makes a remark about 'knowing the difference of opinion'. This (formulaic) remark can be found in the reports of a number of different judicial decisions, throughout the *Fatāwā* of Subkī.[28] It is there for a purpose. The judge is effectively claiming that his decision lies within an area of permitted *ikhtilāf*; within that area his choice of rule is final and cannot be overturned merely because a different judge espouses a different one of the permitted rulings.

[28] Ibid., I, 505, ll.18–9; II, 16, l.5 (*maʿa ʿilmi-hi biʾl-khilāf; maʿa ʿilmi-hi bi-ʾkhtilāf al-ʿulamāʾ*).

(See further below.) In this case, it is not absolutely clear where the area of *ikhtilāf* lies. Also unclear is the judge's intention in citing that remark by the founder 'siblings by two parents sharing with siblings by the father only'. In the case at issue, we are faced with siblings who share a mother only. If the judge intended to read the word 'father' as meaning parent, then he had at least an argument on his hands (though he could probably make some kind of case since the words at issue are *abawayn* – two fathers/parents – and *ab* – father/?parent). The summary raises at least one other problem. The Ḥanbalī judge gave his ruling when neither Alatī nor her agent was present. Since she was effectively or presumptively the one ruled against (*al-maḥkūm 'alay-hā*), normal rules of procedure specify that the judicial decision (*ḥukm*) should have been issued in her presence.

Alatī or her agent, with all these objections available as legal recourse, has now appeared before another judge and demanded the annulment of the Ḥanbalī judge's decision. We may assume that Alatī has gone before a Shāfiʿī judge who is a deputy of Subkī. (All the judges of Damascus and the surrounding regions were technically deputies to Subkī, by virtue of his post as *qāḍī al-quḍāt*; the exceptions were the judges of the other three schools who existed only in Damascus.) The deputy judge has prepared the summary and presents it now to Subkī, asking for a fatwa. This is the *masʾala* translated above.

Subkī's response effectively states that it is permissible to overturn the ruling of the Ḥanbalī judge. His fatwa is long, and tortuous in places. Like the fatwa about the Juwāniyya mosque, it presents first a basic response and then a series of arguments in Q and A format (*in qulta … qultu …).* He is particularly tortuous on the significance of the founder's phrase 'siblings by two parents sharing with siblings by the father only' and so lays himself open to a witty and cheeky final question: 'Since what you have said about this phrase is too subtle for the understanding of most people, how can it possibly be used to assess the intentions of the founder?' Again the suspicion emerges that some fatwas by Subkī are not simply the product of private thought and study. They are a managed record of oral debate, and they preserve some of the qualities of the original debate.

The ultimate aim of Subkī's argument is to establish that the rule adopted by the Ḥanbalī judge – that daughters who share one parent, the mother, or two parents, the mother and the father, are all equally 'near' to one another – is outside the area of standard, permitted *ikhtilāf.* The tenor of his argument is sufficiently indicated in the opening paragraphs of his *jawāb*.

1. *Jawāb*: The *madhhab* of Shāfiʿī, Mālik, Abū Ḥanīfa and Aḥmad in relation to a waqf dedicated to 'the nearest of his relatives'or 'the nearest person to him', if he has a full-brother and a half-brother, whether the half-brother is by the father or the mother, is that the full-brother is given precedence.

By agreement of the majority. It is said,[29] there is a dispute (*khilāf*) derived from the rules of marriage, but this is rejected on the basis of the difference between marriage and waqf. In fact this dispute can scarcely be established and, furthermore, it relates only to a half-brother by the father. No dispute has been transmitted in relation to a half-brother by the mother. Someone may wish to establish a dispute on the basis that i. a half-brother by the father and a half-brother by the mother are equal and ii. a half-brother by the father is equal to a full-brother, according to some; therefore a half-brother by the mother and a full-brother are equal, in their view. To do this he must first establish that those who declare the half-brother by the father and the half-brother by the mother to be equal also believe in the equality of a full brother and a half-brother by the father. This will be difficult to do for it is a weak argument on a weak argument based on a supposition. The result of all this is that what is transmitted in all four law-schools is the precedence of the full brother over the half-brother by the mother. No other view is transmitted, not as an opinion, an argument, a transmission, nor from any well-known scholar, nor from a jurist who has expressed it clearly.

2. Q. Some have said that all siblings are equal in 'nearness' though the full brother is stronger.

A. This is muddle. The linguistic form *aqrab* ('nearest') is an expression of what is superior and necessarily implies an increase in nearness. The full-brother possesses two factors of nearness, and so exceeds the half-brother who possesses only one. It is true that a half-brother by the father is stronger than a half-brother by the mother because he belongs to the male lineage (*'aṣaba*), and there is agreement that the word 'nearness' can be applied to him absolutely, whereas there is dispute on this in relation to the half-brother by the mother.

It is necessary to note that the topics of the law are not all the same in this respect. They are in fact varied. In inheritance laws, the full-brother is given precedence, absolutely, over the half-brother by the father. In relation to marriage there is dispute. In relation to testamentary bequest and waqf, the established view (*al-mashhūr*), according to us, is the decisive affirmation of the precedence of the full-brother over the half-brother. It is said,[30] there are two views as in marriage, but this is rejected. In the Mālikī school there is dispute in relation to testamentary bequests, but there is no dispute in relation to waqf; they too decisively affirm the precedence of the full-brother. All of this relates to the full-brother and the half-brother by the father. As to the half-brother by the mother, we know of no dispute in any of the four schools; they all affirm that the full brother is 'nearer'.[31]

[29] *Qīla*. This is an established formula for introducing a minority view.
[30] See previous note.
[31] Subkī, *Fatāwā*, II, 11.

In the final section there, Subkī makes the basic point that full-brothers (those that share two parents) are 'nearer' to one another than half-brothers (those who share only one parent). In the case at issue, Dunyā and Alatī are full sisters, and so are Zaynab and Malika. The point is relatively simple, but Subkī's exposition is diffuse; it is not, however, casual. All the concessions he makes here are going to be picked up later. He has to acknowledge and distinguish areas of dispute in order to preempt their use against him. There are real (established) disputes: In different topics of the law different views prevail. And there are unreal (non-established) disputes: Any general claim that half-brothers are equal in nearness to full-brothers is rejected, as based on 'a weak argument on a weak argument based on a supposition'. The point is elaborated in the preliminary statement, and the interlocutor's first question provides an excuse to say it all again. Full-brothers are nearer relatives than half-brothers and, while there are areas of the law where that is not the prevalent view, or where there is acknowledged dispute, there is no dispute on this issue in relation to waqf. In any case, if anything at all be conceded to the argument that a half-brother by the father is equal to a full-brother (on the assumption that it is only the father who counts for nearness), this does not apply to a half-brother by the mother.

The diffused and repetitive elements of this argument might be explained as reflecting the teaching function of the mufti. Though the issues are complex, the language is simple. Complexity is resolved through repetition and digression rather than tightly controlled structural and grammatical form. The audience, however, must already be well advanced in juristic science; this fatwa is not aimed at the masses. The general qualities of language and structure and, sometimes, the specific content of the Q and A items, however, offer a more precise suggestion as to the origins of this material: the *masʿala* has been presented to an audience for debate and Subkī's final writing up retains some of the qualities and some of the specific content of the actual debate.

3. As Subkī develops his argument, the question emerges as to how the phenomenon of established *ikhtilāf* impinges on the inviolability of a judicial decision. Again, the issue is explored in diffuse language and dialectic form, without much effort to define and state precisely the universals that lie behind the issue.

1. Q. Conceding that the established view in the four *madhhab*s is as you say, and that no dispute is found to contradict this view, can a jurist not derive a dispute, inferring it from the equality of the half-brother by the father and by the mother and the established dispute relating to the former and the full-brother?

   A. I have already replied to this. The distinction is clear and it prevents any such derivation. And even supposing the derivation could be established, it would be a weak view.

2. Q. If the qadi gives judgement on the basis of a weak view, why should it not be put into effect (*yunfadh*)?
   A. God says, 'Judge between them on the basis of God's revelation' [Q5:49]. And the Prophet said, 'A qadi, even if he judges right, if he lacks knowledge, is in Hell.' When a qadi proceeds to judgement (*ḥukm*) and does not believe in his own judgement, then he fails to judge on a basis of revelation, and he lacks knowledge; therefore it is not permitted for a qadi to give a judgement until he believes that it is a true judgement.
3. Q. This relates only to the *mujtahid*. As to the *muqallid*, when he adopts a view, it is permitted whether the view be weak or strong.
   A. That notion is true only in *taqlīd* that relates to one's own actions. In matters of fatwa or of judicial decision, Ibn al-Ṣalāḥ has indicated consensus that it is not permitted.
4. Q. If two opinions are equal in his view, is it permissible for him to give a fatwa or a judicial decision based on one of them without establishing a preference (*tarjīḥ*), in the same way as the *mujtahid* when faced with two indicators (*amāratayn*, sc. in a revealed text) which he considers equal; he simply chooses, according to one view?
   A. The difference between them is this. In a case of conflict between two revealed indicators, the rule of choice is given from God. In the case of variant opinions from one Imam, Shāfiʿī for example, if there is conflict and no way of establishing a preference and no date [which would establish the preferred, later, view], it is prohibited to declare that his school comprises all of these views, or just one of them to be established by simple choice.[32] The only resourse is suspension of decision until a factor of preference arises (*laysa illā al-tawaqquf ilā ẓuhūr al-tarjīḥ*).
5. Q. If the judge has the capacity to establish a preference?
   A. When he has the capacity, and establishes a preference for a view which is transmitted with a sound proof, it is permissible and his judgement will be put into effect (*nufidha ḥukm-hu*), even if it is a view rejected by most jurists, as long as it is not outside the *madhhab*.
6. Q. If he does not have the capacity to establish a preference?
   A. Then he must follow the view which is known to be preferred in the *madhhab*.
7. Q. If he gives judgement based on a view which is outside the *madhhab*, while being convinced of its being the preferable view, and having the capacity to establish preference?

[32] For *bi-ʿaynihi* read *yuʿayyinu-hu*.

A. If his post as qadi is not based on the condition that he follow a particular *madhhab*, it is permissible. But if that condition is imposed, either verbally, or by custom (*bi 'l-'urf*), or by virtue of the formula 'I appoint you to judgeship according to the such and such *madhhab*', as happens in some investitures, then it is not valid for him to issue a judicial decision on any other basis. This is because the appointment does not include that possibility. If the appointment is valid, he is restricted to that *madhhab*; if it is not valid then he may not give any judgements at all.

8. There is dispute amongst the jurists on a judicial appointment that includes a condition that judgements must be related to a specific *madhhab*: either the appointment is invalid, or the appointment is valid but the condition invalid, or the appointment is valid and the condition likewise. The view that the appointment is valid but the condition invalid relates only to the *mujtahid*, and not to the *muqallid*. People today are *muqallids* so this view has no application. My view, in respect to present times, is that anyone at all who takes up the post of qadi, if the Sultan specifies appointment to judgeship by the established tradition of a *madhhab* if he is *muqallid*, or by his own opinion if he is a *mujtahid*, or if the Sultan says, 'I appoint you to judgeship according to such-and-such a *madhhab*', then he may not go beyond the bounds of the established tradition of that *madhhab*, whether he is *muqallid* or *mujtahid fī 'l-madhhab*. He may give judgements based on opinions that are preferable to him and based on strong argument. He may not go beyond the bounds of the *madhhab*, whether he is *muqallid* or *mujtahid*, because the terms of the appointment restrict him. Nor may he give judgements based on eccentric and far-fetched views within the *madhhab*, even if they are preferable to him, because they are the equivalent of views outside the *madhhab*.

9. Q. If a judge gives judgement that a full-brother is equal to a half-brother by the father or to a half-brother by the mother, may that judgement be annulled?

A. The apparent situation (*al-ẓāhir*) is that it may be annulled. This is because the evidence that 'nearness' requires precedence for the full-brother is a revealed text (*naṣṣ*), and it is as if the judge had opposed a revealed text. If the founder of the waqf has made it a condition, and he gives judgement otherwise, then he has opposed the founder's condition, and the jurists say that the conditions of the founder are like the texts of the Law-giver. I say, by way of instruction, the conditions of the founder are a part of the texts of the Law-giver because of the Prophet's words, 'Believers are bound by their conditions'. Just as opposition to a revealed text requires

> annulment of a judgement, so likewise does opposition to the conditions of a founder.[33]

The essential point made by the interlocutor in his opening gambit is that there is a possibility here, since there is so much acknowledged dispute, and in spite of all the objections (so neatly formulated by Subkī, who had the advantage of writing up the final version), of deriving a new ruling. Subkī immediately categorises this view as either not permitted or weak (para. 1). The question then becomes whether a judicial decision based on a weak view can nonetheless be put into effect (*yunfadh*). Subkī says not (para. 2), but uses the device of the interlocutor to draw out the details of why not. The interlocutor now has the task of presenting arguments that will enable a judge to make a final and non-revocable decision based on a weak or eccentric ruling. Subkī aims to limit the judge to the established *madhhab*, and insists that a judgement based on an eccentric ruling can be annulled.

A judge may be *mujtahid* or *muqallid*. These terms here refer, apparently, to the absolute *mujtahid* (founder of a *madhhab*) and to an affiliated jurist. When the judge is *muqallid*, in the sense of being affiliated to one or another of the major *madhhab*s, it is suggested that he may simply choose amongst the views that have emerged and been acknowledged within that *madhhab*. Subkī draws on the authority of Ibn al-Ṣalāḥ to reject this idea: a judge or a mufti, when engaged in his official capacity, must find reasoned grounds for a preference (Paras. 3 and 4). If he has an appropriate capacity, he may establish a preference for any one of the positions acknowledged within the *madhhab*. If he does not have the appropriate capacity, he must embrace the position promoted within the *madhhab* – that is, as established within the textbook tradition (Paras. 5 and 6). The interlocutor then pushes the question to its logical end: A judge may have the appropriate capacity and prefer a ruling that is outside the *madhhab*. Subkī has to admit that such a judge has the right to base his judgement on his (genuine and reasoned) preference, but at this point brings in a new issue, namely that the judge's post may be conditional upon his following the established *madhhab*.

The transition, whether it recalls Subkī's intervention in a real debate, or represents thought and consideration that emerged in the course of written composition, gives Subkī a chance to expound those difficult terms *mujtahid* and *muqallid*. Used absolutely, the term *mujtahid* refers to an independent creative thinker (like Shāfiʿī), and there are none such today. People today are *muqallid*. They may, of course, be *mujtahid fī 'l-madhhab*, that is capable of rational preference within the sphere of established *ikhtilāf*. But whether *mujtahid* in this sense,

[33] Ibid., II, 12–13.

or *muqallid*, a judge (today) may not go beyond the bounds of the *madhhab*. An eccentric and far-fetched view is counted as outside the *madhhab* (para. 8).

The distinction between qadis who are *mujtahid fī 'l-madhhab* and qadis who are *muqallid* deserves amplification. Subkī was a qadi, appointed by the Mamluk sultan, subject to a condition (whether expressed or implied) that he was to restrict himself to the Shāfiʿī *madhhab*. He was certainly, in his own opinion and in that of most of his contemporaries and successors, *mujtahid fī 'l-madhhab*, that is, capable of establishing rational and reasoned preferences for elements of *ikhtilāf* within the *madhhab*. The subordinate judge who had written to Subkī asking for his view on this case can probably be considered as *muqallid* – he did not have the knowledge and skills that would enable him to decide on this case. That was why he wrote to Subkī. Subkī, in his capacity as mufti, was now giving his opinion and justifying it by the rational arguments that were required. The subordinate judge would proceed to issue his ruling, which would (probably) be based on Subkī's fatwa. This judicial ruling would not be a blind ruling based merely on choice, for Subkī had provided him, at great length, in clear language, in dialectical format, with all the relevant factors of preference (*tarjīḥ*). The judge would no doubt proceed, first to annul the *ḥukm* of the Ḥanbalī judge, then to issue a *ḥukm* in favour of Alatī; and his *ḥukm* would be put into effect (*yunfadh*).

When Subkī responded to the popular saying that the mufti rambles and the qadi rules (above), one of the points he made was that a *ḥukm* is binding (on the litigants) whereas a fatwa isn't. But in this case the *ḥukm* of the Ḥanbalī qadi is found to be not binding, because it is subject to annulment. The fatwa of Subkī, by contrast, is definitive (not, in the technical sense, binding – *mulzim* – because not issued in the form of a judicial decision). As Subkī said there, a fatwa cannot be evaded – unless either the petitioner or the qadi involved has some knowledge which outweighs it. In this case Subkī's fatwa is not to be evaded, because of the considerable deployment of knowledge that both justifies and constitutes it. Theoretically, of course, the children of Zaynab and Malika might go back to the Ḥanbalī qadi and ask him for a fatwa which would have a sufficient weight of knowledge to match that of Subkī. The reality of Subkī's post probably made it unwise, but the quality of his learning was the decisive factor. Not every holder of a judicial post, even a very senior post, could manipulate argument as he could. Throughout Islamic history, even in the century of Mamluk power that preceded Subkī's death, a majority of judges would be content to act as *muqallids*, and to pass difficult cases to the acknowledged scholars of the age, who were as likely to be teachers in a madrasa as judges. (A judge could, of course, solicit a number of fatwas if it was important, academically or practically, to establish a variety of options. This had varied practical results depending on the social realisation of judicial and muftis' positions. The combination of roles – chief judge and influential mufti – in Subkī was not characteristic of all Islamic societies. The Ottoman experience was broadly such as to ensure the institutional separation of these roles.)

4. I have signalled on a number of occasions that the form, content and structure of this fatwa (and the one analysed in Section 1 above) suggest origins (partial origins) in oral debate, as if the question, submitted to Subkī by a deputy judge, was submitted then by him to students or companions for general discussion. The evidence for this can be found in the cumulative effect of certain features: the Q and A format, the specific content of questions which could hardly have been formulated in private, the diffuse and slightly rambling structure, the drafting technique that brings to the beginning an anticipatory pre-judgement of objections to be raised, and so on. The point is worth reiterating in respect of this passage. The sequence of Q and A items that begins it is in fact a diffuse and partial restatement of a conventional item of *uṣūl al-fiqh*, cast into dialogue format. Here is a scholastic version of the rule (taken from the *Jamʿ al-Jawāmiʿ* of Subkī's son, Tāj al-Dīn).

> A *ḥukm* may not annulled in *ijtihādiyyāt*, where there is agreement that they are *ijtihādiyyāt*. But it may be annulled if it is opposed to a revealed text, or a clearly manifest rule, even if established by *qiyās*, or if a judge gives a decision opposed to his own *ijtihād*, or if he opposes the text of his Imam, while not being *muqallid* to someone else where that is permissible.[34]

In the case at issue, Subkī argues that the question – the meaning of 'nearest' in relation to full sisters and half-sisters – does not belong to the category of agreed *ijtihādiyyāt*, and so annulment is possible. The interlocutor tried first to establish that there were grounds here for establishing an acceptable variant view, that is for bringing the question into the category of *ijtihādiyyāt*. This move was preemptively rejected ('a weak argument on a weak argument ...'). The interlocutor conceded the point, but introduced the idea of a judge who has the capacity to establish a preference, and happens to prefer, in good faith, an eccentric view. It is a hypothetical judge, deriving from and illustrating a principle of *uṣūl* – a sound move by the interlocutor, since, as the above quotation shows, a judge may not (normally) give a decision opposed to his own *ijtihād*. Subkī concedes the point (as he must): A fully competent judge has the right to base his judgement on reasoned and genuine preferences, without incurring danger of annulment. But only if his official position is not based on the requirement that he follow the *madhhab*. And Subkī now has a different question to assess: Is it valid

[34] Quoted in Badr al-Dīn al-Zarkashī, *Tashnīf al-masāmiʿ bi- jamʿ al-jawāmiʿ* (Cairo: Maktab Qurṭuba, 1998), IV, 591.

and legitimate that a judge's competence may be limited, in this way, by the terms of his appointment?

Subkī obviously did not need to hear this issue debated in order to write up his fatwa. As far as it goes, the interlocutor and his partner enact a fairly conventional version of this particular argument. On the other hand, the formal re-enactment of standard debates was not just a part of the teaching programme of those days, but also a standard component of leisure and recreation. The skills of the interlocutor here are working against Subkī's desires; for, to a degree, the interlocutor has won his case. He has established a condition under which a qadi might be able to produce an irrevocable judgement in favour of, effectively, the children of Zaynab and Malika. Subkī (the proponent of annulment) intervenes to transfer the focus of interest to a different question. It is noticeable that the discourse type here, briefly but perceptibly, changes. The dialogue format (Q and A), evident in paras. 1 to 7, gives way to the formal exposition of a juristic dispute (para. 8), whether a judicial appointment is valid if it includes a condition that the judge must base his decisions on the established *madhhab*. This dispute is not enacted as dialogue but as juristic analysis. Subkī manages to finish his account of this question with a decisive statement of the relevant, the winning, position: a judge may not 'give judgements based on eccentric and far-fetched views within the *madhhab*, even if they are preferable to him, because they are the equivalent of views outside the *madhhab*'. This conclusion is effective because the judge is bound by the terms of his appointment, not because it is absolutely out of the question in terms of *uṣūl* theory. In *uṣūl* theory, a judge with the appropriate degree of competence is required to rule in accord with his own *ijtihād*. It is to be noted that the Q and A elements translated here do not explore all the issues that are contained in the general rule of *uṣūl* theory, but only those that have a possible bearing on this particular case. This is not an attempt to express or elucidate a universal, but to show the relevance of a universal to a particular case.

It is the transition in discourse type that confirms the general impression that the *jawāb* element of this fatwa is a managed record of a real debate. There was some kind of interlocutor who put forward the arguments which Subkī here records. The transition to formal exposition reflects either an intervention by Subkī in the debate, or an argument devised by him subsequently.

5. About judicial decisions in an Islamic context, there was then an element of unpredictability. A judge would normally follow the dominant view within a *madhhab*, thus offering general predictability in the law. However, where there was established *ikhtilāf* (or when a clever jurist could argue a case into an area of *ikhtilāf*) then a fully competent judge could establish his own preference, within the area of acknowledged *ikhtilāf*, based on reasoned argument. A less competent judge was fully bound to the preferred view within the *madhhab*, meaning the

one promoted and established by the literary tradition. In either case, a judicial decision, once issued, was binding on the litigants and safe from annulment. However, if a judicial decision could be shown to be based on a view that was not an established component of *ikhtilāf*, it might be annulled. There were available a number of practical resources for increasing the predictability and the security of the law – for example, if the governor appointed a qadi with a condition of appointment that specified which item of *ikhtilāf* he was to use in a case of established *ikhtilāf*. The permissibility of such a condition of appointment had been affirmed, for the Shāfiʿīs, in precisely those terms, by Māwardi.[35] In Subkī's version, the need for predictability in the law is implicitly conceded, as is the need for security after a decision. Predictability and security, however, depend not on the governor's assessment of *ikhtilāf*, but on his choosing a particular *madhhab*. Subkī's version of the relevant rules tends to ensure that the vast majority of qadis (and muftis) were fully bound by the textbook tradition of the *madhhab*. Only the highest ranking could exploit the flexibility of established *ikhtilāf*. (That, of course, is one reason why, in works of *furūʿ al-fiqh*, it was important to establish both what was the established *madhhab*, and what was the range of acknowledged *ikhtilāf*).

In the context of the present fatwa Subkī returned to the issue of annulment at a later stage, to restate in near universal terms, the general position.

1. Q. They say that the judicial decision (*qaḍāʾ*) of a qadi should not be annulled except if it opposes a revealed text, or consensus, or a clear analogy. Qarafī, for the Mālikīs, adds, or a general principle. And the Ḥanafīs add, or if it is a judgement not backed by revealed evidence.
A. I say, in this case, this is opposed to a condition stipulated by the founder, and so is opposed to a revealed text; it is a judgement not backed by revealed evidence; it is opposed to what we know of the four *madhhabs*; it is a matter on which we know of no *khilāf* and so is as it were opposed to consensus. If dispute should be established, it is eccentric and an eccentric view is of no significance, just as a far-fetched possibility does not pre-empt the decisive status of a revealed text. It was in consideration of this that the Imām al-Ḥaramayn[36] counted a whole bundle of interpretations void. This is also what the Ḥanafīs say about an eccentric *khilāf*. They say it is a *khilāf* not an *ikhtilāf*, meaning by that that only an established and reasonable *ikhtilāf* is taken into consideration, while an eccentric and far-fetched *khilāf* is an opposition to the people of truth. This is what I say. In order to

[35] See Calder, 'Friday Prayer and the Juristic Theory of Government: Sarakhsī, Shīrāzī, Māwardī', *Bulletin of the School of Oriental and African Studies*, 49 (1986): 35–47.

[36] The title given to the Shāfiʿī jurist and theologian al-Juwaynī (419–78/1028–85).

> be taken into consideration it must be a dispute, or a possibility, that has currency as such. If a judge gives judgement based on such a view, it cannot be annulled by one who thinks that a different view is better, because there is a possibility, which he acknowledges, that it may be right, as in the established school traditions. But an eccentric view and a far-fetched possibility, one that he considers to be an error [a judicial decision based on this kind of view may be annulled].[37]

Subkī's argument that judges were bound by the terms of their appointment to work within the boundaries of established *ikhtilāf* was understood, in his time and subsequently, to mean that in practice all judges were so bound.[38]

6. In a different case, Subkī showed more concern for the permanence of a judicial decision.[39] A certain Bahādur ʿĀṣ owned 18 1/3 shares in a village which, in its totality, constituted 24 shares. The remaining 5 2/3 shares were held in waqf for the Madrasa Amīniyya in Damascus. The *qāḍī al-quḍāt* Jalāl al-Dīn, the Shāfiʿī qadi who had preceded Subkī, had given permission to the Ḥanafī qadi, Ṣafī al-Dīn al-ʿAttāl, to make a formal division of the property. This formal division had been validated by judicial decree (*ḥukm*) first by the Ḥanafī qadi, then by Jalāl al-Dīn and then by 'those who came after him' (Subkī himself?) – *wa-ḥakama bi-ṣiḥḥat al-qisma ṣafī al-Dīn, wa-baʿda-hu qāḍī al-quḍāt Jalāl al-Dīn thumma man baʿda-hu*. Division here means that there had been a clear apportioning and distinguishing of the properties.[40]

Bahādur ʿĀṣ died and left two wives, five sons and a daughter. One of the wives died, leaving as her sole heir her son, ʿAlī, one of the five sons of Bahādur ʿĀṣ. ʿAlī sold the totality of his portion of the village. Subsequently, another son of Bahādur ʿĀṣ, Nāṣir al-Dīn, appeared before Subkī seeking permission to plead for a judicial declaration that ʿAlī had died without making any testamentary

[37] Subkī, *Fatāwā*, II, 19. The text is garbled in the last line, but the meaning seems clear.

[38] The Ḥanafī tradition adopted the same broad position with regard to muftis and qadis. Ibn ʿĀbidīn expressed it thus in his poetic recapitulation of the mufti's task:

To act or to respond to a petitioner
  Using a view that's weak is not allowed.
Save one who acts under necessity
  And one whose skill and knowledge is renowned.
But not a qadi, he can't judge this way;
  And if he does his judgement will not stand.
Especially qadis now; they are restricted
  To school-established rules when they're appointed.

Norman Calder, 'The *ʿUqūd rasm al-mufti* of Ibn ʿĀbidīn', *Bulletin of the School of Oriental and African Studies*, 63 (2000): 215–28.

[39] Subkī, *Fatāwā*, I, 291–7.

[40] Hiroyuki Yanagihashi, 'The Judicial Functions of the Sultān in Civil Cases According to the Mālikīs up to the Sixth/Twelfth Century', *Islamic Law and Society*, 3;1 (1996): 72, for another example of co-ownership and division.

bequests. His intention was thereafter to plead before a Ḥanbalī or a Ḥanafī judge for a declaration that the sale had been void.

If it could thus be established that the sale was invalid, and that ʿAlī had not otherwise disposed of his property (i.e., by testamentary bequest), then all of ʿAlī's share in the village would revert to his legal heirs – that is, his brothers and sister. Subkī, here, had been approached, in his official capacity as a judge, to give permission for a litigant to make his appeal, that is, to become a *muddaʿī* – a claimant in a judicial process. Subkī did not give permission, and later wrote up his reasons, which constitute the present fatwa. Strictly speaking no question had been posed. Nāṣir al-Dīn did not want this fatwa. The fatwa accordingly differs formally from many in this collection in not displaying the components *masʾala* and *jawāb*. It is in fact a fatwa initiated by the mufti himself who, in this case, has refused to accept the role of a judge, and has issued a fatwa which, though it functions as a kind of apologia for his actions, relates to a matter which had not been brought before him. Nāṣir al-Dīn had wanted Subkī to rule on the absence of a testamentary bequest. Subkī chose to give a fatwa on the validity of a sale. The case illustrates the remarkable interventionary powers of a Muslim judge.[41]

The fatwa begins with conventional formulae of prayer and praise for the Prophets followed by the words, 'A case has arisen amongst the judicial proceedings of our time namely …' and he proceeds to give the details of the case which I have outlined above. The summary, in this case, is by Subkī himself. Subkī then indicates that he would have given permission to Nāṣir al-Dīn to plead if he had discovered that there were grounds for declaring the sale void. He had required that the document of sale be brought before him. On inspecting it he had discovered that the Amīr ʿAlī son of Bahādur ʿĀṣ had sold the whole of his portion, which he held in ownership, of the village, namely 4 1/16 shares, out of the 24 communal shares (*sahman shāʿiʿan*) that are the whole of the village.

Subkī distinguished two points that had to be clarified if the sale was to be safeguarded. The first related to the question whether ʿAlī owned precisely 4 1/16 shares in the village. This depended on the rules of fixed proportional inheritance and arithmetic.

1. BA left two wives; each inherited 1/16 of the property (i.e., 1 7/48 shares).
2. The remainder was divided amongst the children, sons receiving twice the share of daughters. There were five sons and a daughter. (18 1/3 – 2 × 1 7/48 = 16 1/24; 2/11 of 16 1/24 = 2 11/12. ʿAlī inherited 2 11/12 shares.)
3. ʿAlī subsequently inherited the whole of his mother's share. (2 11/12 + 1 7/48 = 4 1/16.)

[41] For the interventionary powers of Muslim judges, Yanagihashi, 68.

Clearly ʿAlī had correctly computed his share and sold only what he rightfully owned.

The second point became the nub of the problem. ʿAlī's document of sale had specified that he was selling 4 1/16 shares out of the 24 communal shares (*sahman shāʾiʿan*) that are the whole of the village. The problem is that the word 'communal' here implies that the whole of the village is held in co-ownership. But in fact Bahādur ʿĀṣ had held in ownership only 18 1/3 shares; the other part of the village was held in waqf. Ideally ʿAlī should have specified that he was selling 4 1/16 of the 18 1/3 shares that were held in common by the descendants of Bahādur ʿĀṣ. His brother Nāṣir al-Dīn was now claiming that the sale was invalid because it represented a claim to sell something in which ʿAlī had no rights of ownership (or only partial rights of ownership). Subkī, while acknowledging some force to the argument, in the end disagreed and felt that the words of the sale could be read in a manner that permitted the validity of the sale. The fact that there had been a formal division of the village, validated by a series of judgements was one relevant factor. A second factor was: that a judge had previously given a judicial ruling on the validity of this sale, and the preservation of a judicial ruling from annulment was mandatory as far as possible – *ṣiyānat ḥukm al-ḥākim ʿan al-naqḍ wājiba mā amkana.*[42] The various aspects of the case, and numerous possible objections, were rehearsed giving rise to one further expression of this principle. 'This case is related to a judicial declaration by a judge; it is thereby preserved from annulment until it becomes manifest that the declaration is opposed to a revealed text, or consensus, or a clear analogy, and none such are found in the present instance.'[43]

7. There was no need for a case to come before a qadi for the validity of a *ḥukm* to be questioned, and subject to scrutiny by muftis. The Jew, ʿAbd al-Qāhir b. Muḥāsin b. Manja, in the year 720/1320–1, constituted a waqf in favour of his descendants, incorporating a condition that if any of them left the Jewish faith they would lose their right to participate in the waqf. ʿAbd al-Qāhir's declaration, and the establishment of all the relevant particulars, took place before the Ḥanafī qadi Shams-al-Dīn Muḥammad b. Muḥammad b. Abī ʾl-ʿIzz who recorded his judgement approving the waqf in a judicial document (*naṣṣ isjāl*). Subsequently the document (and the supervision of the waqf) fell to the Ḥanafī qadi's son, ʿAlā ʾl-Dīn, who took over from his father. The latter (presumably after carrying out a review of his father's documents) sought a fatwa regarding the validity of that clause which excluded a descendant who converted (sc., for the purposes of this argument, to Islam). He received one response from a Ḥanbalī judge, and then one from Subkī, in the year 747/1346–7, both judges in this instance acting as

[42] Subkī, *Fatāwā*, I, 293, l.21.

[43] Ibid., I, 295, l.2.

muftis. Neither the Ḥanbalī nor Subkī liked the clause in question, though the grounds and conditions of their dislike were not the same.[44]

In this case, no judicial process has been started. There is no evidence that any of the descendants of ʿAbd al-Qāhir had abandoned their Judaism. The Ḥanafī qadi had initiated the problem and had sought opinions from two of his colleagues. Subkī's concluding remarks throw the ball back into his court.

> This qadi [i.e., the original Ḥanafī] has given a judgement in favour of this condition. So let there be an investigation of his *madhhab*. If there is something there that requires the validity of this condition, then it is not permissible to annul it, and the situation continues in accord with his judicial decision. But if his *madhhab* requires the annulment of this clause, or if there is no transmitted view, granted that we have now demonstrated the invalidity of the clause, then it should be annulled and a judicial decision should be issued affirming the nullity of this clause, and the continued rights of one who converts to Islam. God knows best.

What the Ḥanafī qadi now required was a learned exposition of the Ḥanafī tradition. If he was sufficiently learned he might attempt this for himself, or he might ask a more learned Ḥanafī jurist for a fatwa. Depending on the result of that investigation, he might or might not initiate an annulment of a clause in the original waqf document.

8. The task of the qadi involved an investigation of the details of a case, and the issue of a *ḥukm* which was binding on the litigants. The mufti did not initiate any investigation. He issued a statement of the law in relation to the particulars that were brought before him – frequently accompanied, in the case of a high-ranking mufti like Subkī, with lengthy arguments. This was not binding (*mulzim* – that is on the litigants), in the sense that a *ḥukm* was binding, but it could be decisive.

Subkī's fatwas were decisive partly because of his position as chief judge. But that is not an adequate explanation. There were many chief judges whose fatwas were forgotten – it is his capacity to produce arguments that counted. The question whether an argument was decisive was, of course, itself a matter of argument. There are numerous instances in Islamic history of cases which lasted for generations as subsequent qadis or muftis questioned the arguments of their predecessors. It is important to note that as fatwas became more and more learned, incorporated more and more argument, they were moving from the strict category of fatwa towards the category of *fiqh*. As Subkī had explained elsewhere, a fatwa was inextricably involved with particulars and might not be a correct reflection of the *madhhab*. Only appropriate consideration by fully qualified jurists could pass judgement on the value of a fatwa as a reflection of the *madhhab*. Many of the fatwas of Subkī contain juristic argument aimed at

[44] Ibid., I, 505.

explaining and justifying his ruling and so ensuring that it will be recognised as a correct reading of the *madhhab*.

In order to secure their judgements against the possibility of an annulment, judges would solicit fatwas prior to giving judgement. This was a way of establishing the possibilities of the *madhhab* – or possibly of the law in a wider sense. If the fatwas did not establish a clear and single ruling as that of the *madhhab*, they would usually establish at least an acknowledged area of *ikhtilāf*, and a fully competent judge could argue that within that area he was permitted to establish a preference (*tarjīḥ*) which would be final and not subject to annulment.

Section 3. Custom, welfare and administrative decree: Divine law and secular legal practice

1. Works of Islamic law display a concern for precise details and fine distinctions. They also imply (and some jurists directly express) an aspiration to cover all human eventualities. This implication is misleading. For there are limits to the detailed provisions of the law (see Chapter 1 above), and there are principles and terms of law which are broad and permissive, leaving space for human initiative, and for differential patterns of historical and social development. Nowhere is the need for these principles and terms greater than in matters that relate to government and its relations with judicial authority.

The management of the waqf of the Madrasa al-Shāmiyya al-Juwāniyya had presented problems when the value of the waqf grew considerably beyond what had been the expectations of the founder. The problem, we have already seen (Section 1.1, above), came to the attention of Subkī. But it had already been dealt with at an earlier date (in 727/1326–7, when the Governor of Syria was Tengiz), and those who objected to Subkī's new rulings tried to establish that the earlier decisions had some permanent value. The focus of discussion related to how many jurists could be maintained from the waqf, and how they were to be paid.

Q. The situation was established in the days of Tengiz, in the presence of the qadis, at 60 jurists, in three degrees, receiving respectively sixty, forty and twenty [dinars].

A. It has not been established in our view that any one of the qadis declared a further increase not to be permissible, or that the number was restricted to just that, or that he issued a decree to that effect (*rasama bi-hi*), or that Tengiz issued a decree to that effect (*rasama*). In fact Tengiz subsequently increased the number beyond sixty. They limited themselves to sixty at that time because they saw that as being in accord with *maṣlaḥa*, and *maṣlaḥa* varies with the passage of time. If their action at that time constituted an argument that the number of jurists should not increase beyond sixty, then the action of those before them would be an argument for an increase, for they had allowed an increase in numbers beyond two hundred. ... In fact we do not know the beginning of this practice, and it is well known in *fiqh* that we cling to custom (*ʿāda*) if we do not know its beginnings; so clinging to that principle is best.[45]

The custom that Subkī wanted to cling to was the custom, in this case, of allowing the numbers of jurists who were to benefit from the waqf to rise and fall in accord with its income and other circumstances. This was a principle of general welfare or *maṣlaḥa* – and *maṣlaḥa* varies with the passage of time. The actions of the earlier qadis and Tengiz were not binding because they were not formulated as a decree (*rasama*). Here are three new factors that affect our assessment of the law: welfare, custom or habit and the presence or absence of a decree.

The last of these terms indicates an administrative or executive ruling, issued with the backing of the secular authorities. It is evident from this instance that decrees can be issued by qadis (in so far as they possess administrative and executive authority), as well as provincial governors. We have come across a related instance previously: Subkī noted that decrees (*marāsim*) had been issued by kings and qadis permitting Christians to repair their churches, though he was convinced the practice was *ḥarām*. 'Many jurists have given fatwas as to its being permissible; and the *marāsim* of kings and qadis have been issued with permission to build.'[46] The jurists gave fatwas; the kings and qadis gave a *marsūm* (pl. *marāsim*). Although the term *rasama* was not used in the discussion above (Section 2) about the governor's right to limit judicial freedom by the terms of appointment, it illustrates another area in which the sultan's decree had a decisive influence on the actual realisation of the law. The appointment of a qadi necessarily included, in the terms of appointment, either verbally, or by virtue of custom, a restriction in the free play of *ijtihād* by the appointee.

The terms *ʿurf* and *ʿāda* convey equally the notion of custom, convention, habit. Custom, as used in these contexts (it could be used differently), was a factor which, acting alongside the specific rules of law, allowed the emergence of different realisations of the same law. When Subkī wanted to make some generalising assertions about the management of waqfs in Syria, he explicitly contrasted the Syrian system with that which had emerged in Egypt. The difference was due to differential development of *ʿurf* and *ʿāda*.[47] In this case, divergent practice had emerged in spite of the common history of Syria and Egypt, a common allegiance to the Shāfiʿī *madhhab*, and a common system of government which had been in place for at least 100 years. The assertion then of Islamic law that it aspires to control every event or every possibility of human life requires considerable qualification. For, effectively, the law could be presented as delegating management

[45] Ibid., II, 122.
[46] Ibid., II, 369.
[47] Ibid., II, 154–8.

of details, in some areas, and in some conditions, to various human agents. One such agent was the governor: His administrative powers included the right to make executive decisions in areas of the law where there was no precise, or no final and binding rule. An executive decision would be binding on the people until a different executive decision emerged. Subkī denied that the judicial commission that had taken place under Tengiz in relation to the waqf document of the Juwāniyya had been backed by an executive decision. He also maintained that the judicial commission had taken into consideration *maṣlaḥa* – the general welfare of the community (or possibly of the waqf), and custom, both of which were flexible concepts permitting considerable local variation across time and space.

The functions of a qadi in different Islamic societies varied. The extent and limits of his competence depended on the terms of his appointment by the sultan or governor. The sultan might choose to restrict the functions of the qadi to the strictly judicial, and limit his decision-making capacity to a particular *madhhab*, or even to a particular item of *ikhtilāf* where there was acknowledged *ikhtilāf*. In Mamluk times (and under many other Islamic dynasties) the qadis had, in fact, considerable administrative and executive power as well as judicial authority. The spheres within which they could exert executive authority varied. It depended largely on specific delegation from the governor, though, in some areas (e.g., the administration of waqfs), delegation could be assumed, even where no specific delegation was given. The diverse patterns of appointment, authority and activity of judges were often described in terms of *rasm* (decree), *ʿurf* and *ʿāda* (custom) and *maṣlaḥa* (general welfare), all of them concepts that were associated with regional and historical variability in the realisation of the law.

2. Subkī, like all other Sunni jurists, accepted that it was a condition of the validity of a judicial post that it be the result of appointment by the actual governor.[48] A special factor affecting the judicial system as it existed in Subkī's time and place was the presence of four judges, one for each *madhhab*, in the two major centres of Mamluk power, Cairo and Damascus. The decision to create this situation lay with – and within the legitimate authority of – the Sultan, and had been effected by the Mamluk Sultan, Al-Ẓāhir Baybars, in 664/1266, as a result of a case that came before the Maẓālim court of the Sultan in the Dār al-ʿAdl in Cairo, in 663/1265.[49] Almost a century later, in the year 754/1353, Subkī, pondering the nature and the extent of judicial authority in his own time, in an

[48] Cf. Schacht, *Introduction*, 188. '[The qadi] is appointed by the political authority, but the validity of his appointment does not depend on the legitimate character of that authority – one of the matter-of-fact features in Islamic law.'

[49] Jørgen Nielsen, *Secular Justice in an Islamic State* (Leiden: Nederlands Historisch-Archaeologisch Instituut te Istanbul, 1985), 116–7.

expository fatwa (not a response to a question) that focused initially on judicial supervision of waqfs, still saw the emergence of four qadis as the beginning of his own situation.

1. The institution of four qadis [in Damascus] took place in the year 664/1265–6. The waqfs which had been established prior to that date, including those of Nūr al-Dīn, Ṣalāḥ al-Dīn and others, all of them, since there was only one qadi, were subject to his supervision, either by virtue of a specific condition [laid down by the founder] or by virtue of his [the qadi's] general authority. In the year 664, that qadi was not deposed, nor did he die. What happened was that three further qadis took office alongside him. Hence his supervisory authority continued, by virtue of the specific condition when it had been specified that supervision belonged to the judge, or by virtue of his general authority where no condition had been specified. That authority would continue to be his, none of the other three being appointed in his place, until the situation changed [e.g.] in the manner discussed before, namely that another single judge who did not share his *madhhab* might take his place. What in fact happened here is that three judges were added to the original one judge. The fact is that their supervisory authority was not made general; it excluded matters related to waqfs, orphans, the appointment of deputies, and the treasury. These four matters were made specific to the Shāfiʿī judge. All four shared in judicial affairs, excluding these. This is how the situation emerged, and this is what was decreed (*rusima bi-hi*) under the Ẓāhiriyya household.[50] Subsequently custom continued according to this pattern (*wa-ʾstamarrat al-ʿāda ʿalay-hi*). As each qadi died, another took his place, of the same *madhhab*, and it was mentioned in the terms of his appointment that he should follow the custom of the one before him (*yudhkar fī tawliyyati-hi anna-hu ʿalā ʿādāt man qabla-hu*). The requirement of the Law (*muqtaḍā ʾl-sharʿ*) in these circumstances is that the authority that was transferred to him included nothing that did not belong to the previous judge in the same *madhhab*; there was no increase in his sphere of authority. Hence no one of the three extra judges gained anything of the supervisory authority which had previously belonged to the Shāfiʿī judge, neither by virtue of the Law, nor by the terms of appointment of the Sultan – may God most high support him.
2. The situation has remained thus up to the present. Therefore judicial authority in relation to the old waqfs, all of them, is as we have described

[50] *Al-dawla al-ẓāhiriyya* – i.e., the reign of al-ẓāhir Baybars, 1260–1277; cf. P.M. Holt, *The Age of the Crusades* (London: Longman, 1986), 90–8.

it. The situation in respect of the waqfs which have emerged after the institution of four qadis is as follows. If the terms of the waqf make a condition that supervision belongs to a specific qadi, then the condition is to be followed in this respect, that special supervision belongs to him in accord with the condition of the founder. But the Shāfiʿī qadi will have general supervision. This is for two reasons. First, convention (*al-ʿurf*) requires this. Secondly, the Shāfiʿī qadi is superior, in virtue of convention, and in virtue of the habitual practice of the Sultan (*ʿurfan wa-bi-ʿādāt al-sulṭān*); and the superior possesses general supervisory authority over the inferior. If the terms of the waqf do not include a condition [specifying who is to have supervision] then supervision belongs exclusively to the Shāfiʿī judge, because of what we have said, and because he is the judge in an absolute sense [i.e., in the general usage of the term in Damascus].

3. This situation remained established under the Nāṣiriyya household[51] when there was discussion of these matters, with the effect that when the word 'qadi' was used without further specification, it meant the Shāfiʿī qadi. This was how the term was understood by those around the Sultan. If he intended some other, then he added suitable qualifications. The Sultan's understanding and that of his entourage became established in accord with these principles. We in the lands of Egypt have always recognised this both as coming from the Sultan, and from those who receive executive orders (*marāsim*) from him … .[52]

The aim of Subkī's argument here is to establish, for Damascus only, and for his time, that the Shāfiʿī qadi has a higher and more general authority than the other three qadis. This is not due to any specific principle of Islamic law. It is due to the pattern of events that had subsisted in Damascus prior to 664, as modified by governmental decree (*rusima bi-hi*) in that year, when three extra qadis were appointed alongside the single (Shāfiʿī) qadi who had previously held independent judicial authority in Damascus. The decree(s) that created the new judges had also specified and limited the range of their authority but did not imply the removal of the Shāfiʿī qadi, nor any reduction in the general authority he was deemed to hold. Custom (*ʿāda*) had been affected by decree (and had undoubtedly achieved its previous form also by decree, since only governmental decrees could validate and define any type of judicial appointment), and the resultant new custom should be assumed to have continued to the present day. The requirements of the Law itself (i.e., the universals that covered the

[51] *Al-dawla al-nāṣiriyya* – i.e., the reign of al-Nāṣir Muḥammad, 1293–1341; cf. Holt, *The Age of the Crusades*, 107–20.

[52] Subkī, *Fatāwā*, II, 23–4.

appointment and succession of judges) did not invalidate the custom, and the terms of appointment of individual judges had implied no change initiated by the government.

Subkī's specific concern was the general supervision of waqfs. In respect of the old waqfs, those created before 664, the right of supervision belonged clearly and absolutely to the Shāfiʿī judge. Marginally less clear was the situation in regard to waqfs created after that date. Subkī argues that, even when a non-Shāfiʿī judge has been specified in the foundation document as supervisor, a right of general supervision continues to be vested in the Shāfiʿī judge, by virtue of custom/convention (*ʿurf*) and the habitual practice (*ʿāda*) of the Sultan. These conclusions too do not relate to any universals of *fiqh*. What is implied here is that the specific rules of law, those that are articulated in works of *fiqh*, in so far as they relate to the appointment, dismissal and succession of qadis, do not in themselves create a unique possible realisation of the law. Rather, the actual realisation of the law will vary according to the contingencies of history and political power, these being the realities that lie behind Subkī's appeal to governmental decree (*rasm*), terms of appointment (*tawliyya*) and custom (*ʿurf* and *ʿāda*).

These points are worth elaborating. It is clear that the conceptual distinctions available to Subkī, which were partially realised in the political structures of his time and place, were flexible, sophisticated and open to varied development. Consider the hypothetical case that a sultan might wish to appoint in Damascus a single Ḥanafī judge. In one sense this was clearly within the defined legal capacity of the governing power. But there would be strong arguments of expediency against any such policy, and these would be translated, at the theoretical level, into arguments of *maṣlaḥa* and *ʿāda* (the people of Syria had long been predominantly Shāfiʿī, etc.). Consider now the case that the sultan might wish to separate the judicial functions of his appointee from an established administrative function, say that of supervising waqfs. Again, this would be clearly within his legal competence. This is demonstrated by his appointment of the three extra qadis who were not given (according to Subkī, who does not question this principle) any of the administrative powers that were traditionally associated with judicial office (para.1). The question whether the people of Syria would be better served by a separation of judicial and administrative functions would be debated primarily in terms of *maṣlaḥa*, *ʿāda* and governmental decrees. The *sharīʿa*, as reflected in works of *fiqh*, provided no definitive answer to this set of problems. It did, however, provide some of the rules, principles, and general concepts through which the question could be articulated and explored. The answer could not but vary with the particular historical and political circumstances of a given community.

Given the historical and social circumstances of Mamluk Syria (not to mention the personal circumstances of Subkī's life and training), it may be assumed that Subkī would not appreciate any argument for the separation of the administrative and judicial tasks that were traditionally associated with the post of the Shāfiʿī qadi in Damascus. He himself was a very considerable pluralist: He added to his post as a judge several posts as a teaching jurist; he acted freely as a mufti, including in cases where he was, or was expected to be, the judge; he exploited all the established possibilities of administrative authority that were associated with a judge's post; and he certainly aspired to, or actually acquired, even wider administrative powers.[53] He was delighted when his son gained a post in the governmental administration, and he subsequently made that son also a deputy judge under his own jurisdiction, thereby blurring the distinction between secular governmental functions and *sharʿī* ones. None of this is surprising given the historical realities of the period. It is important, however, to note that the conceptual disentangling of all these functions was already achieved. Some of the potential benefits of separating these various functions were worked out in the later Mamluk, and more specifically, in Ottoman times (when, in particular, the appointment and ranking of muftis by the government became established). On the other hand, and reflecting again the varied development of historical realia, the position of qadi probably became even more intricately involved with administrative and governmental affairs under the Ottomans than had been the case in earlier social and political circumstances.[54] The advantages and disadvantages of separating the judicial and administrative functions of qadis, of increasing or decreasing their participation in routine governmental administration, of effecting clear separation of juristic and judicial functions, of permitting or prohibiting the combining of secular administrative office and judicial office, and so on, were all matters on which the *sharīʿa* had little to say. They had to be worked out in terms of *maṣlaḥa*, *ʿada*, and governmental decree, and were differently realised in different temporal and geographical situations.

Subkī's arguments about the particular situation of qadis in Mamluk Syria could not be translated into the universals of the law. These were already fixed and established. He was, however, convinced that his arguments were binding upon the people of that time and region, subject only to the usual limits of juristic debate.

4. There is a point to be made in relation to these matters. If one of the three [non-Shāfiʿī] qadis should read these words of mine, then either a different view will be manifest to him based on proof, in which case he should adopt a procedure consistent with his view. Or, he will agree with my

[53] See the fatwa on Friday prayer; ibid., vol.1, 178–81.

[54] Uriel Heyd (ed. V.L. Ménage), *Studies in Old Ottoman Criminal Law* (Oxford: Clarendon Press, 1973), 215–9.

> argument, or, be in a state of uncertainty. In either of these last two cases he should rejoice, because God has preserved him from the supervision of affairs in which he has no authority, and preserved him from dealing in appointments and financial receipts to which he has no right while excluding those who have rights, and from perpetrating other corrupt acts. He should thank God for this preservation. In the case of a Shāfiʿī qadi who reads these words, if he agrees with my argument, he should not rejoice but realise that he is subject to a divine trial. God has charged him to undertake judicial office, including the supervisory authority that is a part of that office, and he should carry out his duty accordingly. As to the secretaries of state and scribes who write on behalf of the Sultan (*kuttāb al-sirr wa-ʾl-muwaqqiʿīn al-muballighīn ʿan al-sulṭān*), they should consider the implications of my words in relation to what they write on behalf of the Sultan, ensuring that their work conforms to the path of the Pure Sharīʿa and to the conventions that have been established (*al-ʿawāʾid al mustaqarra ʿalay-hā*; *ʿawāʾid*, sg. *ʿāda*), rather than to conventions which have no foundation. Conventions of the latter type arise from the desire to please or flatter, or from shame at carrying out a praiseworthy act. In such a case no duty of obedience emerges, and nor should the decrees of the Officers of State (*marāsim wulāt al-umūr*) make them binding.[55]

The first part of that passage concedes the possibility that a non-Shāfiʿī judge may well have a view different from Subkī's and may be able to defend it by proof, in which case he must act in accordance with his view. It is in fact quite likely that Subkī's fellow judges did over time gain supervisory control of waqfs and tried to maintain that control independently of the Shāfiʿī judge. Subkī not only holds a contrary opinion, but offers to the governmental administrators the advice that they should act in accord with his view. Clearly, since his words imply that this is a legitimate area of *ikhtilāf*, the officers of state might not always act in the way he wished. The primary argument available to him to constrain their activities is the argument of established conventions (*ʿawāʾid*, sg. *ʿāda*). The neat parallelism of 'the Pure Sharīʿa' and 'established conventions' is not an empty parallelism. It distinguishes again between the divine law (which provides overall guidance, including some precise and pointed limitations) and a broad area of practice (where a number of potential systems might, by virtue of custom, convention and governmental decree, with equal validity, be realised). Any dispute that might emerge – for example, if a Ḥanafī judge deemed

[55] Subkī, *Fatāwā*, I, 25.

himself to have greater powers than were conceded to him by Subkī – could be resolved by governmental decree (subject to *maṣlaḥa* and *'āda*) since all parties agreed that decrees which did not actually contravene the established law were effective and binding. Nothing, however, of Subkī's assessment of the particular situation of Syria could affect the rules of the *sharī'a* as set out in works of *fiqh* (though, no doubt, some niceties of expression might ease or block particular developments). The administrative conventions of a particular place and period did not affect the expression of the law, even when, as in this case, those conventions were deemed to be binding and (in a very extended sense) in line with the *sharī'a*. Subkī's last two sentences point to the possibility that conventions might emerge which do not have the same validity. He would wish to ensure that these were not given the sanction of administrative action.

Subkī's argument establishes certain broad distinctions between judicial authority, which, controlled ultimately by the universals of the law, finds a particular realisation based on custom, welfare and governmental decree; and governmental authority, which is constrained by its own conventions as long as these are not opposed to the universals of the law. The task of distinguishing governmental and judicial authority was continued in the immediately succeeding paragraphs.

5. There is a further point to be made here, for the sake of clarifying knowledge, though I have the greatest possible distaste for initiating it. The question arises in relation to the Sultan, may God most high support him, though he is of the highest rank and the most elevated status, though he is the one who appoints the major qadis, whether he has supervision over waqfs. If we simply specify that supervision belongs to the *ḥākim*, does that mean the qadi alone, or is the Sultan too contained within the meaning of the term? It appears to me that if a condition is laid down that supervision belongs to the *ḥākim*, this does not include the Sultan; and likewise if there is a condition that supervision belongs to the qadi. In the case of the qadi this is an explicit reference to the representative of the Law (*nā'ib al-shar'*). As to the *ḥākim*, there is a possibility [that it includes reference to the Sultan], but convention (*'urf*) requires that this term is like the term qadi. The people of Egypt and Syria know no *ḥākim* except the qadi. This is different from the convention (*'urf*) of Iraq. Hence, for any waqf established in Egypt or Syria, if it contains a condition that supervision belongs to the qadi or to the *ḥākim*, supervision in that waqf belongs to the official who is the representative of the Law (*nā'ib al-shar'*), and does not imply any authority for the Sultan. It is just like a condition that supervision belongs to Zaid; it cannot extend to anyone else.

6. If this is acknowledged, does the Sultan perhaps have the right of general supervision over the qadi? It is a possibility, since the Sultan is the one who appoints the qadi. And the opposite is also a possibility, since general supervision means nothing other than the supervision of the law (*naẓar al-sharʿ*), for it is the supervisor of all. If any of the special supervisors offends in any respect, in any duty of supervision, the Law will deal with the matter and repair the offence. The qadi is the representative of the Law and hence he has the right of general supervision over every special supervisor, from the Sultan downwards; and likewise he has the right to exercise judicial authority over them. If the qadi, by virtue of the founder's words, is the special supervisor, then the functions of special and general supervision are conjoined in him, and there is no requirement of general supervision over him. If we suppose that the duty of supervision has been specified to someone other than the qadi, then there is no doubt that the qadi has the right of general supervision in his capacity as representative of the Law (*nāʾib al-sharʿ*).
7. Shall we say then that the Sultan too has the right of general supervision? There is no doubt that the Sultan is higher in degree but – may God support him – he does not have the free time to oversee particular affairs or the needs of *sharʿī* rules. His duty is to look after the generality of his power; he is the shadow of God on earth; his noble supervision requires him to appoint a representative of the Law (*nāʾiban ʿan al-sharʿ*) to undertake the burdens of the *sharīʿa* and to supervise its rules and regulations. He transfers to him the reins of the *sharīʿa* so that he, the Sultan, may be free to carry out his own duties – i.e., to consider the burdens and the welfare of the community, to struggle with the kings of the earth, to organise armies, to administer the country and the welfare of its inhabitants, to promulgate wars against the enemies of God's religion and to repulse them, to establish communications within the kingdom, to suppress the wicked, and other such like great activities which neither qadis nor all the rest of creation can undertake. Likewise the Sultan – may God most high strengthen him and his followers – should not occupy himself with judicial authority in the fields of marriage or divorce or sale, for his supervision extends to things higher than that.
8. All of this is relevant if the founder of a waqf specifies that supervision belongs to the qadi or to the *ḥākim*. But if he fails to specify that supervision belongs to anyone, and given that the jurists claim that the valid view is that supervision belongs to the qadi, I used to hesitate on the question whether the Sultan shares authority with him or not. Now, however, my

view is established that he does not share authority with the qadi. The qadi holds it alone, as the jurists have said, and the Sultan has no authority over him. Unless the Sultan is of the type of 'Umar b. 'Abd al- 'Azīz, for he and his like are the caliphs of the Law (*khulafā' al-shar'*), greater than the qadis. The words of those of our companions who have declared that supervision belongs to the Imam should be interpreted as referring to rulers of this type. As to those who gain office through force, their regulations are effective, and their general appointments which relate to the needs of the people are valid, including appointments to judicial office. They set up a man in the place of the Lawgiver (*fī makān ṣāḥib al-shar'*), and give him the symbols of the *sharī'a*. As to particular appointments [of lower rank] the people do not have the same need of them, and they belong to the representative of the *sharī'a*. But God knows best. Written on the 16th of Ramaḍān, seven hundred and fifty four/15 September, 1353.

Paragraph by paragraph that argument points towards a practical and effective demarcation of the different spheres of duty of the Sultan and the qadi. Not, of course, in the sense that there will be no areas of argument, or areas of uncertainty – there are bound to be such; but in the sense that there is an established core of activities that belongs to the sultan and a different established core of activities that belongs to the qadi. In para. 5, Subkī argues that the Sultan has no rights over the supervision of waqfs. This is an exclusive prerogative of the qadi. Even in arguing the case, however, he shows that this distinction is not as clear as he might wish. The basis of his argument lies in the convention (*'urf*), here the linguistic convention, of the peoples of Egypt and Syria. The convention of Iraq, apparently, permits a different consideration, namely that the governing power at least shares in the supervisory authority of the qadi. It is more than likely that the Mamluk government and at least some of its juristic advisers might disagree with Subkī on this matter. The Mamluk government certainly made periodically some claim to intervention in the administration of waqfs; this is why Subkī has to argue against such a right.

Subkī also claims that the Sultan 'should not occupy himself with judicial authority' (para. 7). But the Mamluk Sultan and some of the major figures of the administration did associate themselves with judicial authority, through their participation in the *maẓālim* courts. We see Subkī here developing arguments that will permit of clear demarcation of the administrative and executive sphere from the judicial sphere which includes a special concern for the administration of waqfs. He was writing in opposition to the actual realisation of these spheres of authority in his own time. And his ideas were constrained by the possibilities of his own time: He might want to separate the Sultan from the legitimate spheres of the judge but he would be unable to see any advantages in separating the various possible areas of activity of a judge – at least in the case of the Shāfiʿī judge; though he was quite happy about the removal of traditional administrative authority from the three extra judges appointed in 664/1265–6.

The working of the *maẓālim* courts is better documented for the Mamluks than for many other dynasties.[56] They were not generally a means for the Sultan to assert independent judicial authority in matters pertaining to the *sharīʿa*. There at least, he was careful to ensure that the qadis and muftis present in the court participated in, or indeed were fully responsible for, the decisions that emerged. Subkī himself, as Shāfiʿī qadi of Damascus, must have been present regularly at the *maẓālim* sessions of the Governor of Syria, and must have offered advice that ensured a general prevalence of *sharʿī* values in those areas of activity that were securely governed by the *sharīʿa*. In areas that were not governed by the *sharīʿa*, the governor and his administrators had presumably more scope. What these areas were is broadly indicated by Subkī in para. 7 above: to struggle with the kings of the earth, to organise armies, to administer the country and the welfare of its inhabitants, to promulgate wars against the enemies of God's religion and to repulse them, to establish communications within the kingdom, to suppress the wicked, and so on. Within these areas there were no doubt disputes and legal machinery and conventions for their resolution, but they were not governed by the *sharīʿa* (save in the sense of overall general supervision).

There were disputes between the governor of Syria and his chief judge. The most famous related to waqf supervision and reached a climax in the year 752/1351, two years before Subkī wrote the present document. The Mamluk governor, Arghun al-Kāmilī, objected to a judicial decision by Subkī (relating to a long-running dispute about the status and ownership of land in the region of Baalbak) and had the matter referred to the Sultan's court in Cairo. There, the Sultan, in consultation with his qadis, made provision for continued consideration of the case.[57] The outcome of the case is not known, but it, and numerous other cases that relate to waqf, demonstrate the tensions that existed, precisely in this area, between judicial and governmental authority. Again, it is worth noting that the conceptual possibilities for a clear, practical separation of judicial and governmental authority, both in respect of purely judicial matters, and in respect of the administration of waqfs, was in place. Subkī was capable of making all the required distinctions; their realisation depended on developments in the political and administrative reality of governmental administration, developments

[56] Nielsen, *Secular justice*.

[57] Ibid., 118–9.

which were not covered by precise rules of the law, but rather by considerations of custom, welfare and governmental decree.

Consideration of the various *maẓālim* cases documented by Jørgen Nielsen demonstrates also that the Mamluk Sultan did have considerable judicial authority, either independently, in things related to administration or the army, or with and through his qadis and muftis, in matters related to the *sharīʿa*. That distinction between matters that belong to the sphere of governmental authority and matters that belong to the *sharīʿa* is not arbitrary (though, as in the present instance, it might be disputed) but reflects a genuine sense of the different spheres of activity of qadis and governors. The qadis are representatives of the Law. The governor has different, and in some respects higher tasks.

Subkī picks his way through the necessary distinctions in paras. 6 to 8 above. In para. 7, he introduces the idea that the qadi is representative of the law (*nāʾib al-sharʿ*), and that he has, on that basis, a general right of supervision over more limited or 'special' (the key terms are *khāṣṣ* and *ʿāmm*) appointments, including that of the Sultan himself. The idea of the law as supervisor of all (*nāẓir ʿalā kulli aḥad*) is not problematic and must be associated with any legal system that sees the government as subject to the law. One of the functions of the *maẓālim* courts was to provide a forum for complaints against state officials, whether of the administration or of the army. The activities of the Sultan himself could be discussed in that forum, even if its practical power was necessarily limited by the presence of the Sultan as participant in judicial decisions. The idea that a governor might appear before a qadi, or require a judicial (*sharʿī*) declaration, in an area that was an established and central component of *sharʿī* authority, was not unknown in Islamic civilisation, and had been enacted on various occasions.[58] Subkī's perception of the law as representing a general supervision over all officers of the government, including sultans and qadis, was not exceptional, nor absurd, nor divorced from practical reality. The law was above both qadis and governors, and there are plenty of examples of both, in Mamluk times, and elsewhere, being required to submit to some form of legal (and *sharʿī*) process of law. (And, of course, numerous examples of unjust governors and corrupt qadis who managed not to be brought to any kind of judicial questioning.)[59]

[58] Inter alia, Ignaz Goldziher (ed. S.M. Stern), *Muslim Studies* (London: Allen and Unwin, 1967), II, 38–88 (though the details of his argument are now dated).

[59] The list of *maẓālim* cases presented by Nielsen includes examples of judicial process of some kind being executed against qadis (nos. 26, 61, 72, 81), government officials (nos. 25, 33, 38, 40, 41), and even the Sultan (nos. 22, 32, 34, 35, 37). Consideration of these cases also shows that a distinction was made between administrative and military affairs (which did not require the involvement of the jurists), and affairs that were related to the *sharīʿa* (which did).

That broad distinction between affairs of government and affairs of the *sharīʿa* is spelt out by Subkī in para. 7. He begins by reaffirming what he had said in the first paragraph about the high rank and status of the Sultan (higher than that of the qadi). This high rank relates to the great activities (*al-umūr al-ʿaẓīma*) which are his concern and could not be carried out by qadis or any other of God's creation. Though the basic list of these activities is (perhaps necessarily) vague, it is a list and it offers a basic concept of the sphere of activity of governors: they fight wars, organise the army, administer the country, look after the welfare of its inhabitants, establish communications, suppress the wicked, and so on. The concept of war here is not the religious concept of jihad, but rather a struggle between kings (*mughālabat mulūk al-arḍ*). Subkī has in mind the actual activities of contemporary rulers, and in his concept of the *sharīʿa* and how it works he finds space for their activities, even, or, precisely, their secular activities. These are the areas in which (save, as usual, for certain broad limits) the *sharīʿa* does not have detailed provision. The most important of the duties of the Sultan, for Subkī, is his duty to appoint a representative of the Law (*nāʾib al-sharʿ*), the qadi, who will undertake the supervision of the rules and regulations of the *sharīʿa*. There is a sphere of activity proper to the Sultan and a sphere of activity proper to the qadi. Central to the latter are matters of marriage, divorce and sale. A disputed area of authority, as is evident from the process of argument, is the supervision of waqfs.

In para. 8, Subkī's argument again shows how uncertain is his claim that the Sultan has no share at all in the supervisory authority of the qadi. He himself had once been uncertain about the matter. And the writings of earlier jurists have to be interpreted in a particular way in order to conform to his claim. In particular the word Imam, when used by earlier authorities, in a context where they say that the Imam has some share in the supervision of waqfs, has to be read as referring only to the ideal Imam, such as is represented by ʿUmar b. ʿAbd al-ʿAzīz. These Imams are the caliphs of the Law, and the two separate spheres of authority, that of the qadi and that of the governor, which are now separate, were conjoined in them. In the meantime, the regulations and appointments of the *de facto* powers are valid and effective, and that includes their appointment of judges, who take the place of the Law-giver, establish the symbols of the *sharīʿa*, and are representatives of the law.

The distinction between the ideal and the actual governor is of immense importance. It could become, as in the present instance, an interpretative principle whereby previous articulations of the law could be interpreted in a particular manner. But it had a much more general importance, because it was by virtue of the distinction between real and ideal that Subkī was able to assert two spheres of authority – that relating to the *sharīʿa* which was the sphere of authority of the judges, and that relating to governmental matters which was the sphere of authority of the actual power. The distinction is not new and is present even in

Māwardī whose work has (too often) been seen as a statement of caliphal absolutism. In fact, his assessment of the Abbasid caliphate as centre and focus of all aspects of political authority, *sharʿī* and otherwise, was symbolic. His theory has some analogies with a theory of constitutional monarchy.[60] The actual bearers of power and authority, including the qadi, derived their authority from the amir, who, as executive head of state, by whatever means, possessed delegatory powers. But, though appointed by the head of government, the qadi's first loyalty was to the law: and as a representative of the law it could be asserted that his authority had a general or universal aspect which made him the general supervisor of all (para. 6 above). But, at the time of Subkī, the question whether the Sultan had a share in this general supervision remained an open question, though one on which Subkī himself had developed strong opinions (para. 7).

Section 4. Conclusions

1. In Section 1 of this chapter we have used the writings of Subkī to insist that the law has three functionaries: the scholar-jurist, the mufti and the qadi. The relationship between these three is hierarchical, the scholar-jurist being unequivocally the highest rank, the one that controls and passes judgement on decisions at a lower level. This observation is opposed to the conclusions of Wael B Hallaq, who, in his 'From *fatwā*s to *furūʿ*',[61] perhaps because he does not distinguish clearly and directly between the scholar-jurist and the mufti, gives to the mufti that degree of authority which belongs in fact to the scholar-jurist.[62] Hallaq associated his claims with a general belief that Islamic law was capable of development and change 'commensurate with the changing needs of Muslim societies',[63] and that the mufti was both the initiator and the manager of change, *fiqh* being 'little more than the sum totality of *fatwa*s that had entered the body of *furūʿ*'. [64]

It is possible to agree with Hallaq's thesis at its most general – that in some sense or another Islamic law was capable of responding to social change – without feeling that he has characterised well either the basic structures of the Islamic legal system or the modality of its accommodation to change. Subkī's work

[60] Cf. Calder, 'Friday prayer'.

[61] See n. 3.

[62] 'It was the mufti – not the qadi or anyone else – who was responsible for the development of the legal doctrine embodied in *furūʿ* works.' (55) 'Discovering and applying the law was the responsibility of the mufti, for he alone, in the final analysis, determined whether or not a ruling is valid.' 'Standing at the top of the legal hierarchy, [the muftis] saw themselves as the guardians of the law and of the community at large.' (59).

[63] Ibid., 30.

[64] Ibid., 55.

reminds us that there is no reason in principle why certain types of accommodation and change should not be effected by any one of the three functionaries. But the ultimate control of change must lie with the scholar-jurist whose work necessarily responds to and passes judgement on the work of muftis and judges (and this remains true when all three functions are fulfilled by one person, as is the case with Subkī himself). Furthermore, Chapters 1 and 2 of the present work have shown that works of *furūʿ* do not in fact show significant signs of responding to the changing patterns of practice in Muslim societies. Generations of jurists re-stated the *madhhab*, using broadly the same topics, rules and terminology for a thousand years. What was important for the possibility of accommodation and change was the necessarily oblique relationship between the law as preserved and the law as practised. A first observation about Islamic law and its response to the flux of social events must be that flexibility is provided in the hermeneutical space that lies between the literary tradition and the social practice. Subkī's fundamental and much reiterated assertion that *fiqh* is concerned with universals, *iftāʾ* with particulars, makes the point more than adequately. It is a matter of negotiating the space between the literary expression of the law and the social realisation of a legal system, of applying universals to particulars. While that task is, in some respects, shared between the jurist *qua* jurist and the jurist *qua* mufti, real authority is achieved only as arguments are developed and modulated and so present the function of the scholar-jurist rather than the mufti. It is possible for a legal system, in its literary manifestation, to remain (on points of detail) near-stable – and that is what we find in the tradition of *furūʿ* – while being (arguably, hermeneutically) compatible with a wide variety of social practice.

2. In Section 3 of this chapter, we have followed Subkī's thoughts on the relationship between secular authority and judicial authority. It is clear that there was available an adequate and potentially discriminating terminology to express the different ranges and qualities of authority as it belonged to a judge and to a secular power. If that depended broadly on the perception that there were different spheres of activity appropriate to qadis and to governors, the elaboration of detail depended more precisely on acknowledgement of three principles which affected the local and contingent realisation of divine law: decree (*rasm*), custom (*ʿurf* and *ʿāda*) and social welfare (*maṣlaḥa*). These three principles can all be analysed as principles of delegation and indeterminacy in the law, in the sense that the law recognised areas of policy within which the social realisation of the law depended not on the law's provision of detail, but on the law's acknowledgement of variant possibilities governed by historical and regional circumstances, or the nature and conditions of secular power.

The application of universals to particulars on the one hand, and the recognition of broad areas of delegation and indeterminacy on the other represent two distinct modalities for permitting diversity and development in the social realisation of the law. Since neither of these requires that the inherited literary expression of the law – the topics, rules and terminology – should change, they may be more successful (or more subtle) ways of accounting for Islamic law's accommodation to social change than mere assertions about adaptability and change in the law. The problem is that 'the law' is radically ambiguous in an Islamic context, since it might refer to literature or to practice. The organic processes of change and development in the local and regional realisation of legal structures (of all kinds) were related only obliquely to the literary depiction of God's law. The latter was preserved, explored and expressed, with the utmost refinement, by scholar-jurists. The former depended upon more factors than can be easily summarised here, the interaction of qadis with governors, administrators and armies being only a small part of the dynamic social complex. A work of *fiqh* does not describe an executive legal system. On the contrary, the explorations of *fiqh* are compatible with numerous different realisations of practical legal systems; and, further, express concerns of a higher moral, social and religious kind than are relevant to the lesser task of merely acquiring an efficient legal system (important though that undoubtedly is).

3. In Section 2 of this chapter, the focus of interest was on the relationship between fatwas and judicial decisions. Subkī was not in doubt that judicial decisions, formally enacted, were binding and had to be preserved – as far as possible. There were, however, limits, occasions when the higher authority of muftis and jurists could be brought to bear on a particular judicial decision in such a way as to render possible annulment by a different judge (maybe by the same judge), and the promulgation of a new judicial decision. In very broad terms, a judicial decision was safe unless it was opposed to a revealed text, a consensus, or a clear analogy (Section 2.5 above) – but to establish that could itself be problematic and might require the highest and most subtle of juristic argument. In the case presented above, Section 2. 3–4, Subkī's concern to set aside a particular judicial decision led not only to arguments about the sources, but to arguments about the *madhhab*, the status of the qadi (*mujtahid* or *muqallid*) and the conditions governing his appointment. While this complex of issues had been acknowledged to be relevant since as early as Ibn al-Ṣalāḥ, Subkī gave them a new and clearer articulation.

Referring only to the contents of the passage translated in Section 2.3 above, we note the following. A qadi and a mufti, acting in their official capacity, are bound to issue rulings in accord with their *madhhab*.[65] If sufficiently skilled (i.e.,

[65] This is implicit in para. 3 and in the argument of paras. 7 and 8. Though Subkī finds a partial authority for his view in Ibn al-Ṣalaḥ (para. 3), he was himself cited by later writers as authority for this position, no doubt because he did much to work out and demonstrate in practice its implications. See Muḥammad b. Aḥmad Ramlī, *Nihāyat al-muḥtāj* (Beirut: Dār al-Kutub al-ʿIlmiyya, 1993), I, 47, and below.

mujtahid fi 'l-madhhab), they might establish a reasoned and justified preference for any view that was familiar within the *madhhab*. If not so skilled, they must follow the generally preferred view (and could discover that, where necessary, by appeal to a higher authority). Under no circumstances could a jurist, when acting as a mufti or a qadi, promulgate a view which was outside the *madhhab*, or a rare and eccentric view within it. In his private life however – that is, when not acting in his official capacity as a mufti or a qadi – a jurist of sufficient status could, for his own private purposes, establish preferences which were outside the *madhhab* and a product of his own analysis of the arguments.

That complex of ideas shows how the historical development of Islamic law and practice, in particular the development of *madhhab* loyalty, impinged upon and clarified a general principle which, in its earliest formulation, did not take account of *madhhab* affiliation. A judicial decision could be annulled only if it was opposed to a revealed text, a consensus, or a clear analogy, and so on. In Subkī's time, and subsequently, this was understood to mean that a judicial decision could be annulled only if it could be shown to be outside of the mainstream of *madhhab* thinking. It was the *madhhab* which passed judgement on the existence of a revealed text, a consensus, or a clear analogy.

This complex of issues relates again to the question of change and development in the law. Social change could be accommodated either through creative and practical manipulation of the idea of applying universals to particulars, or by exploitation of the broad areas of delegation and indeterminacy implicit in the notions of general welfare, governmental decree and custom. But change in the sense of asserting that a rule previously established in the *madhhab* had been replaced by a new and different one is not easy to demonstrate – as we have seen in Chapters 1 and 2.[66] Of course, new and productive discriminations might be introduced and, in spite of all caveats, there were in fact acknowledged reversals of the law, but these became more difficult to effect with the passage of time. The juristic tradition itself was not less interested in the phenomenon of change than modern Western scholarship, and was often better able to provide a detailed and fully discriminating account of where change had occurred,

[66] Hallaq claimed to demonstrate for a fatwa by Ibn Rushd that it changed the Māliki *madhhab*. In fact, what he showed was that it was preserved and admired. Hallaq can conceive of no reason for preserving it other than because it had changed the *madhhab* – but there is no evidence that it had done so or that it ever did so. There were of course plenty of good academic reasons for preserving and enjoying the play of thought and argument by Ibn Rushd, as a significant example of *ikhtilāf*. Whether it was ultimately perceived to be within the area of acknowledged *ikhtilāf*, or preserved and proffered as an example of an eccentric view is not clear from Hallaq's analysis. Hallaq, 'Murder in Cordoba: Ijtihād, Iftāʾ and the Evolution of Substantive Law in Medieval Islam', *Acta Orientalia* (Oslo): 55 (1994): 55–83. Subkī too produced many interesting arguments, all of which were preserved, to demonstrate views only some of which were eventually allowed to affect the *madhhab*.

and why.[67] Subkī himself was perceived to have changed a great deal in the Shāfiʿī *madhhab*.

Subkī's son, Tāj al-Dīn, in the biographical notice of his father, pointed to and listed the innovations his father had achieved. These were of two types. The first type consisted of views which Subkī embraced though they were unequivocally outside the *madhhab*, or weak and eccentric (*ḍaʿīf, shādhdh*) views within it. Subkī's preferences here were interesting, might be relevant to his private life, but could not be used by Subkī himself, or anybody else, in his professional capacity as a mufti or a qadi. The second type consisted of views which were well-established within the *madhhab*, where Subkī simply changed the balance of preference.

> These [are] opinions which he has established as valid in the *madhhab*. This list includes items where Rāfiʿī and Nawawī together preferred an alternative view; and where Nawawī alone preferred an alternative view. ... We do not mention here those items in which he agrees with Nawawī while opposing Rāfiʿī, because this is evident, and because action is based on Nawawī, especially if he is supported by the Shaykh Imam [my father]. The views that are attributed to him here, those where he opposes both the earlier shaykhs, or Nawawī alone, are such that they must, clearly, be embraced. For I do not doubt that it is not permissible for the transmitters of our time (*naqalatu zamāni-nā*) to oppose him, since he is an imam, well-versed in the arguments of Rāfiʿī and Nawawī, in the texts of Shāfiʿī, and in the words of our companions. He had the perfected capacity to establish a preference (*tarjīḥ*). Hence, those who have not reached his high status, whose status in the sphere of fatwas (*fī ʾl-futyā*) is mere transmission, they have a duty to limit themselves on the basis of his views. As to one who has insight and the capacity to establish a preference, the whole matter is transferred to his own investigation, and not to the opinion (*futyā*) of Rāfiʿī or Nawawī or the Shaykh [my father].[68]

That passage makes familiar distinctions. Generally, the *madhhab* is that which was established by Rāfiʿī and Nawawī together, or by Nawawī alone in opposition to Rāfiʿī. Where Subkī has now re-asserted a different (but familiar) view in opposition to Nawawī, then, it is argued, because of his great authority, the view preferred by Subkī should prevail, and be recognised as the *madhhab*. Low-ranking scholars, working as muftis and qadis, should merely accept the *madhhab* as thus established. Higher-ranking scholars, those capable of establishing a reasoned preference, should analyse the matter for themselves – but may not go beyond the familiar range of *ikhtilāf* within the *madhhab*. Subkī's achievement here is that of a *mujtahid fī ʾl-madhhab*: the knowledge he wielded relates to the arguments of Rāfiʿī and Nawawī, the texts of Shāfiʿī and the words of our companions.

[67] See Ibn ʿĀbidīn's treatise on custom for an assessment of change within the Ḥanafī tradition. 'Nashr al-ʿarf fī binā al-aḥkām ʿalā al-ʿurf', *Majmūʿa rasāʾil Ibn ʿĀbidīn*, n.p (n.d.): 114–47.

[68] Subkī, *Ṭabaqāt*, X, 235.

The list of new rules that were appended to this heading was perceived by Subkī's son, and by his contemporaries, as being a remarkable achievement, a weighty product of learning, experience and illumination. It is not difficult, even in the late twentieth century,[69] to participate in the sense of mastery, insight and fulfilled learning that was Subkī's when he discovered a new argument or a new preference. Since he wrote up many of his arguments, we can share his experience – to a degree. But this list of discrete rules can hardly be presented as an emblem of development. There are less than 150 items in total, all of them isolated reformulations of established rules, none of them (by definition) going beyond well-established options within the *madhhab*. This is a drop in the ocean of the law. Nor were these innovations accompanied by appeal to general principles of development. There were no such principles. In promulgating a new rule, Subkī was re-establishing the *madhhab* in the form it should always have had.[70] Consideration of the rules that he changed does not suggest that Subkī responded more to practical problems than he did to theoretical and other problems.

Development of the law, in the sense of changing rules or terminology in response to contingent events, is not then particularly characteristic of the literary tradition. But we have already seen, in Chapters 1 and 2, that various forms of literary development did take place reflecting the larger meaning of the law within Islamic society – for the law was not merely practical. Furthermore, increasingly refined thinking about the place of the law in the structures of Muslim belief, or in Muslim society, led to new and important conceptions which might have ramifications at various levels. The three areas of thought which we have seen Subkī explore in this chapter were all areas in which he significantly refined and advanced, perhaps transformed, the perceptions of jurists about their own tasks and their position in society. No scholar prior to Subkī had so clearly stated, or so discriminatingly assessed, the significance of the three functionaries of the law. No scholar prior to him had so embraced, acknowledged and expressed the consequences of *madhhab* loyalty in relation to the promulgations of qadis and muftis. (In both cases the ability to write clearly about these things depended, at least in the Shāfiʿī tradition, upon the seminal work of Ibn al-Ṣalāḥ who had made revolutionary attempts to understand the

[69] These words were written in 1996–97.

[70] 'The *sharīʿa* is like an ocean, forever giving up its jewels. If a proof is valid, then its concealment from the people for long ages does not harm its validity.' (Subkī, *Fatāwā*, II, 586) 'It is perfectly possible that a particular totality of events may result in a judicial decision (*ḥukm*) which would not be appropriate to any one of them. … We do not say that legal rulings (*aḥkām*) change with the changes of time, but rather through the variety of emergent forms (*bi-ʿkhtilāf al-ṣūra al-ḥāditha*). If an event occurs which has a special characteristic, we must give it due consideration, for it may be that the totality of the event is such that the Law requires for it a particular ruling (*ḥukm*).' (Subkī, *Fatāwā*, II, 572).

special role of the mufti in Muslim society.) Finally Subkī's thoughts about the nature of judicial authority in relation to and in contrast with secular authority depended directly upon his own experience of Mamluk power. He was a powerful and innovative thinker but he was also a thinker within a well-established and homogenous literary tradition. His academic achievements are those of a hard-working scholar, participating in the thought and arguments of generations, advancing by small degrees and consensual effort the community's appreciation of divine law and its role in society.

4

The Social Function of Fatwas

Introduction

1. For each of the three functionaries of the law there is a corresponding body of literature which exemplifies their activities. For the academic jurist, it is the literary genres of *furūʿ al-fiqh* and (to a lesser extent) *uṣūl al-fiqh*. For the judge, it is the court records (*sijill*s). The latter had a practical importance as a record of decisions and judgements, but had no direct significance as an articulation of divine law; they did not constitute precedents; they were not a part of the training of jurists or judges. Works of *furūʿ*, on the other hand, were a record of the *madhhab*, of *ikhtilāf* and of the arguments that grew out of these; they were the measure of the law, and the prime means of education for judges and jurists. They were also the major component of a 'liberal' education, in so far as that was known to pre-modern Islamic societies. The literary products associated with the mufti were the fatwa, the fatwa collection and the analytic works, or manuals of conduct (*adab al-muftī*) which explained and justified the mufti's task.[1] This chapter is concerned with the fatwa, its functions and its transformations.

Section 1. The basic fatwa

1. Standard juristic discussion of the mufti and his function – of the type for example that is contained in a manual of *iftāʿ* – refers to two types of fatwa: the

[1] For more on the *adab al-muftī*, Muhammad Khalid Masud, '*Ādāb al-muftī*: The Muslim Understanding of the Values, Characteristics and Role of a *Muftī*', in Barbara Daly Metcalf (ed.), *Moral Conduct and Authority: The Place of Adab in South Asian Islam* (Berkeley, Los Angeles, and London: University of California Press, 1984), 124–51; Muhammad Khalid Masud, Brinkley Messick, and David S.Powers, 'Muftis, Fatwas and Islamic Legal Interpretation' in Masud, Messick, Powers (eds.), *Islamic Legal Interpretation: Muftis and their Fatwas* (Cambridge, MA, and London: Harvard University Press, 1996), 15–20.

fatwa issued to a layman (*ʿāmmī*), and the fatwa issued to a judge. The former type predominates and I will refer to it as the basic fatwa. It consists of a question (*masʿala*) posed by a layman, and a *jawāb* given by the mufti. As described by Nawawī in the seventh/thirteenth century, the question is ideally written by the petitioner (the *mustaftī*), or his agent, on a piece of paper – the *ruqʿat istiftāʿ*, and the answer written by the mufti, on the same piece of paper. The paper belongs to the petitioner and the mufti does not have the right to keep it. There is a presumption that a question will deal with a real issue. 'One should ask the mufti [only] when the event occasioning the question happens.'[2] 'If a layman (*ʿāmmī*) asks about what has not happened, it is not necessary to respond.'[3] For analytic purposes, a layman is normally presumed to be the source of a question. Hence the mufti is required to write clearly[4]; (Subkī, we have seen, also specified that the mufti should use clear and uncomplex language). He might write, along with the answer, a proof, as long as it consisted of a Quranic verse or a hadith; but not an argument based on *qiyās* and not a method of *ijtihād* – because this might confuse the unlearned reader. Conversely, if the fatwa was not for a layman, but for a qadi – this is the second type of fatwa generally acknowledged in the manuals – then it was acceptable to indicate the method of *ijtihād*.[5] On these criteria, a fatwa is of two types, aimed either at a layman or at a judge, and may differ in content, depending on its recipient. In both cases the fatwa is practical in the sense of searching for information about how to act in response to an event that has already happened.

A mufti should not write in his answer words or phrases of the type, 'There are two opinions on this matter' or 'two views' or 'dispute' for none of this represents a valid answer, as it does not procure the required end, which is to explain how to act (*bayān mā yaʿmal bi-hi*).[6] In other words the mufti is not expected to write like a jurist. He should aim at precision, relevance, a practical answer. Further, he should not write on the basis of what he happens to know about the case, unless there is reference to it in the question; he should limit himself to the question as phrased. If he wants to add a qualification, he should write something like, 'If the matter is thus-and-thus then the answer is thus-and-thus.' Since there is a possibility, even a presumption, that a petitioner will present his *ruqʿa* to more than one mufti, it is a matter of convention that the first mufti will write on the left side of the paper, thereby leaving space for subsequent replies.[7] (On the other

[2] Nawawī, *Rawḍat al-Ṭālibīn* (Beirut: al-Kitāb al-Islāmī, 1985), XI, 103.
[3] Ibid., XI, 110.
[4] Ibid., XI, 106.
[5] Ibid., XI, 113.
[6] Ibid., XI, 113.
[7] Ibid., XI, 113.

hand, if the mufti notes spaces at the end of lines in the *mas'ala* component, he should scribble in the gap – to prevent deception.[8]) All of these details confirm that by the mid-seventh/thirteenth century, a clear and well-understood procedure had emerged whereby the masses had access to juristic guidance in matters that occurred in their daily lives; and this procedure was paralleled in the more sophisticated world of judges, who also required, if for slightly different reasons, juristic guidance.

The conventions governing judicial fatwas differed from those of the basic fatwa. These might contain argument, and, in different administrative contexts, might be subject to official management. In practice, at both levels, for the layman and for the judge, the vast majority of fatwas must have been of very little interest.[9] Most of the questions that reached a mufti from a layman would be dealt with, immediately and briefly, on the petitioner's paper, which would then be returned to the petitioner and forgotten. Questions that came from qadis might have greater juristic interest, since an experienced qadi would not ask merely routine questions. But even qadis' questions had a routine aspect. It was a matter of professional common sense that they should secure appropriate backing for their decisions in order to guard against the possibility of annulment. Questions from qadis might nonetheless elicit interesting answers, as the mufti was permitted and, for practical reasons, might consider it advisable, to provide relevant arguments. In difficult cases a mufti might be concerned to see his interpretation of the law made effective, or might simply be proud of his arguments. In such circumstances, he would try to ensure the preservation of his fatwa. In the case of a high administrative appointee (a Chief Judge, like Subkī, or, later, a Grand Mufti, like Abū al-Su'ūd[10]) the basic needs of administrative efficiency required a record of the decisions that had been issued and the reasons for these decisions.

2. The evidence of the great collections shows that these two types do not adequately account for the forms or the content of the fatwas that have been preserved. The process of asking questions and getting the answers of the learned went considerably beyond a concern with the merely practical. Even the uneducated were not without imagination and intellectual curiosity, and they used whatever access they had to the learned as a means of inquiring about all matters of religion and law. Qadis, students and fellow jurists used the device of the formal question in search of education, instruction, advice, recreation, amusement

[8] Ibid., XI, 106.

[9] Cf. Uriel Heyd, 'Some Aspects of the Ottoman *Fetva*', *Bulletin of the School of Oriental and African Studies*, 32 (1969): 54; Brinkley Messick, *The Calligraphic State: Textual Domination and History in a Muslim Society*, (Berkeley: University of California Press, 1993), 150.

[10] Ottoman Grand Mufti, held office 1545–74.

and play. The central and basic mode of education, for all grades of society, was *fiqh* and its structures and concepts were available in varying degrees to all members of society, and might be used in varying ways. A standard method for initiating a session (of education, instruction, advice, etc.) was to formulate a question and put it to one of the learned.

Closely related to the processes of question and answer which together constitute the literary form of a fatwa was the process of debate or *munāẓara*. Inside the madrasa this was a formal and structured part of the curriculum;[11] outside the madrasa, it was a mode of cultured education, recreation and play. The younger Subkī tells the following story about his father.

> We foregathered one night I and some others. One of those present said, 'We would like to hear [your father, Taqī al-Dīn al-Subkī] debating (*munāẓara*) and none could induce him but you.' So I said to my father, 'The company would like to hear you debate according to the conventions of juristic dispute (*'alā ṭarīq al-jadal*).' 'In the name of God', he said, complying, and I realised that he had agreed only out of love for me and desire to teach me. 'Look out a question', he said, 'that has as many different opinions as you are in number, and let each one of you support his chosen opinion and sit with me to discuss it'. I chose the question of *ḥarām*. 'Go off', he said, 'and let each one of you study and prepare the position he will defend'. So off we went. …
>
> Each one of us took the role of defending his opinion, while my father opposed it, revealing the weakness of his argument, until my companion was silent. He dealt with each in turn, until all had been silenced. 'Where then is the truth?' one asked. 'I shall take up the position that so-and-so defended', he said, and he defended it until we said, 'Yes, that is the truth.' 'I shall now take up the position of so-and-so', he said. In this way he defended each view in turn until we said, 'So where is the false view?'
>
> 'Now the truth will become clear', he said. 'The chosen view is that of Shāfi'ī; and the refutation of this other view is such-and-such; of this other view such-and-such; of this other view such and such.' And so he completed the argument in all its aspects, to our astonishment, for each of us knew that the Shaykh had not looked into this problem for many years.[12]

This was a matter of education, as the younger Subkī makes clear, but it was also simply a way of passing an evening. The participants, including Subkī himself, were required to adopt and argue for positions they did not believe in. Facility in argument was admired, even if there was also a desire that the correct answer should in the end be reached. (That the correct answer, from Subkī's point of view, in spite of his facility in arguing equally well for and against all views, should correspond to that of Shāfi'ī is instructive.) Games of this type ('games' not in any disparaging sense) were a part of the educational and cultural system

[11] George Makdisi, *The Rise of Colleges: Institutions of Learning in Islam and the West* (Edinburgh: Edinburgh University Press, 1981).

[12] Subkī, *Ṭabaqāt al-Shāfi'iyya al-Kubrā* (Cairo: 'Īsā al-Bābī al-Ḥalabī, n.d.), X, 203.

of every Islamic society where *fiqh* was the basis of education – and that is every Islamic society from the ninth to the nineteenth century, everywhere. If Subkī chose to record the results of a debate of the type just described, he would almost certainly be constrained by the literary format of the fatwa. He would formulate the question under the heading *mas'ala*, and he would give the reply under the heading *jawāb*. He would perhaps incorporate into the *jawāb* element the best and most interesting of the arguments that had been produced in session – including his own (which, in this case, both for and against every possibility, had been the winning arguments).

These considerations have a bearing on the question of how to classify and analyse fatwas. It is obvious from a great many of Subkī's *Fatāwā* that he used questions that came to him, from whatever source, to initiate debate. When he subsequently came to write up his response to the question he would incorporate much of what he had learned from the debate, including the to and fro of argument. But the end product was no longer a basic fatwa of the type that was described in the manuals. It had become an element of juristic discussion. The audience anticipated for this material was learned, even if the first presenter of the fatwa was not. Conversely, it is clear (as we shall see) that questions which started as debate were written up in the literary form of the fatwa. Fatwas became debate, debate became fatwas; it is not always easy to separate the processes. In either case, the result was a written document with some of the formal characteristics of the fatwa and some of the formal characteristics of juristic debate.

3. A complex and nuanced transformation of a basic fatwa into juristic debate can be seen in the following case. The events took place while Subkī was still in Cairo, prior to his becoming judge in Damascus. In the Ṭaylūnī mosque, on a Friday, he received a petition relating to a carpet-maker who had entered into a contract with Zaid for the manufacture of carpets. He wrote his reply on the petition, as usual. On the following day, as he was going into the Manṣūriyya to give a lesson, a question was brought before him. He recognised it as a different wording of the case he had already dealt with. On this occasion the petition already contained an answer from another authority. Subkī neither liked the answer nor acknowledged the status of this other – incompetent, he claimed – mufti. He handed it back to the bearer with no reply, indicating thereby his opinion of this presumptuous mufti (in accordance with an established rule: If a mufti sees on a *ruq'a* the reply of one who is not qualified to give fatwas, he should not give a fatwa with him[13]). Subsequently, in class, one of the students asked for an explanation of the affair. Subkī records that he did not disclose the name of the person

[13] Nawawī, *Rawḍa*, XI, 106. Nawawī adds, 'Al-Ṣaymarī adds that he may cross out this fatwa with or without the permission of the owner of the *ruq'a*.'

whose competence he had impugned, but he built a lesson around the two items of law that had thus come before him – the question which had been asked (it related to the provision of payment in advance for the manufacture of goods, a practice known as *istiṣnāʿ* and not approved of by the Shāfiʿīs, though permitted under certain circumstances by Mālik and Abū Ḥanīfa) and the question of who had a right to give an authoritative fatwa.

In the latter context, he noted that there were people who, having learnt their *fiqh* from some small *mukhtaṣar*, like the *Ḥāwī*,[14] thought they were *fuqahāʿ*. However, while such books were fine and good and useful, they were not an adequate training in *fiqh*. The utmost that was attained by a student of such a book was a certain virtue or excellence (a *faḍīla*), but not a knowledge of *fiqh*. Subkī then distinguished three types of excellence. Those who had a knowledge of *sharʿī* rules and of how to derive them from Qurʿan, sunna and the words of the acknowledged Imams; these knew *fiqh* and were known as the *fuqahāʿ*. Those who had a general knowledge of the religious sciences, such as *tafsīr*, *ḥadīth* and *uṣūl al-dīn*, but did not apply themselves to the arguments of *fiqh*; these were known as the *ʿulamāʿ*. Finally there were some who had acquired various excellences but fell short of either of these two ranks. They were known as the *fuḍalā*. Many people, because they fail to distinguish between the three groups, fall into error in believing that this last group are either *fuqahāʿ* or *ʿulamāʿ*. Those who have studied only the *Ḥāwī* belong – of course – to the third group.[15]

The event did not end there. A third version of the case was produced, permitting a different analysis of the legal facts. On this analysis, the (allegedly incompetent but by no means unskilled) rival authority had a much stronger case, and seems to have persuaded other authorities to support his ruling.[16] Subkī, faced with this situation, which is now a debate between jurists (it was not the carpet-maker who re-formulated the legal facts), responded to the final version of the question with the *jawāb* which was preserved, from which these details have been extracted. In response to the re-phrased *masʿala*, he gave a complete account of the whole affair and his part in it (including the story of his classroom discussion with his students, and his disparaging reference to the rival authority as one who knew only the *Ḥāwī*) and maintained a negative attitude to the point of law at issue. However, he now conceded some (qualified) force to the alternative view.

[14] By Muḥammad b. Saʿīd Abū Aḥmad, known as Ibn al-Qāḍī, Ṣāḥib al-Ḥāwī, d. after 340/951.

[15] Subkī, *Fatāwā*, I, 447–9. There is an excellent analysis of the legal aspects of this fatwa in Nissreen Haram, 'Use and Abuse of the Law' in Masud, Messick, Powers, *Islamic Legal Interpretation*, 72–86.

[16] Subkī, *Fatāwā*, I, 448, ll.22–5. Subkī is both vague and not a little abusive about those who might have supported the third version of the case. This was hardly justified in relation to the possibilities of the law, as Haram's analysis shows. She attributes Subkī's continued negative attitude to the petitioner as arising out of concern to forestall abuse of the law.

The legal points can be studied elsewhere.[17] What I want to stress here is that, of the three versions of the petition that were produced, we only have the last one; we have it only in Subkī's (rewritten) version; and we only have Subkī's version of the events, not that of the rival authority. The first two versions were basic fatwas, representing an effort by the carpet-maker to establish his rights and obligations in law. The third version, the one that has been preserved, reflects a debate between two jurists, a debate that had acquired some notoriety, for it was a focus of dispute, involved personal rivalries, and had become the subject of a classroom discussion. The form and contents of the fatwa reflect its real audience, who are jurists and trainee jurists, no longer the carpet-maker (he retained an interest, of course, in the conclusion, but not in the juristic details). It is an example of a basic *mas'ala* being transformed into a juristic debate, and being preserved only in its last, and most juristic, phase. The *mas'ala* in its final format had been contrived by a jurist whose skills were of a higher order than Subkī was willing to concede, and the *jawāb* is aimed at that jurist and at a broader audience of students and jurists.

4. The collection of materials then which are called the *Fatāwā* of Subkī is not representative of the typical business of a mufti. Like most other collections of fatwas, it is the tip of an iceberg: The vast majority of fatwas have not been preserved. While there are some basic fatwas contained in the *Fatāwā*, it is highly probable that, precisely as in this case, the basic fatwas have been more frequently than not omitted. Subkī's written response on the original *ruq'a* is not preserved. The collection is neither a statistically useful bundle of fatwas, nor is it a precise and uncompromised representation of the forms of a fatwa. From a literary point of view, however, it is probable that the collection is typical – not of the fatwa but of the fatwa collection. It is the more interesting, the more problematic, the more educational, or the more amusing fatwas that have been preserved for posterity. A fatwa collection is not governed by the same criteria that govern the production and issue of individual fatwas, and cannot be taken as representative of fatwa production in society.[18] The criteria of selection, needless to say, may vary for different fatwa collections.

5. Subkī's remarks to his students apropos the carpet-maker have a further usefulness in that they remind us of the educational reality of traditional Muslim societies. A true knowledge of *fiqh* was the highest peak of educational possibilities. But this necessarily meant that those who aspired to understand and to

[17] Haram, 'Use and Abuse of the Law'.

[18] See also Messick on the scholarly features of the collection of fatwas by Shawkānī, *The Calligraphic State*, 150–1; and Seth Ward on the problem of determining the audience of Subkī's collection, Seth Ward, 'Dhimmi Women and Mourning' in Masud, Messick, Powers, *Islamic Legal Interpretation*, 87–97.

share, in whatever degree, in the great cultural achievements of such societies required at least a preliminary training in *fiqh*. Such a preliminary training, in Subkī's time, consisted, for the Shāfiʿīs, in study of the *Ḥāwī*. Though that was inadequate as a training in *iftāʾ*, it was a sufficient training to provide general competence, and it was probably enough to ensure that a person with this degree of education could understand, formulate and enjoy juristic debate, at a number of different levels. Indeed someone who had studied the *Ḥāwī* might under certain circumstance claim a sufficient competence (based on low-grade *taqlīd*) to give fatwas on uncomplicated issues (*pace* Subkī).

It is a characteristic of Subkī's writing, as it is a characteristic of the intellectual tradition that formed him, that when problems emerged related to the authority of fatwas, he introduced distinctions based on a hierarchy of knowledge and skills. The hint may be useful for the present project of classifying fatwas. They can usefully be classified, initially, according to the educational and professional competence of the questioner-recipients. (History and the processes of literary selection have already ensured a classification according to the grade of the mufti: For practical purposes, only the works of high ranking muftis are preserved.) The lowest class of recipient is the (relatively) uneducated, the layman or *ʿāmmī*. Of the more educated, it is useful to distinguish those who have a professional and practical need for authoritative fatwas – judges (also the supervisors of waqfs, the guardians of orphans' wealth, government administrators on occasion) – and those for whom fatwas function as part of the educational/recreational sphere – students and jurists. (This distinction is not intended to imply that judges and administrators do not sometimes ask hypothetical questions, or use the fatwa as an instrument of education, nor that students and jurists do not ask questions that are practical and directly related to the conduct of life.) Finally, it is useful to think of the mufti as a formulator of questions to himself, as initiating a personal account of the law in fatwa format. This gives a basic four-part typology, based on identifying the questioner-recipient: the basic fatwa, delivered to the layman; the judicial and administrative fatwa; the educational/academic fatwa, initiated by and delivered to students or jurists; and the personal, self-initiated fatwa.

The basic fatwa, we have already seen, consists of two components, the *masʾala* and the *jawāb*; it is written on a separate piece of paper belonging to the petitioner. It has, by preference, no or little intellectual or artistic content. It has in itself no status as authority (since it ought to conform simply to the *madhhab*, and where it does not it will be dismissed by academic jurists, Chapter 3, Section 2). A fatwa that relates to judicial business, whether to a specific judicial case or the administration of a waqf (or the property of orphans or other official duty of a judge), will usually have the same basic format. The *jawāb* element may, however, be expanded to include at least some argument. The document will certainly have administrative importance, as a justification of a judicial decision, or as a record of policy and preferred strategies, and might have juristic importance because it is (or is not, for that is also useful) a practical (elegant, compelling, witty, etc.) statement of the *madhhab*. Questions which come from students and jurists will also conform initially to the standard format. They are likely to betray their origins and their intentions by use of technical terminology, academic references, contrived form, elegance, wit, cultural allusion, and so on. Hypothetical questions are not impossible in relation to strictly judicial matters; and questions about real practical mundane matters might be initiated by students or jurists wrapped in a flurry of recondite textbook references. As a question becomes more interesting juristically it is likely to lose its specificity (its quality of being tied to particulars) and might lose its format. Questions formulated by a mufti for himself can be either public or private. In so far as they are public, they must be directed at either the common man, or the judge/administrator, or the student/jurist, in which case they will be assimilated to the former types. Only in so far as they imply a private meditation directed at the self will they be distinguished in the following analysis.

Section 2. A typology of fatwas

1. There are a great many fatwas in the *Fatāwā* which correspond to the conditions of a basic fatwa. Their presence in a collection is a little surprising since this necessarily means that the question has been removed from the original *ruqʿa* (which remained with the petitioner) and preserved by the mufti. There has to be a reason for this. Some fatwas might be interesting in themselves. But even the most uninteresting fatwa could become significant if it was combined with others in such a way as to become a more general study, having more of the character of a jurist's work than a mufti's.

I composed a booklet called *ʿIqd al-jumān fī ʿuqūd al-rahn wa-ʾl-ḍamān*, and later produced a shorter version called *ʿIqd al-jumān fī ʿaqd al-ḍamān*, in which I included certain *masʿalas* transcribed as they were received and others formulated according to my own thoughts. It is my desire to give an abstract of (*mujarrad*) those *masʿalas* here, in abbreviated form, without attribution [to authority/tradition, etc.] in order to be useful. I have called it *Nathr al-jumān*. …

Masʿala. Two people say, 'We will guarantee (*ḍaminnā*) what is owed to you by so-and-so. There are two views (*wajh*) on this question. One, that each may be required to pay [only up to] a half of the debt. Two, and this is the valid one, that each may be required to pay [up to] the whole. …[19]

[19] Subkī, *Fatāwā*, I, 299–301.

The treatise consists of sixteen *mas'alas*, none of them much longer than the first, given here, and all related in one way or another to the use of the dual in relation to either pledges (*rahn*) or the provision of guarantees (*ḍamān*). There is no juristic argument, just firm statements of how to interpret grammatical duals in this context. The longer forms of the work, mentioned by Subkī, presumably contained argument and authority. Clearly, Subkī either collected or remembered *mas'ala*s related to this issue, brought them all together, subjected them to a greater or lesser degree of editing, added some *mas'ala*s of his own invention to clarify or complete his analysis, and produced his treatises. There is no doubt that, in some form or another, the finished documents were 'published', primarily perhaps to judges or administrators who dealt with merchants' affairs, but also to lesser muftis, students and jurists. As in the case of the carpet-maker, the basic fatwas emanating from and aimed at the layman have been transformed into juristic material. In their present form these 'fatwas' are of interest primarily to students, jurists, muftis, to that part of the educated public who took an interest in the law as literature (or play for some of the problems are linguistic games), and, possibly, to merchants. In relation to its potential audience, the treatise does not relate to what has happened but to what might happen. Its origins lie in real events that generated fatwas, but these have been combined with juristic material which was selected so as to offer, in the end, an intellectually and aesthetically satisfying exploration of an area of law. The whole has been recast so as to recall the fatwa format even where the point at issue was derived in fact from the juristic tradition.

Many of the relatively uncomplicated *mas'ala*s preserved in the *Fatāwā* were perhaps preserved for this, or analogous, purposes.

Mas'ala. Someone absent in a distant country owes debts to a group of people. He sends to one/some of them a portion of the debt he owes. Can those to whom he has not sent anything make a judicial claim against him?[20]

Mas'ala. A man hires his divorced wife to suckle his daughter by her, in a specified town, but she travels with the girl, without his permission, to another place. Is the contract of hire cancelled during her journey?[21]

Mas'ala. Concerning a scribe hired by a man to make a copy of the Qur'an at a specified fee. The scribe delayed for a year, during which time his writing improved and his prices went up. May he demand an increase over the specified fee, or should he choose cancellation of the contract?[22]

In each of these cases, and in many others, the form of the question and the answer is of sufficient simplicity to suggest that this is a fairly precise note of a

[20] Ibid., I, 338.
[21] Ibid., I, 445–6.
[22] Ibid., I, 437.

real case. This of course may not be the precise, original form of the question, but nothing about the question or the reply suggests, in these cases, that any serious modification has taken place. There are many other instances where questions of an equal simplicity have become an excuse for a longer and more complex juristic analysis, suggesting that they have been transferred from their original context to a teaching or debating context. The carpet-maker's question is an example.

The three examples above are all practical, redolent of reality, and potentially judicial (in the sense at least of preempting or preparing for a judicial claim). Questions, however, were addressed to muftis covering all points of law, and included questions which searched for knowledge without reference to action. In the following case the questioner wanted to know not how to act but why the law was as it was.

Mas'ala. I was asked (*su'iltu*), on Saturday the 15th of Rabīʿ al-Ākhir, 752/11 June, 1351, about the reason for the prohibition against reciting the Qurʾan during the *rukūʿ* and the *sujūd* [sc. during these phases of ritual prayer]?[23]

In the following case too there is no suggestion that a particular event had occurred to elicit the question; the questioner was asking for knowledge about the law.

Mas'ala. He was asked (*su'ila*) about the status of a magician, about what is necessary in respect of such a one, and the hadith that have arrived.[24]

This question is incorporated under the general heading of apostasy (*ridda*), and generates an answer which is formally juristic ('Some of the learned hold the view that he should be killed etc.'), while being also an opportunity for display of relevant items from Qurʾan and hadith.

Subkī also received questions which related to familiar theological issues.

Mas'ala. What do the noble *'ulamā* say about the Prophet's words, 'Every child is born in the *fiṭra*; it is his parents who make him a Jew or a Christian or a Majūsī'? And what is the chosen view on the children of idolaters, are they in Paradise, or Hell, or Limbo?[25]

This is a conventional theological question which, in spite of the basic knowledge implied by the question, might be formulated by almost anybody in a traditional Islamic society. Subkī gave it a fairly extensive answer, liberally decorated with hadith, and finished with an admonition not to talk too much about these problematic matters. The following question belongs to the same broad category.

23 Ibid., I, 142.
24 Ibid., II, 323.
25 Ibid., II, 360–5.

Mas'ala. What do the noble *'ulamā'* say about the words of the Imām al-Ḥaramayn,[26] that the faith of a *muqallid* is not permissible? What was Shāfi'ī's view on this and is it compatible with the view of the Imām al-Ḥaramayn? And if the situation is as the Imām al-Ḥaramayn says, then what can be done by a layman who does not know the proofs for the validity of his faith?[27]

Again the question is a standard item of theology (also of *uṣūl al-fiqh*). It is perhaps less generally known than the first, and the liberal garlanding with references to academic authority might suggest a questioner who has more than a modest education. Its function of course was to elicit a virtuoso display of learning from the scholar to whom it was addressed. The basic components of an appropriate reply would be easy to find, for even the modestly educated; the ability to remember, elaborate and display *ex tempore* these components was what was being tested. The fossilised plural of the question (*mādhā taqūl al-sāda al-'ulamā'*), a frequent formula, perhaps indicates that the question was not specific to a single mufti, but was put to several on the same or on different occasions.

Subkī's *Fatāwā* contains a large quantity of *tafsīr* type material arranged in relation to specific, but apparently randomly selected, Quranic verses. These are not usually presented with the terms *mas'ala* and *jawāb* and may have origins in private devotion. On the other hand there is no reason to doubt that Subkī was presented with questions about the meaning and significance of Quranic verses and these may be a record of some of his replies. He was also asked questions about hadith.

Mas'ala. What do the noble *'ulamā'* say concerning the hadith which states, The quest for knowledge is a duty (*ṭalab al-'ilm farīḍa*)? Is it established as valid or not? Someone says it is in Bukhārī, and another it is in Muslim, and yet another that it is not established as valid, and he relates this view from the Imam Aḥmad.

At first sight the question implies simple ignorance in the questioner, so untrained in the religious sciences that he cannot investigate this matter for himself. Subkī's early training and fame came from his studies in hadith, and this would be an invitation to display his memory and erudition. However, the question is elementary, and the reasons for its incorporation into a collection like this not immediately obvious. The answer given by Subkī, though it has a routine factual element, is not without an elegant irony which may account for its preservation, and hints at an educational context.

Jawāb. This hadith is related by Ibn Māja, from Hishām b. 'Ammār from Ḥafṣ b. Salmā from Kathīr b. Shanzīr from Muḥammad b. Sīrīn from Anas b. Mālik from the Prophet, who said, 'The quest for knowledge is a duty for every Muslim; and one who offers

[26] The title given to the Shāfi'ī jurist and theologian al-Juwaynī (419–78/1028–85).
[27] Ibid., II, 365–8.

knowledge to someone unsuitable is like one who garlands a pig with diamonds, pearls and gold.' There is dispute on Kathīr b. Shanzīr as to whether he is a reliable or a weak transmitter. God knows best.[28]

The quest for knowledge was a duty. It was sometimes a practical necessity (as when a scribe tried to avoid a contractual obligation, or a debtor proved selective in repaying his debts), sometimes a measure of curiosity (as in the exploration of reasons for ritual obligations, or in abstract consideration of the status of magicians), and frequently a pleasure, a good in itself. Questions were put to jurists in order to gain a practical advantage, or simply to gain knowledge, or to initiate a debate, or a display of learning, or to provoke, amuse, annoy, or distract. In addition to all this, and sufficiently different, is the specific motive implied in the hadith just cited. The quest for knowledge was a religious duty. In formulating questions and listening to responsa, a Muslim was carrying out an act of worship, for the sake of God – not even, simply, for the sake of knowledge. Subkī himself was aware that his lifetime's devotion to miscellaneous writing, so much of which conformed to the literary format of the fatwa, was also an act of worship, deriving its value, not from its practical and social functions (though it had, frequently, such functions), nor from the pleasure or the recreation that he found in this activity, but from its being a response to a divine command, and constituting therefore, in itself, an act of worship (*'ibāda*). (Chapter 3, Section 1)

This brief survey of the basic fatwa, as it is preserved in the *Fatāwā* of Subkī, suggests a three-fold subdivision of the type. A basic fatwa can be juristic and practical (searching for instruction about how to act in relation to an event that has already happened); juristic and educational (searching for knowledge and understanding of the law, without any immediate consideration of how to act); or theological and miscellaneous (searching for theological and other religious knowledge). While only the first type could be motivated by a strictly practical concern for how to act, all these types share in varying degrees the educational, recreational and ritualist qualities of the fatwa. By 'ritualist', I mean here the process of seeking and giving fatwas as, in itself, an act of worship.

2. The judicial fatwa. The basic type of the judicial fatwa consists of a summary of the facts of a case, by a judge (or his assistants), usually in such a way as to focus on a particular point of law. The summary and question is then presented to the mufti, or to several muftis. The judicial case may be at an early stage, it may be a case of appeal, or it may be a long-running case which has been through several appeals and counter-appeals. One typical example has been studied above (Chapter 3, Section 3.2); several examples have been published by

[28] Ibid., II, 545.

modern scholars. Formally similar material was produced when Subkī refused to hear a case, and, wishing to formulate the reasons for this, summarised the situation in the form of a *mas'ala* and used the *jawāb* element to justify his decision. In this case, the characteristic formal elements of a fatwa were used to produce a document which was, in both parts, the work of one author (Chapter 3, Section 3.6).

Closely related to the strictly judicial fatwa is the category of expository fatwas relating to waqfs. The (special as opposed to general) supervisor (*nāẓir*) of a waqf, if he was in doubt about the interpretation of the provisions of the foundation document, might present it to the mufti for his opinion on how to implement the provisions. The replies would be important to the supervisor at a personal professional level, as a justification of his activities, and at a judicial level, if his activities were, for whatever reason, brought before a qadi. Subkī, combining the functions of a judge (who had general supervisory authority over waqfs in the Damascus region) and a mufti (a powerful and respected mufti) was naturally a recipient of inquiries about the management of waqfs. The basic format of the *mas'ala* element in such cases was a summary (citation and paraphrase) of the relevant parts of the foundation document, combined with an invitation to respond to particular issues and difficulties. Amongst the expository fatwas preserved in Subkī's *Fatāwā* and related to waqfs are some that he has summarised himself[29] and some summarised by others, usually provincial judges. On one occasion, Subkī, not satisfied with the summary of a waqf document that was put before him, urged a reconsideration of the original document, but gave an interim reply based on the question as formulated.[30]

As in the case of the basic fatwas preserved in the *Fatāwā*, there is some evidence that judicial fatwas too were variously subject to transformation if they were offered as or otherwise became subject of juristic debate, or if they became a locus of juristic display. Some argument, of course, was necessary to establish, in the case of a judicial fatwa, that a particular view corresponded to the *madhhab* (or to acknowledged *ikhtilāf* within the *madhhab*), and so was protected from annulment. But, in many cases, the multiplication of argument and learned reference, the free play of digression and formal features such as extensive Q and A material, all combine to suggest that the final version of a judicial fatwa might preserve some elements of juristic debate, implying a learned and juristic (not merely judicial) audience, and having broad educational as well as strictly administrative ends.

[29] Ibid., II, 52 (*intahā mā aradtu naqla-hu min kitāb al-waqf*).

[30] Ibid., II, 59–60; a judge had written from Safad with an enquiry about a waqf document.

In certain quite specific cases, it is difficult to believe that the document preserved is the one that was originally returned to a judge who had requested a fatwa. 'There are four problems (*masāʾil*) which need to be explicated (*dāʿat al-ḥāja ilā al-kalām ʿalay-hā*)', said Subkī, and proceeded to clarify and explain. The first problem he described as *manqūla*, transmitted from the juristic tradition, the second as deriving from a fatwa of Ibn al-Ṣalāḥ,[31] and the third had a general juristic flavour. Only in the fourth *masʾala* did he mention 'the event which had caused [his] mentioning these problems', namely a case that had come before the courts in Jerusalem. The case in question was solved by referring back to what had been established in the first three problems. The form of the document and the quality of argumentation are not ideal from an administrative point of view; they simply delay the answer that the judge required. It suggests, again, the transformation of a relatively simple judicial problem into a juristic display piece.

In general, it can be said that, while the category of judicial fatwas has a certain homogeneity deriving from the nature of the problems cited and the practical aspect of the petitions, they are not necessarily free from those tendencies identified above which transform a practical question into an educational, recreational, or ritual process.

Closely allied to judicial and waqf orientated fatwas are those that emerge from the secular administration. In the year 754/1353–4, the governor of Safad wrote to the Governor of Damascus about a group of Christian traders who had indulged in public demonstrations of their faith on the occasion of Palm Sunday, in the old city. This had created problems amongst the local population, and the Mamluk had to summon the qadi and local administrators to decide what to do. On seeking a fatwa, he found that the local *fuqahāʾ* only prolonged the dispute, and so he sent to Damascus. The question came before Subkī, who gave a characteristically negative response, based on a presumption that the Christians had broken their contract (*amān*) and were subject to punishment at the discretion of the Sultan and in accord with the *maṣlaḥa* of the Muslims.[32] We do not know whether the same question was put before other muftis, nor how the governor reacted to Subkī's ruling.

Some of the independent treatises in the *Fatāwā* which have almost lost the appearance of being responses to questions or to particular situations may have origins in secular administrative affairs, for example, his treatise on the prohibition of the repair of churches, his ostensibly self-initiated defence of the death penalty inflicted on an Imāmī who had cursed the Companions, perhaps also his

[31] A Shāfiʿī jurist and scholar (577/1181–643/1245).

[32] Ibid., II, 317–21.

treatises on water rights in Damascus, and the lengthy treatise on the status and functions of the Shāfiʿī qadi in Mamluk Damascus.

3. The educational/academic fatwa. The case of the carpet-maker, cited above, demonstrates one way in which a basic fatwa could be transformed into an educational fatwa. As preserved, the *masʿala* was written by an educated and skilled jurist (*pace* Subkī), and the *jawāb* was directed at an audience of students and jurists. When a fatwa was formulated and proposed by a scholar, or even a layman with some taste for scholarship, it necessarily generated the characteristics of juristic discourse, rather than those of a basic fatwa.

Masʿala. I was asked about a person fasting [for Ramaḍān] who utters some slander or abuse and then repents. Is the deficiency in his fast cancelled [by the repentance] or not? My first thought was that it was not, but the questioner, a man of knowledge (*dhū ʿilm*), debated with me and broadened the argument. … This question of his, and his review of it, contains a number of issues which we must now respond to. …[33]

There follows a long juristic argument, about major and minor sins, their effect on acts of worship, directly relevant juristic opinions, analogical opinions and incidental insights (Subkī even has the subheading *fāʾida ʿāriḍa* = incidental insight). The whole is a juristic and educational display piece. It is reasonably called a fatwa only because there was an initial *masʿala*. The final polished reply is a record of a debate, recalled and managed in tranquillity. The presentational format recalls its origins as a fatwa, but it is the characteristics of juristic discourse that predominate.

Classroom discussions were perceived by Subkī as *masʿala*s and prompted from him lengthy juristic display pieces, which might, in practice, be extremely valuable, though their practical aspect does not account for the format, was not the immediate cause of the debate, and does not exhaust the value of the material.

Masʿala. A problem produced in the discussion at a study session in the Ghazāliyya in the year [blank] – *antaja-hā al-baḥthu fī dars al-Ghazāliyya*. It took place in the presence of the Qadi of Bilbīs, and I wrote something on it in Ghazza in the year 734/1333–4. The situation concerns a man who makes a formal avowal that he owes X one thousand and ten dirhams. Subsequently he pays four hundred dirhams of the debt, and then dies. X then goes before a qadi and claims six hundred and ten dirhams. Is it permitted for the witnesses to affirm before the judge the avowal of the deceased for the original sum without rendering their testimony void? Or is their testimony rendered void in so far as they bear witness to something that is not claimed by the claimant, or is more than is claimed by the claimant? If it does not render their testimony void, then is it recorded [in the court records] that it was established before the judge that the deceased made an

[33] Ibid., I, 220–32.

avowal of the original sum, or just the remainder of the debt? Inform us, may you be rewarded.

Jawāb. This is a problem which has disturbed the jurists of our age. I have even seen the Shaykh Qutb al-Dīn al-Sinbātī – who, when he had just taken up the post of deputy judge in Cairo, appointed Sirāj al-Dīn al-Maḥallī and me to attend his session in case any difficult problems arose so that we could deal with them – I have seen him oppose the view that the witnesses should testify to the whole of the debt, preferring that they should specify the sum mentioned by the claimant. ...[34]

Subkī goes on to cite the words and opinions of Ibn al-Rifʿa,[35] from which he deduces, gradually, his own view:

There are two possibilities. One, and this is the majority of actual cases, is that the claimant should make a claim for six hundred and ten out of a total of one thousand and ten which had been formally avowed as owing to him. He should bring a document, for example, recording the avowal for the whole sum and backed by a list of witnesses. We will then ask them to bear witness to that. ...[36]

Subkī goes on to defend this position with reference to two juristic analogies and a number of Q and A problems which he resolves in favour of his preferred position. The second possibility which permits the witnesses to confirm a debt of six hundred and ten by reference to their having heard an avowal of one thousand and ten, but without reference to a document, is aired and, on balance, dismissed.

The discussion is of practical importance in so far as it indicates to judges within Subkī's jurisdiction his preferred way of dealing with this situation. It has distant origins in actual cases: Subkī recalls how he first came across the issue when he was acting in a consultative capacity to a practising judge. Since that time he has written on the problem, and the immediate cause of the present discussion is a classroom session in a madrasa. The length and complexity of the discussion, the references to juristic texts, analogy, argument, Q and A difficulties, all confirm that the value of the discussion is not merely practical but juristic, and aimed at students and jurists (and the educated public), as well as at judges.

In this case, as in so many, the fatwa format is a literary device for the contextualisation of juristic discourse. Though the *masʾala* might recall a formulation by somebody else, Subkī intrudes his own presence by first person reference, and does so again in the *jawāb*. He is responsible for the final version of the *masʾala* as also for the final version of the *jawāb*.

[34] Ibid., II, 477–82.

[35] Shāfiʿī scholar (d. 710/1310).

[36] Ibid., vol.2, 479.

A *mas'ala* might be formulated without any reference to reality, as a result of study in and consideration of juristic texts.

A *mas'ala* from Egypt in the month of Muḥarram 755/January–February, 1354.

Mas'ala. What do the noble jurists say, the leaders of religion, the learned of the Muslims, those granted his guidance because of their obedience ... about the following. A man is in a state of purity as to *wuḍū'* (i.e., minor ritual ablutions) and then becomes *junub* (i.e., incurs major ritual impurity), without touching his penis, or sleeping [or any other act that could cancel his *wudū'*; it is conceded that, in these circumstances, according to the valid view within the *madhhab*, his *wudū'* is not cancelled. Then the time of performing ritual prayer comes upon him but he cannot find water [with which to perform *ghusl*, required because he is in a state of major ritual impurity – *janāba* – though not minor – *ḥadath*], and all the conditions of its absence are fulfilled. Accordingly, he performs *tayammum* (uses sand instead of water). He then performs that prayer. The time arrives for the next prayer, and the next, and so on. In such a case, he remains in a state of *wudū'* by virtue of the prior state which preceded his becoming *junub*. Is he permitted to pray each subsequent ritual prayer on the basis of the prior *wudū'*, thus making the single *tayammum* act in place of a *ghusl*, or should he repeat the *tayammum* on each occasion. And what is the answer to the Shaykh Muhyī al-Dīn al-Nawawī's opinion, given as follows in the *K. al-Adhkār*? 'A person who is *junub*, or menstruating [and therefore *junub*], cannot find water, while it is permissible for him [or her] to recite from the Qur'an. He subsequently suffers a *ḥadath* (a cancellation of minor purity). It does not become *ḥarām* for him to recite: it is as if he had performed *ghusl* and then suffered a *ḥadath*.' What is the answer? Inform us, may you be rewarded.[37]

The two questions here are linked. In the first case, a man is free from impairment of minor ritual purity, but has suffered a major ritual impurity (*janāba*). He performed *tayammum* in order to obviate the *janāba* and so made it permissible for him to perform prayer. The answer to the question is straightforward: He must perform the *tayammum* for each subsequent prayer. *Tayammum* does not stand in the place of *ghusl* – for *ghusl* would suffice for subsequent prayers. The problem extracted from Nawawī (given a very abbreviated form here) has some parallel features. Initially the man has suffered a *janāba* (requiring *ghusl* or, failing access to water, *tayammum*) but not impairment of minor purity (so, no need for *wudū'*). Not finding water, he has carried out *tayammum* (this is implicit), and so is permitted to recite. On suffering a *ḥadath*, he retains permission to recite because 'it is as if he had performed a *ghusl*'. The questioner wants to bring out an apparent contradiction: In the first case, the *tayammum* is treated as not taking the place of a *ghusl*, in the second case, the *tayammum* is treated as taking the place of a *ghusl*. How so? The noble jurists, leaders of religion, and so on, are invited to explain this conundrum. It requires, of course, distinctions. Recitation of the Qur'an has different rules from ritual prayer: it requires freedom from major but not freedom

[37] Ibid., I, 135.

from minor ritual impurity; hence in the second case the *ḥadath* does not affect the prior status of this person, who remains, by virtue of his *tayammum*, permitted to recite. However, *tayammum* takes the place of *ghusl* in the sense of permission, not in the sense of removing *janāba*. Hence, in the first case, the person remains in a state of *janāba* and must renew his *tayammum* each time. The two cases, Subkī remarks, are in some respects similar, in some respects different. Subkī, in his reply, cites Jurjānī who had also dealt with the passage in Nawawī's *Adhkār*. It had obviously a certain notoriety as a focus of juristic discussion.

This *masʿala* has not been prompted by life, but by literature. Study of the *madhhab*, and the invention of a hypothetical case, has enabled the questioner to bring out an apparent disharmony in the rules of the *madhhab*, and he invites the jurists to display their knowledge and ingenuity in harmonising it. The problem is headed as 'from Egypt' which might mean that it was sent – a written question to tax the muftis of Damascus. Alternatively, a visitor from Egypt posed it *ex tempore* to Subkī to see how he would respond.

Questions which, like this one, had their origins in speculation about the concepts and structures of the law were not uncommon. They were formulated by jurists and students, either in a genuine spirit of inquiry, or with the intention of testing and challenging the jurist, and deriving pleasure and amusement, as well as instruction, from the situation. An apparently innocuous question about the capacity of a cat, under certain circumstances, to cause impurity in water and of clothes to retain impurity, generated an answer from Subkī in which he made the following remark: 'These are rules that I have not found transmitted anywhere, but I wrote a long piece (*kitāba muṭawwala*) on them in a fatwa that a jurist asked me about – *fī fatwā saʾala-nī baʿḍ al-fuqahāʾ ʿan-hā*.'[38] In that case too it was a jurist who had formulated the original question. He had done so in response to his reading in the *madhhab*, which had led him to isolate a number of problems that were not clearly answered by the transmitted law. These he had put before Subkī, who had obligingly written his long reply. Precisely the same questions emerged later, and were again put to Subkī who gave the reply we now have in which he refers to his longer study. Clearly, the questions had acquired some kind of circulation amongst students or jurists because they constituted an amusing, interesting, challenging test-case. To pose these questions to Subkī was not to express ignorance of the answers, but rather to invite a display of erudition. Even when the original jurist posed the question in the form of a request for a fatwa, he was much less interested in the reply, than in the opportunity offered to enjoy argument, debate, display, literary form – literary matters that reflect trained minds.

[38] Ibid., I, 128–9.

The category of educational/juristic fatwas is large and has varied manifestations. Similar to the conundrums just cited, and moving even further towards the condition of recreation and display, is the category of rhymed questions. These are certainly rare but crop up in fatwa collections with sufficient regularity to remind us of the recreational aspect of the process. Subkī offered a *jawāb* to the following *masʿala* which matched it in rhyme and metre.

A girl with her brother buys up their father.
He, being freed, acquires *mawālī*,
Slaves he has freed; then death overtakes him;
And the *mawālī* too, a few days later.
They leave some property, so what is its status?
Does the son take it all, paying no heed to his sister?
Or does the sister share with her brother?
This is my question [to the learned mufti].[39]

The property of freed slaves (*mawālī*), if there is no other claim on the property, is inherited by the master who freed them. In this case the master has died before the *mawālī*. Assuming that there are no other potential heirs except the son and the daughter, who inherits? The obvious complication lies in the fact that the boy and the girl bought the father and so were joint owners, prior to setting him free. They were thus potential heirs both in their capacity as son and daughter and in their capacity as owners who have freed a slave. Subkī's answer is that the boy gets everything, because, by virtue of being the son, he excludes other heirs, in respect specifically to the category of inheritance from *mawālī*. There were four alternative distributions, but they were wrong.

The posing of learned *masʿala*s by educated questioners led to debate and, with Subkī, led frequently to the production of independent treatises. The 'long piece' related to cats and impurity is one example, but there are many more. He had on one occasion a debate with his son on the significance of a conditional clause when it is embedded in a sentence beginning *kāna* as in, 'The Prophet of God, when/if he performed *iʿtikāf* used to … ' – *kāna rasūl Allah idhā iʿtakaf. …* This eventually led to the production of an independent treatise on the juristic significance of sentences with this grammatical form.[40] There was a fatwa element in the origins of this treatise but only fossilised aspects of this have been retained in the final version. Subkī wrote a *risāla* to the people of Makka when the scholars there (*ʿulamāʿ*) had a dispute on a point of law relating to the pilgrimage.[41] Effectively

[39] Ibid., II, 252–3.
[40] Ibid., I, 232–55.
[41] Ibid., I, 255–60.

he treated a point of law that had disturbed the scholars and produced *ikhtilāf* as a question requiring a reasoned juristic answer. In these cases, the process of asking a question and initiating a debate lies some way behind the production of an independent treatise, which retains only vestiges of the formal characteristics of a fatwa.

It is not intended, in referring to this type of fatwa as educational/academic, to preempt the question whether they are also practical. The classification is based, initially, on the ability to identify, for a particular fatwa, a questioner-recipient. What is being suggested here is that there is an extensive body of fatwas which were initiated by the educated, and were answered with a view to the educated as an audience. These had characteristics quite different from those laid down in the manuals (*adab al-muftī*). Some of the fatwas in this category had origins as basic fatwas and had been transformed by diverse processes into academic fatwas – that is, they had been taken out of the hands of the original questioner and finally generated a response aimed at a trained and educated audience. Some had specifically judicial origins and had again been transformed through processes of discussion and juristic writing into academic fatwas. In the process of transformation, what had been practical and a response to real events became juristic, an account of the law, and only potentially practical, relevant to future events not to a specific past event. Many fatwas of this type had their origins not simply in hypothetical cases, but in study and analysis of law-books; they derived from literature, not reality. Some have a pleasantly unserious and essentially recreational character; others become a locus for discussion of serious juristic matters, or for the discovery of harmonised views within the *madhhab*, or generate lengthy juristic treatises. Clearly, the type as a whole displays the same spectrum of possibilities that I asserted for the first type, having qualities that range from the practical, to the educational, recreational and ritual (in the sense of constituting *ʿibāda*, worship). It is worth stressing again what I stressed there: It is the practical aspect of the fatwa which is removable. Even the most practical fatwa has some elements of the educational, recreational and ritualistic. Some fatwas, however, are asked and answered with no reference to any past event, and with relative indifference to the potential emergence of a future event that will require the knowledge asked after.

4. Before proceeding to characterise my final category (the personal fatwa initiated by the jurist and directed only at himself) it is necessary to assess what the study so far implies about the social function of fatwas. Even if it could be shown that a majority of real fatwas had a practical orientation (which is possible, though not measurable in relation to pre-modern societies, because the evidence is selectively preserved), this study must suggest that, as a social process, the fatwa was serving more than merely practical ends. Like works of *fiqh*, the fatwa

was a multi-functional literary form. Once those more than practical ends have been identified, they must be fed back into our perception and analysis of practical fatwas: No matter how practical, they had other functions.

My final example of the academic/educational fatwa offers valuable clues. In this case, a group of sufis (*fuqarā'*) asked Subkī to produce the answers to five questions, on an independent sheet (*waraqa mustaqilla*). The questions had been originally presented to them by a group of jurists, and they wanted Subkī to answer on their behalf. The passage is headed *istiftā al-shaykh Faraj* – a petition from the Shaykh Faraj for a fatwa.

> The noble sufis (*al-sādāt al-fuqarā'*), may God in his mercy and bounty grant them their desires, have an intense desire to respond to certain questions put to them by certain noble jurists (*ba'ḍ al-sādāt al-fuqahā'*), the leaders of religion, may God be pleased with them all. If it is pleasing to our Master, the Qāḍī al-Quḍāt, that he respond to them on our behalf, so that they may benefit, and so that a reminder of him should remain with them, and their holy prayers continue for him and his descendants, let him honour us with his noble words written on an independent sheet, relating to the following five questions.

The first question relates to the linguistic form of a sufi *dhikr*. The second, third and fourth are standard questions of *furū' al-fiqh* and the fifth a standard question of *uṣūl al-fiqh*. Subkī dealt with the questions unevenly (perhaps he tried to restrict himself to a single sheet), answering one question in a single line, while expanding and developing others. With the possible exception of the first one, the questions are not difficult, and only mildly challenging.

Here, there can be no doubt, the process of giving and receiving fatwas, is a symbolic process. Though it may be important to know how to act; though it is admirable to seek knowledge, advice and education; though it is pleasing and amusing and recreational to engage in debate and manifest one's skills; there is something else going on. It is possible to define this something else first in social terms. The process of asking for and receiving fatwas is a reciprocal process of social exchange, practised by all ranks and grades of society. While it may be important sometimes to know, it is important also simply to participate. The terminology and subject matter of the law is transformed into a symbol of social cohesion, solidarity and homogeneity, and a process that articulates that cohesion. By participation in the process the various social divisions of traditional society interact and are fused. At the same time, the diverse modes of actualising this process articulate and reaffirm status and hierarchy. The layman asks questions of the mufti, not just because he wants to or has to know (though he may do both), but because in so doing he marks his participation in the social process, and acknowledges the knowledge and authority of the mufti. In this respect the asking of empty questions, those to which he already knows the answer, or those to which he is indifferent to the answer, is not to be dismissed as pointless. The articulation of status and hierarchy is marked by the fossilised, formulaic items which have a regular (though not apparently a necessary) presence in the question item; formulae such as, 'What do the noble jurists say – may God grant them success? (*ma taqūl al-sāda al-ʿulamāʾ waffaqa-hum Allāh*)' or, 'Inform us may you be rewarded (*aftu-nā maʾjūr in*).'

These considerations can probably be carried over into the category of judicial and administrative fatwas. Something was achieved when a governor simply posed a question to a mufti or (for this was wiser, or more expedient) to a group of muftis, even if he had no need of the reply, or little intention of responding to it. The process of asking and responding became an articulation of the shared authority of the governing and the religious classes. When the learned classes exchanged questions amongst themselves (and again these included empty questions, those to which both parties already knew the answer) they were displaying by the nature of their participation in the process (which differed significantly from the interaction of the layman and the mufti) the special qualities of their social group.

In this particular case, two social groups, the sufis and the jurists, interacted by requesting and delivering fatwas. The jurists had posed the questions. It may reasonably be assumed that their intention was to challenge the sufis, not to find out the answers. Except possibly in relation to the first question, about *dhikr*, there was no great difficulty in that. By accepting the challenge and providing the answers, the sufis acknowledged the symbolic significance of the process. They were willing to participate in the social process and so confirm, by established means, their place in society. By getting Subkī to answer on their behalf, they were fully admitting the symbolic nature of the challenge and winning for themselves all the advantages of his patronage. What they acquired was respect, honor, acknowledgement – and this was true even if they did not themselves, or could not, articulate the replies to the questions.

The social significance of the process should not hide the special religious qualities of this process. For those who participated, the exchange of knowledge was a response to a divine command and a participation in an act of worship. God had after all commanded the search for knowledge, as he had commanded the dissemination of knowledge. The receiving and responding to questions was therefore an act of obedience. Those who participated at the highest levels (the muftis and jurists) were conscious of fulfilling on behalf of the community a duty that was laid on the community, that of preserving and articulating knowledge. Those who participated at the lowest levels (the layman) were enacting some kind of personal engagement with divine law. At intermediate levels, the offering and receiving of questions was reciprocal. In respect of the religious as well as the social significance of the processes of *iftāʿ*, the presence of empty questions (ones to which the questioner already knows the answer) and empty answers (either superfluous or incomprehensible to the questioner) are not surprising, are in fact signs of the religious significance of the processes.

God's self-revelation to Muslims was enacted historically in the lifetime of the Prophet, preserved as revelation in the twin corpus of Qurʿan and hadith, and transformed by the founders of the schools into the structures of the law. What was preserved and articulated by the *fuqahāʿ*, was perceived, by the community at large, and by the *fuqahāʿ* themselves, as a mediation of God's last and highest act of self-revelation in history. To participate in the terminology, rules and structures of the law, was to participate in the divine to the highest degree that was possible for human beings (outside of the mystical sphere). The symbol of that participation was the *sharīʿa*. The *fuqahāʿ* were the guardians and the mediators of the *sharīʿa* to the community. By participation in the processes of *iftāʿ*, the *fuqahāʿ* and those they interacted with engaged in an act of worship which was (presumably) experienced and valued as just that.

In spite of the common (but misleading) cliché that there are no priests, or no clerics, or, even, no mediators, in Islam, between God and his community, it is clear that the jurists functioned precisely as mediators. The most powerful of the terms that connoted God's self-revelation was *sharīʿa*. Though it had a divine aspect (caught in the term *sharīʿa, sharīʿat Allāh*), it had also a human aspect (represented in the term *fiqh, fiqhu Mālik,* etc.). The human mediators of divine law were the *fuqahāʿ*, who acquired their status through knowledge and commitment to the *madhhab*, and had a duty to transmit it to the wider community. Their capacity to mediate, that is to reveal and explain the symbols of divine revelation to the community, was intimately related to their participation in the processes of fatwa. It is necessary here to invoke the usual hierarchies. The highest level of mufti coincided with the highest level of *ijtihād*, and belonged nearly exclusively to the founders of the four *madhhab*s. What Subkī mediated, when he acted as mufti, was the authority of Shāfiʿī. What he preserved and guarded, when he acted as academic jurist, was likewise the authority of Shāfiʿī, symbolised in the notion of the *madhhab*.

The sufis, in responding, in the case before us, to the challenge of the jurists, requested Subkī, an acknowledged jurist of stature, to act on their behalf. They clearly did not expect that the jurists who had asked the questions would be less pleased by this strategy. In fact, the jurists would benefit from the participation of Subkī in a way that they would not benefit if the sufis acted on their own behalf. They would benefit by his more skilled, but also more religiously elevated participation; there was a holiness, a closeness to God, that belonged to the highest ranking muftis. Further, the jurist challengers would have, by virtue of the independent paper, a memento of Subkī's participation. They certainly did not require the paper in order to know the answers to their questions; the value of the paper lay in its symbolic representation of a great mufti. And they would be inspired to offer prayers on his behalf, so Subkī too would benefit from responding on behalf of the sufis. Though there is an inseparable social element to the processes of *iftā*ʿ (when it is a marker of social cohesion and a symbol of hierarchy), there is also a reticulation of purely religious ideas (knowledge as worship) that is embedded in social actions and is the ultimate guarantee of their meaning. Only a consciousness of the religious element offers a complete understanding of the processes of exchanging fatwas, at all levels and of all types. This case in particular throws into relief the social and religious symbolism of the fatwa – for no other value is involved. The learning exchanged is almost trivial. In any case one of the parties appoints an outsider to enact their role, so nothing is proven about the reality of their learning. There is no *ex tempore* display of knowledge, skills, argument, and so on. What is achieved is the common participation of two social groups in the established symbols of social cohesion and hierarchy, common participation in a religious ritual, and, in this case, a common acknowledgement of the value and status of the highest religious dignitary of the day. The symbolism of the 'independent sheet' is not so unusual as it might seem, for the basic fatwa, the one articulated between the layman and the mufti, also involved the retention by the questioner of the mufti's writing. It was a token of his interaction with, his coming close to, the class that mediated between God and the community.

5. The last category of fatwa is that where the mufti himself formulates a question and develops an answer which is directed primarily at himself, where the mufti is his own audience. In many respects the category overlaps with the general category of the educational/academic fatwa. Some of the processes whereby fatwas whose origin was basic (a real question directed by a layman to a mufti) became juristic summaries, or display pieces, or independent treatises, are such that it is difficult to distinguish whether the end product was primarily intended for an audience or primarily perceived as a value to the writer. Subkī was certainly aware of the last type of value, and expressed it when he classified his habit of extensive writing as an act of (private) worship. In small and isolated cases also, it is clear that, by a mental habit, or by virtue of the need for a literary format to think with, he formulated private juristic questions to himself using terminology that recalled the processes of *iftā*ʿ. 'A *mas*ʿ*ala* which I reflected on and did not find reported anywhere. ...'[42] The words introduce a personal meditation on an item of the law, initiated by no outside agency and aimed at no one but himself (albeit available for incorporation at a later stage into a different context). There

42 Ibid., I, 148–9.

are in fact numerous occasions in the *Fatāwā* where a juristic aperçu is reported under the heading *mas'ala*, devoid of any contextual evidence which is revealing of the origins of the thought. Content often suggests juristic meditation but it is impossible, in many instances, even where the familiar two components of the fatwa are present (*mas'ala – jawāb* or *mas'ala – ajāba*), to distinguish securely between a basic, or judicial, or academic/juristic fatwa, and a personal meditation on a point of law. It is only clear that there are at least some examples of the latter.

The following example has the normal format of a fatwa. The question is familiar and might have been generated by any partially educated person, in a number of different contexts. But the reply is directed, quite clearly, by Subkī, to himself. Or rather, in this context, to God. Subkī utilises a conventional format (*mas'ala* and *jawāb*) and a conventional question to introduce a private assessment of his own situation, and this assessment modulates into a prayer directed at God.

Mas'ala. The Shaykh was asked for his opinion about deriving benefit ['eating'] from waqfs in our day – *ra'yi-hi fī 'l-akl min al-awqāf hādhā al-zamān*.

Jawāb. Waqfs are of many types. One such is when a founder establishes a waqf for himself. Another such is when he makes a declaration that the founder has established this waqf for him, while intending by the words 'the founder' himself. In these two cases the waqf is void according to the established Shāfi'ī tradition, and likewise according to the Mālikī school, one of the transmissions from Aḥmad, the opinion of Muḥammad b. al-Ḥasan, and the implications of the opinion of Abū Ḥanīfa. Another type is when somebody transfers ownership to another, and delivers the goods to him, and then that other person establishes those goods as a waqf in favour of the original owner. This is void according to the school of Mālik. These three types of waqf may well be transferred to the benefit of jurists and others, in which case deriving benefit from them is a matter of ambiguity (*shubha*) – for the *ikhtilāf* of the learned is one category of the ambiguous – and so they are not clearly legitimate (*ḥalāl*). If it happens that a judge gives judgement (*ḥakama*) in such cases, declaring that they are valid waqfs, either because he considers them intrinsically valid in the first and third cases, or because he acknowledges the truth of the declaration in the second case ..., then the judgement is effective on the basis of surface appearance (*ẓāhiran*). But whether it is effective in its inner reality (*bāṭinan*) is a matter of *ikhtilāf* amongst the learned. Hence this judicial decision does not exempt such waqfs from the category of the ambiguous, a category which is feared by those who aim at purity in religion and honour. ...[43] So abstention from all three types of waqf constitutes piety [indeed the second type may be totally *ḥarām* under certain conditions ...]. Deriving benefit from the waqf of the Ḥakāriyya is of type three, and many of the madrasas of Syria are of the same kind.

Another type of waqf is one that is initially constituted in favour of another [and in that respect valid] but the founder acquired the property in a manner that constituted

[43] *Man ittaqā-hā istabrā'a li-dīni-hi wa-'irdi-hi* ... Read (?) *ittaqa-hā man istabrā'a*, etc.

an ambiguity (*shubha*). Deriving benefit from such a waqf is also a matter of ambiguity. Many of the waqfs founded by kings, amirs, their followers, and such like are of this type if they are based on property which they were not careful about. Further, there are waqfs which were constituted by kings from the Treasury, and waqfs from the Treasury are a matter of *ijtihād*, so abstention from them is piety and deriving benefit from them is a matter of ambiguity. Another type is a waqf founded by a person on the basis of property which is not ambiguous, for the benefit of jurists and others, but it is subject to a condition which invalidates it according to the tradition of one of the established schools. To derive benefit from such a waqf is also ambiguous and to refrain from it is piety. A further type of waqf. …

Another type of waqf is one which is free from the deficiencies listed above, but its property is mixed with property which is not free from these deficiencies. One such waqf is the Umayyad mosque in Damascus which provides my stipend in relation to my judicial position (*maʿlūmī ʿalā ʾl-ḥukm min-hu*). To derive benefit from it is an ambiguity. I wish, since I have eaten at these ambiguous sources, that I had limited myself to mere necessity, for that would have been an excuse aimed at preserving my physical constitution. But I continue in this position, and a person of this type is far-removed from piety and from talking about it, so how can such as I talk about purity (*ikhlāṣ*) which is of a higher degree? Grant me, O God, forgiveness!

But sometimes I utter words with the tongue of ecstasy, and I have no share in their utterance. And sometimes I speak with the tongue of knowledge, and have a certain share in such a speech. Further, it may happen even to one who is not pious, that he achieves purity (*ikhlāṣ*) in a particular action, and, deriving help from the blessing of that purity, he becomes one of those who, mixing pious and evil acts, may see God incline towards him (*ʿasā Allāh an yatūb ʿalay-him*). I have longed for that station to become manifest in me (*wadadtu law ḥaṣala lī dhālika ʾl-maqām*). I am now 71 years old and I have no faith that this has become manifest in me for even the twinkling of an eye. Alas for all that I have neglected in relation to God! I wish now that the whole of my past life had been built on a bare sufficiency, and so constituted neither a burden nor a benefit; and I wish that there might emerge in me now a single action that was pleasing to God. I am not pleased with myself nor with these words of mine, not even with these very words, nor pleased they should be seen by anyone. I have written them only in accord with my habit of writing, and in the hope that someone may read them who will find benefit in them, and that they will be for me no evil.

Only God knows what is in the hearts of men. You may not know what is in your own heart for it has its intrigues known only to God. Still less will someone else know what is in your heart, nor will he believe what you tell him, but rather accuse you of lying, or not listen to you at all. Do you then strive to purify what is in your heart (*fa-anta ʾjtahid fī ikhlāṣ mā fī qalbi-ka*)? If it is good it will be to your benefit, if evil, then it will be a burden. Nothing avails you but God. If we postulate that some other knows these things and believes you, then this other either loves or hates you or takes up an intermediate position. The one who loves you, in whom there is no doubt – though God knows best – cannot benefit you an atom's weight, nor preserve you from the evil thereof. If it is thus with the one who loves you, then how can it be with the other two? So estimate the capacity of all three as nothing. Be sure that to concern yourself with them or with seeing them achieves nothing. If you become sure of that, you will benefit.

Lay aside all hypocrisy …, be content with the One, and approach nearer to the eternal God. Let your heart not imagine that there is in existence anyone other than He. I do not intend by these words to speak as the heretics speak. Far from it. For they have given consideration to all that is other, while I make it nothing. I see, in every direction I look, only my creator, God, the protector, the comforter. Except indeed if you aim at a religious end, like teaching, and acting according to it. Amongst the totality of religious ends is to see one's shaykh in order to inform him of one's actions and delight him thereby; that is a sound aim.

What I have said about the waqfs is a warning to myself and to many like me. And the same is true in respect of deriving benefit from the Treasury, for the jurists, for the military, and for others. …

These many matters, if they are investigated, are such that you will scarcely find on the surface of the earth a single dirham which is clearly *ḥalāl*. For craftsmen, merchants and peasants, all of them have occupations or incomes which end up at one of the [ambiguous or illegitimate] points we have described. To eat only of what is *ḥalāl* is a cause of every good; to do otherwise is to oppose every good, and to distance oneself from God, from the benefits of prayer, and from purity in action. O God, we ask you that you take our affairs into your hands, and do not leave us to ourselves, nor to any of your creation, nor to any of our works, for we have no works. O you who possess glory and bounty! May God give prayer and praise to our Prophet Muḥammad, the best of prayer and praise, and the most lasting. O you who are noble! Praise be to God, Lord of the worlds.[44]

The discourse type here is ambiguous, and suggests mixed motives. Subkī starts firmly in juristic mode. Asked about deriving benefits from waqfs, he proceeds to categorise them, but in a negative sense: He focuses on the possibility of invalidity rather than on the possibility of validity. This is contrary to the professional constraints on a judge and a mufti. The presence of established *ikhtilāf*, for all practical purposes, for the normal professional needs of a mufti and a judge, is a sign of validity. The established *ikhtilāf* of the schools is deemed to be permissive and will constrain a qadi certainly, and a mufti usually, to acknowledge that a particular ruling, in spite of personal disagreement, is within the parameters of the law, and therefore valid or permissible (or whatever). Subkī here lists not what is permissible but what engenders ambiguity (*shubha*) and, therefore, is to be avoided by one who has a particularly elevated and idealistic view of the law. In all the cases where he finds here a *shubha*, he would, in his official capacity as a judge, be bound to find valid and effective waqfs. Here he considers it a piety (*wara'*) to abstain from these waqfs. The result of his listing the potential ambiguities in all types of waqfs, including the Ḥakāriyya in Cairo where he had worked as a young man, and the Umayyad mosque, which provided the income for his present post, is despair. There would have been

[44] Ibid., II, 100–103.

an excuse if he had provided from these sources only for the bare needs of his physical constitution. By participating in these waqfs (all of which were valid by the normal requirements of the law) he had moved away from piety (*wara'*) and purity (devotion – *ikhlāṣ*). This realisation leads to the first modulation into the discourse of prayer – *Allāhuma ghafran*.

In that mode, he begins to talk about his experience of mystic states (*ḥāl*), and the tongue of ecstasy (*lisān al-ḥāl*). He has turned his thoughts to the sufi way where *ikhlāṣ* and *tawba* are amongst the early stages of the mystical experience and, in a moment of despair, he finds that he has not achieved even the stage (*maqām*) of *tawba* which is the first real step towards mystical progress. Like the play on *ikhlāṣ*, *tawba* and *maqām*, the play on *riḍā* in the next section is an oblique reference to the path. God is not 'pleased' with his actions, nor is he pleased with himself, his actions, or his writings, not even the particular writing in which he confesses himself to be not pleased, and he is not pleased that someone should see this writing. He writes, not with a view to an audience, but out of habit, and in the hope that someone who can benefit will (eventually) read what he has written (*'asā an yaqifa 'alay-hi man yantafi'u bi-hi*). The mood is in stark contrast to, say, the mood of his treatise on the qadis of Damascus. There, he was looking for factors that made for legitimacy; here he is looking for factors that promote illegitimacy. He has focused on the ideals of piety, renunciation and the mystic way, and, measured by those ideals, he finds that it is the ambiguities of the law which manifest themselves to his scrutiny, and reveal to him the imperfections of human experience, and the vast gulf that separates the law as an ideal from the law as a practical and efficient method of legitimising experience. It is not the law that has changed here. It is his subjective experience of the law. The imperfections of human understanding of the law (*ikhtilāf*) offer hope of legitimacy (and as a qadi he was required to recognise every such hope) or despair of fulfilment of God's law (and as an aspirant to sufi experience, he despaired of his own lifetime's commitment to office).

The train of renunciatory thought continues, generating apostrophe and second person reference which is clearly aimed at the self. 'Nothing avails you but God' – Subkī is talking to himself. 'Lay aside all hypocrisy … and be content with the One.' Subkī is talking 'with the tongue of ecstasy' or with only a mixture of knowledge, as he had warned when he felt the state come upon him. The appeal to God, the protector, the comforter, has its effect, for Subkī recalls the benefits of teaching, and the comforting role of a (sufi) shaykh. At that point, he is able to return to juristic discourse, and, following on from the original question, he raises now a related issue – deriving benefit from the treasury (*al-akl min bayt al-māl*). That leads to the same conclusions, that life is a constant, and inevitable, falling short of an ideal. There is no aspect of human relations in the economic sphere (craftsmen, merchants and peasants) which is not contaminated by ambiguity or prohibition. There is no possibility of complete fulfilment of the law. The good that would be caused if one ate (derived benefit) only of the *ḥalāl* is not a real possibility (save perhaps to mystics and ascetics). The inescapable context of social life – where scarcely a dirham can be found on the face of the earth that is *ḥalāl* – is such that the benefits of the *ḥalāl* (which include the attainment of *ikhlāṣ* in acts and favourable answers to one's prayers – *istijābāt al-duʿāʾ*) are not really available, even to Subkī. Though, in the circumstances, prayer cannot achieve all that it might, prayer is all we have, and Subkī again moves from juristic discourse (of a rare type) to apostrophe and prayer.

Here the format of the fatwa, and the strict consideration of juristic details, has become the means for a personal meditation on life and the law as an unattainable ideal. At first sight this text may look untidy or disorganised, but there is a real progress of experience being expressed here. It is an argument. Subkī looks first at the system of waqfs as articulated in the theory of the law and then transformed into social reality, and finds only ambiguity and despair, a falling short of the *sharʿī* ideal, which affects even himself. He moves to prayer and a wish for an experience which he does not have – the experience of renunciation, the experience of the mystic path. His sense of loss, of the unachieved *ikhlāṣ* which he longs for, modulates into an articulation of absolute dependence on God. Through this he re-discovers solace in the thought of his teaching and acting in accord with it (*al-taʿlīm wa-ʾl-iqtiḍāʾ bi-hi*), and in the thought of his shaykh. This leads to a further and wider consideration of the economic realities of social life. Not only the system of waqfs, but the whole system of economic life is contaminated. Though distanced from God by this situation, and deprived of the full benefits, including the benefits of prayer, that would accrue if social life were *ḥalāl*, there remains only prayer. The contemplation of the law as an ideal leads inexorably to a realisation of man's complete dependence on God. In a fully achieved appreciation of what the law means, prayer is the only conclusion – 'for we have no works'.

Subkī wrote this at 71, in the same year as he wrote his appreciation of the role and duties of the Shāfiʿī qadi in Damascus. He looked there upon the world with a very different eye. The realisation that 'we have no works' was clearly no excuse for failing to work. One of the five questions put by the jurists to the sufis, in the 'fatwa' mentioned above was as follows.

> Throughout the land there exist no pure dirhams, nor gold; debased silver is acknowledged to be the normal currency. Is that permissible for economic exchange on the grounds that, 'When the situation becomes difficult, the law becomes generous?' Or is

this situation to be interpreted, as they have declared [in works of *fiqh*], absolutely not permissible?[45]

Subkī replied, with a one-line answer that avoided the difficulties of the question. 'The chosen view, in my opinion, is the permissibility of loans in these debased dirhams.' The full ramifications and implications of the question need not be analysed here. The point is that, as a mufti, Subkī simply declared (or ambiguously declared, but, in either case, declared) that participation in economic exchange was permissible (though the conditions of economic exchange did not conform to what was implied in standard textbook descriptions). It was permissible, however, only as a necessary deviation from an ideal. One of the functions of a jurist/mufti was to preserve and acknowledge the *sharīʿa* as an ideal. Focusing on that aspect of his task, he could only despair at the world as it was, and fall back on prayer and absolute dependence on God. Man's incapacity and dependence was a necessary implication of the study and preservation of the law. Conversely, the jurist/mufti had also the task of taking the world as it actually was and responding in such a way as to facilitate a pattern of social relationships that shadowed if it did not actually realise the ideal. When the situation becomes difficult, the law becomes generous – *idhā ḍāqa ʾl-amr fa-ʾttasaʿa*. (The phrase had a long and complex history, invariably as a means to facilitate a deviation from the ideal.)

The *sharīʿa* is an ideal, known in all its perfection only to God. *Fiqh* is the human expression of that ideal and it is essentially a failure: The evidence of *ikhtilāf* sufficiently indicates the inadequacy and approximations of human expression. The usefulness of that inadequacy is that it opens up an area of permissibility, making it possible to discover and affirm multiple manifestations of legitimacy. This is a benefit, a concession to mankind's weakness. But it is also a symbol of mankind's failure. Looked at with the eye of doubt, all social structures are seen to be inadequate and imperfect realisations of a dimly perceived ideal. In these circumstances, works become useless – man has no works – and man is revealed in his naked dependency on God's mercy, with prayer as his only recourse. The *sharīʿa*, paradoxically, is both highly practical – a facilitator of social life, and highly idealistic – an infinite, and a despairing, search for understanding and commitment to God's law. Continued participation in the search is a communal duty carried out by the *fuqahāʾ*, through the mediation of the great Imams, for its own sake, in response to a divine imperative, irrespective of practical results.

[45] Ibid., I, 144.

It will be obvious that a mufti in his private capacity must sometimes formulate to himself a basic fatwa – a question about an event that has actually happened in his own life and requires an answer. The extension to academic, hypothetical and purely idealistic questions, formulated by a trained mufti to himself, and generating written responses which might have no immediate audience, being perceived as an act of worship, or simply a habit of writing, is also clear enough, though unambiguous cases must be difficult to establish. In this case, Subkī indulged in an exercise of creative writing in response to a familiar question. This was not the familiar (the practical) answer, and not a suitable answer for the general public. It was an answer which put all its stress on the law as an unachieved ideal (not even achieved as an item of knowledge, still less as social practice). For him, this meditation pointed to despair, prayer and the path of sufi renunciation. He certainly had no immediate audience in mind, though he thought it might be useful to some (unspecified) reader at some (unspecified) time. It is an (almost) unambiguous case of a fatwa written for an audience of one, the mufti himself.

Section 3. Summary

The fatwa has a larger range of functions than is usually conceded either by the traditional manuals of *iftāʿ* or by modern scholarship. These sources share a general stress on the fatwa as a practical decision, practical in the sense of responding, with a ruling, to an event that has actually happened. A wider consideration of all the types of fatwa that actually occur in a collection (and I do not believe that the *Fatāwā* of Subkī is unusual in its typology, though no doubt unique in its particular preferences and proportions) suggests that the process of giving and receiving fatwas reflects (completely) all the functions of the law. The law is a religious structure, its preservation and dissemination a religious duty, and the implementation of that duty incorporates educational, recreational and aesthetic ends, as well as the merely practical. I have proposed an initial typology based on the questioner-recipient: layman, judge (or administrator), student or academic jurist, the mufti himself. At all four levels the practical fatwa coexists with clearly non-practical fatwas, those whose most obvious functions relate to education, recreation, display, or simply to worship (*ʿibāda*). These are typological categories only in a Weberian sense (ideal types): It seems unlikely that any fatwa at all, even the most practical-seeming, will be entirely free from all the other elements. The only element that can, consistently, with security, be discovered sometimes to be absent is the practical. I do not mean by this that an educational fatwa – one that responds to a quest for knowledge about the law – is not practical, merely that its practical aspect is measured against a potential and future contingency, as opposed to the actual and past event which I have incorporated as a condition of my category of the practical. The differential presence of these elements in the elaboration of a single fatwa and in the compilation of a collection must vary from jurist to jurist, and from compiler to compiler, and accounts for the variety and the distinctive qualities of the many collections that exist.

The distinctive qualities of an individual fatwa do not fully account for its social function. For the process of giving and receiving fatwas was also symbolic, in two different (if deeply interrelated) ways. In a (merely) social sense, the fatwa was part of a system of reciprocal exchange whereby a traditional community achieved unity and cohesion, while marking status and hierarchy. In a sense that the participants would recognise as a higher sense, the process was a communal expression of participation in divine revelation. The value, at the social level, of cohesion was repeated, at the religious level, by the value of divine revelation, experienced in and through community. The mediation of the divine message was hierarchic. No participant after the – mythic – days of the great Imams, founders of the *madhāhib*, was acknowledged to have a full and direct experience of revelation (a category whose prime function was to be translated into *sharīʿa*). The highest ranking muftis acquired their understanding of *sharīʿa* from the founders of their school, and mediated it, under authority, to the lower levels of muftis, and to the populace at large. The enactment of mediation was sacramental: it was the primary symbol of divine presence in the community – and did not depend on the real content of fatwas. To mediate what was superfluous (because already known to the recipient), or useless (because it was an unattainable ideal), or incomprehensible (because the recipient had only a partial understanding of the message) was still to enact the formal affirmation of the divine command in the community.

None of the standard collections of fatwas is merely a collection of fatwas, repeating the qualities and the mix of socially realised fatwas. The collection necessarily involves selection, organisation and transformation. In the category of basic (practical) fatwas, the original question is always lost, because the original *ruqʿa* stays with its owner. A sociological study of a mufti and his practice would not necessarily produce the same results as a literary study of the collected fatwas of the same mufti. The great administrative collections of the Ottoman period, which reflect the special conditions of a period when there were government-appointed muftis (as there were not in Subkī's time), have their own special characteristics, but are not the less selected, managed and transformed, perhaps with more concern for system and bureaucracy than for, say, piety, aesthetics or education such as marks the collection of Subkī.

These reflections lead to questions about the definition of a fatwa. A possible recourse, but it would be a travesty of linguistic usage and social reality, is to so limit the term that it applies only to the documents that are generated by and respond to a particular event that has actually happened. This type has a special status, and it is the type that is discussed, almost exclusively, in the manuals. But the manuals are not describing social practice. They are laying down rules for the provision of guidance to those who need it. They are not describing the fatwa or its function in society, they are describing a social and religious need and how it can be resolved by exploiting the social phenomenon known as the fatwa. The self-imposed limitations of that tradition of writing should not affect the efforts of modern scholarship to describe the whole social and religious function of the fatwa. An assessment of the law, based merely on the practical fatwa, would not be an assessment of the law as a complete system, but rather, by a vicious if inevitable reduction, of the law in practice. And all the analytic observers agree, with Subkī, that, in this sense, the mufti was a derivative and subordinate position, subject to control and qualification by the academic/teaching jurists. Subkī offered a wider definition when he proposed that the mufti was one who applied the universals of the law to particulars. That too has problems. It has the equal disadvantages of including those of his long treatises which, though they lack all other qualities of the fatwa, have (sometimes distant) origins in, and reference to, a real event; and of excluding all those 'fatwas' which relate to law (or theology) at the level of universals and without reference to a given set of particulars. A practical middle position (offered undogmatically, for definitions have to serve, not constrain, academic tasks) is to define the fatwa in literary terms, as a document which clearly exhibits some realisation of the *masʿala – jawāb* format. This would not eliminate problem cases, but it would create a body of core fatwas, exhibiting all the types I have described in this chapter. In proportion as the fatwas lost these formal attributes they would be re-classified as examples of *furūʿ* type (or other) discourse. Many of the longer treatises of Subkī can be classified either as *furūʿ* type discourse, or as belonging to the genre of *tafsīr* or hadith commentary. The fact that they frequently contain reference to a specific reality would not affect this classification: We have seen that reference to reality does occur in *furūʿ* type discourse, and even, though much more rarely, in *tafsīr* and hadith commentary.

Afterword

Scholarly Priorities and Islamic Studies: The Reviews of Norman Calder

Robert Gleave

> Why does the law matter anyway? For a student it is easy to enjoy *fiqh* ... more difficult to account for this pleasure, and extremely difficult to re-express the theological message that is there encoded.[1]

The pleasure Norman Calder derived from reading *fiqh* texts is clear from the chapters in this book; his skill in re-expressing their theological message is evident here also. And although I am not convinced that all students would agree that *fiqh* is 'easy to enjoy', anyone who studied with him will detect in this volume of studies a characteristic precision of expression and depth of insight. Norman's book reviews are packed with revealing comments (such as that cited above), and though academics do not always consider their book reviews their greatest achievements, in Norman's case, they repay closer inspection, both individually and collectively.

Like works of *fiqh* and *uṣūl*, academic book reviews have a 'stability of form and content'.[2] There is the obligatory summary of the reviewed work's contents, followed by an account of its position relative to other scholarship on the subject, and, finally, the reviewer's critical evaluation of the work's contribution to the field. Within the last of these, reviewers will engage both with the content of the work (the account it offers and the thesis proposed by the author), and the stylistic and technical merits of the book (the quality of prose, the utility and

[1] 1993: Kohlberg, 63. The following footnotes referring to Calder's book reviews cite the date of publication, author's name and page number. Full bibliographical information for each review is listed at the end of this chapter (The Book Reviews of Norman Calder).

[2] N. Calder, *Sharīʿa*, *EI²*, 324.

accuracy of the critical apparatus and transliteration, etc.). The order of these elements is not fixed, though perhaps the most common presentational scheme is the one just outlined. Standard elements of a book review might be combined into a single passage. For example, the content summary may include commentary and evaluation of scholarly merit integrated within it.[3] Usually, the criticism of transliteration (and, on many occasions, writing style and editorial thoroughness) is shunted towards the end of a review, thereby avoiding the appearance of petty nitpicking, while simultaneously promoting the impression of scholarly diligence. Demoting technical comments to the conclusions of a review 'reveals' an eagerness to engage with intellectual content rather than superficial presentation.[4] Within these broad generic boundaries, reviews can be innovatory, challenging, engaging and humorous. They can also be dull and perfunctory. Reviews can, on occasion, make a more significant contribution to the field than the reviewed work itself.

Most academics do not choose which books to review. They are asked by a journal's editor. An academic can, of course, turn down requests to review a work, but he or she has to have been solicited in the first place. A reviewer can approach an editor with the title of a book and ask to review it, but this is considered rather gauche (and can raise the editor's suspicions of the reviewer's motives – Does he or she have an axe to grind?). If a reviewer produces a review that fits a journal's house style and is an intellectual contribution, he or she will, in all probability, be asked again when another book in the field is submitted. Often, however, the most important factor in determining who is approached is the extent of the editor's confidence that the scholar will submit a publishable review within a reasonable timeframe. Once an editor finds a reviewer he or she can trust, the reviewer is likely to be approached for further reviews.

From the reviewer's perspective, entering into a 'reviewing' relationship with a journal and its editor is, in a sense, a statement of one's assessment of that journal: Academics have preferences over where their reviews appear. Some of these preferences are based on expediency, but mainly they are expressions of the reviewer's assessment of quality. Loyalty is a major factor, but which journal one is loyal to is, in a sense, an evaluation of quality. Furthermore, as the volume of

[3] Calder uses this presentational technique when reviewing collections of papers (by either a single author or many – see 1983: *La Notion*; 1983: Lazarus-Yafeh; 1985: Vajda; 1985: Stern 1; 1985: Stern 2; 1986: Warburg; 1987: Stern; 1987: Martin; 1990: Rippin; 1991: Burrell; 1993: Kohlberg). He also uses it for integrated monographs though, giving his assessment of particular chapters in the course of a description rather than simply describing the work, and then embarking on an assessment (see 1983: Cook).

[4] Calder uses this technique in his reviews 1986: Leaman, 107, and 1991: Amin, 115.

publications increases and the time for simply reading recent work in the field decreases, reviewing a recent publication in one's chosen field is a convenient way of ensuring that one's research has currency. One is under an intellectual obligation both to read a book received for review and to allow oneself to be educated and challenged by it.

With these thoughts in mind, a number of points emerge from an overview of Norman Calder's book reviews. First, the vast majority of the reviews (all except three of the forty-three I have located) were published either in the *Bulletin of the School of Oriental and African Studies* (*BSOAS*) or the *Journal of Semitic Studies* (*JSS*). This fact, of course, is no accident: It reflects (partially) Calder's academic career. He studied at SOAS for his doctoral research under John Wansbrough and A.K.S. Lambton between 1976 and 1979, and became a natural contender for relevant reviews in the *Bulletin* in subsequent years. Similarly, the *Journal of Semitic Studies* was (and continues to be) anchored in the life of the Department of Middle Eastern Studies at the University of Manchester, where Calder taught between 1980 and his death in 1998. His inclination to publish reviews in these two outlets was not solely due to parochial convenience. Rather it reflects his commitment and contribution to the intellectual life of both SOAS and the department in Manchester. Scholarly journals were, for him, among the most important academic legacies of an institution. Since these two institutions had contributed to his own academic development (not only in terms of employment, but more importantly, in the opportunities they provided for scholarly exchange), it was natural for him to contribute to their journals. For Calder, the journals' importance is reflected in their being his preferred place of publication. This does not, of course, mean that he was uncritical of the institutions in which he worked (anyone who worked with him knows his incisive wit could be turned against the leviathan of institutional bureaucracy). Rather, his choice to publish in organs attached to institutions to which he was committed, and with which he had a personal history, should perhaps be interpreted as a measure of his dedication to the notion of a scholarly community rooted in the idea of a university. For Calder, his local academic community was an important venue for testing of ideas. These institutions were the context in which his ideas emerged, as he engaged in conversations and exchanges with colleagues from diverse disciplinary backgrounds. This is acknowledged in the dedication of his ground-breaking monograph *Studies in Early Muslim Jurisprudence*, where he thanks his colleagues Alexander, Samely and Imber.[5]

[5] 'All three, at various times, have read and commented on substantial drafts of this work, invariably to my benefit.' N. Calder, *Studies in Early Muslim Jurisprudence* (Oxford: Clarendon Press, 1994), x.

However, supporting local endeavours was not the only reason Calder accepted books for review. Seen collectively, and totalling over 50,000 words, Calder's reviews are his assessment of the discipline of Islamic studies and its various subdisciplines. He hoped, through reviewing individual works, to set out his own view as to the current state of the field, and its potential future direction(s). He had, then, a broad audience in mind when he composed his reviews. The chapters in this book, which constitute Calder's final unpublished writings, also indicate his wide-ranging vision for the future study of Islamic law rooted in detailed analysis of specific texts, assessed to be both representative and important. Norman would probably pour scorn on my attempt to piece together an intellectual history from the scrappy evidence of book reviews, but this, ironically, was his own chosen method in his analysis of the development of early Muslim thought. What follows should not, though, be taken too seriously. It may lead to an enhanced understanding of the scholar and his contribution, but most importantly, it gave me the chance to read and in many cases re-read his frequently amusing, always thoughtful and often challenging reviews. The style of reviews is usually less formal than that of monographs and articles, and this can be seen in most of Calder's reviews (reading them prompted in me melancholic smiles and nostalgic nods of recognition, as Norman's personality and mannerisms jumped off the page). Calder was fully aware that the works he was reviewing were the products of an individual's (or groups of individuals') industry. He therefore had a duty to allow himself to assess a book, taking into account the contribution it made to the field, and whether or not the scholarly enterprise as a whole had been progressed through these efforts. These were his criteria for quality, and when he judged a work to have failed to meet them, his intellectual honesty compelled him to say so.

I think it would be true to say that works which attempted to review available evidence and thereby produce convincing narratives or working hypotheses excited Calder most. Such works led to his most expansive and detailed reviews (cf. reviews of Cook, Crone and Hinds, perhaps also those of Hawting and al-Azmeh). However, if we are to stay honest to Calder's approach, one needs to build in caveats before proceeding to analysis. He had a dislike for hasty generalisations in a field that was, in his view, still in its infancy; he is probably wringing his hands in desperation at the large number of half-baked introductory books on Islam produced in the last decade. So, here are the caveats. From the date of publication of a book review, it is far from an automatic indication either of when the author was asked, or of when he or she received the book, or of when he or she wrote the review. Journals do not always receive books for review at the time of publication; editors do not find a reviewer instantly; reviewers do not begin writing the review on the day of the book's receipt; space to publish a review is not always available in the next issue. All these factors – and others (such as proofreading the reviews and making subsequent changes) – can mean that characterising the history of a scholar's intellectual interests from the reviews he is offered, accepts, composes and are eventually published is not a scientific exercise. The following assessments are, then, tentative. To reduce the effect of these caveats, one can add that Norman appears to have been quite a reliable reviewer. The vast majority of his reviews (more than 75%) appear in print within two years of a book's publication. Many review editors would, I am sure, be pleased if they could hit this target in their review sections with such frequency.

Calder's reviews: A diachronic assessment

The works Calder was asked to review reflect his own interests and expertise within the field of Islamic studies. His early reviews, in 1980 and 1981 cover works on Shīʿism and the notion of authority in early Islam (cf. reviews of McDermott, Tabātabāʾī/Chittick, Sachedina and the interdisciplinary *La notion d'autorité au Moyen Âge*). His reputation as an expert in these areas emerged out of his doctoral research at SOAS and his ground-breaking thesis on Shīʿī jurisprudence.[6] Later in the 1980s, he reviewed works in other areas, but his interest in Shīʿism and questions of political/juridical authority remained (cf. reviews of Khomeini/Algar, Momen, Arjomand, Crone and Hinds, Kramer, and in the early 1990s, Kohlberg). Beginning in 1982, he published reviews in the distinct but related fields of hermeneutics and the interpretation of the Qurʿan (cf. reviews of Böwering, Pouzet and later Rippin). Also from this time, he began to review works in the area of Islamic theology (cf. review of Cook, but also that of Lazarus-Yafeh). From 1984, works with greater philosophical focus began to interest him (cf. reviews of Shehadi, Platti, Leaman twice, Goodman and Netton). In the late 1980s and into the 1990s, he was the obvious choice as reviewer for *BSOAS* and *JSS* in the field of Islamic law, though interestingly he did few reviews in this field (cf. reviews of Amin, Saleh and Johansen, Weiss and earlier Peters).

His greatest scholarly contribution in terms of his publications was in the study of Islamic law; however, he completed few reviews in this field. It was not because he was not asked – I remember him passing on books for review to postgraduate students (myself included), and arranging the switch with journal editors. He arranged for me to review one work, saying, 'I know him; he is a good friend; I disagree with him on many points; he knows this and I have already

[6] N. Calder, 'The Structure of Authority in Imami Jurisprudence', unpublished PhD thesis, University of London, 1979.

written about it. I do not think a review from me would be either helpful or a contribution.' It seems that Calder was more willing to take on reviews in areas outside of his own specialism, and though he never wrote anything substantial in the field of Sufism, *kalām,* or *falsafa,* his interests were broad and included these subdisciplines. However, he had views on the state of Islamic studies generally – views which he made known through these reviews. Scanning the subjects of his reviews and the eighteen years of his career they span, one gains the impression of a scholar increasingly willing to take on new areas of research; he develops new angles as he agrees to take on new works for review. He begins with Shīʿism, moves on to theology, history, Sufism and Quranic hermeneutics; finally, he deepens his interest through extensive readings in philosophy. In his major field of Islamic law, he remained highly selective throughout, concerning himself only with Peters, Johansen, Saleh, Amin and Weiss. By the end of his career, his intellectual curiosity had led to a creditably eclectic range of review subjects, including not only those topics already mentioned, but also mediaeval Arabic and Hebrew writings, Jewish and Christian philosophy, scriptural interpretation generally and the methodology of Islamic studies. Perhaps he preferred to review works on subjects in which he was not expert because they stretched and challenged him; also he may have felt able to comment as an informed consumer of secondary literature (some of the works he reviewed aimed to be surveys of their topics).[7] Furthermore, he felt he had an outlet to comment on Islamic legal scholarship in other publications (articles and monographs) – there was no need to do it again in book reviews. He was the sort of interested intellectual that many authors hoped would read their work, be affected by it, and comment on it. As Samely nicely puts it, Calder's 'intellectual personality has given important features to the ideal scholarly reader whom I take into view when I write'.[8]

In terms of review output, the mid-1980s was Calder's most prolific period. In the eight years between 1982 and 1990, he wrote thirty-one reviews; in the next eight (1991–1998), he composed only eight. For the later years, this may have been due to his illness, but another reason is likely to be his wish (perhaps combined with external factors) to concentrate on his own compositions. The increasing pressure on British academics in the 1990s to publish items that could be realistically returned on the Research Assessment Exercise (a tyranny which remains with us) made writing book reviews a low priority. The time lag between the

[7] He hints as much in his review 1995: Goodman and Netton, 123, when he states that the works under review are (unsuccessful) attempts to transform 'philosophical discourse into general (academic) culture'.

[8] A. Samely, 'From Case to Case – Notes on the Discourse Logic of the Mishnah', in G. R. Hawting, J. A. Mojaddedi, and A. Samely (eds.), *Studies in Islamic and Middle Eastern Texts and Traditions in Memory of Norman Calder* (Oxford: Oxford University Press, 2000), 233.

publication of the works and the appearance of Calder's reviews also increased somewhat, though this was in part due to Calder's penchant in later years for bracketing works together in a single review (cf. reviews of Johansen and Saleh, Fox and Leaman, Goodman and Netton). In any case, book reviews have never received much recognition by university employers, and it is no coincidence, I am sure, that when academics were most pressured to produce monographs and articles, Calder's book review productivity slowed down. For example, Calder's longest review (of Cook's *Early Muslim Dogma*, running to around 3,500 words and seven pages of the *Journal of Semitic Studies*) would not (and probably could not) have been written in the early 1990s. Not only would an editor not indulge a reviewer in this way (though the emergence of the 'Review Article' might have provided an alternative outlet, outside of the reviews section), but a scholar would be unlikely to commit the effort and time necessary to compose such a detailed piece of research which was to be 'merely' a book review. Finally, there is, of course, a natural tendency to be more selective, and in his later years, Calder clearly chose books to review that held a particular interest for him, and on which he felt he could make a meaningful comment. Irrespective of whether his assessment was positive or negative, the authors of these later works (Fox and Leaman, Netton and Goodman, Weiss, Chittick and Frank) had already passed one test – their work was sufficiently interesting to deserve Calder's attention at a time when his energy was required elsewhere.

Calder's reviews: A thematic approach

A review is, perhaps, the only time an academic's work receives detailed and thorough treatment by peers in the field. If one is talented enough to write a work that becomes the touchstone for subsequent scholarship (as Calder did with *Studies*), one sees the scholarly community's reaction not only in reviews, but also (and repeatedly) in footnotes specifically designed to refute or augment one's hypotheses. For those whose work may not have this immediate impact, reviews are of great importance. Indeed, university careers are enhanced (or damaged) by reviews. Reviewing a book is then an unavoidably ethical enterprise. Any criticism must be tightly argued and one must avoid, at all costs, slipping into *ad hominem* denigration. This was Calder's standard, even if one senses, at times, a frustration with the review genre and a wish to say more than it permitted. Occasionally authors considered his reviews overcritical and responded in like fashion (cf. Arjomand's response to Calder's review of the *Shadow of God and the Hidden Imam*).[9]

[9] 'Arjomand to Editor', in Correspondence, *Middle Eastern Studies*, 24;3 (1988): 383.

Before examining Calder's detailed comments on particular subfields within Islamic Studies, a few general remarks concerning his priorities within a review (as far as they can be ascertained from the textual evidence) are in order. An overwhelming concern is with scholarly method: How is one to 'do' Islamic studies? How is one to convey the content of the tradition one is analysing to a wider audience? To sum up his own methodological position, one can quote one of his early reviews:

> For the study of the intellectual superstructure which sustains and organizes a traditional system of religious belief, the only mode of investigation available (at least in a historical context) is the precise and discriminating elucidation of religious texts. This is a task which, I would suggest, demands initially a literary critical approach and a sensitivity to the genuinely creative aspects of religious literature.[10]

This 'literary critical approach' was (of course) inherited from Wansbrough and pervaded Calder's published work. At times, his commitment to this approach prevented him from positively assessing works in which this approach was not utilised. On the subject of the writing of Umayyad history, specifically, Calder notes in his review of Hawting's *The First Dynasty of Islam*:

> What it was one had missed in the braver and grander and wilder histories of the Umayyad period (which have not been few in the last decade) is discovered here to be a diffidence appropriate to the sources. Style matters if a historian is to create something other than a catalogue of historiographical clichés which may hide not only the reality he is searching for but also the struggle he has had with his materials.[11]

In carefully worded introductory sentences such as these, Calder sets the scene for the reviews that followed. He praises Hawting's work partly because it is a careful working-out of the literary critical approach, where the connection between *topos* and fact is never inevitably causal. His criticism of Mottahedeh's approach in his *Loyalty and Leadership* stems from this perspective:

> Mottahedeh has perhaps not sufficiently distinguished between the 'facts' … and the social myth which underpinned historical (literary) reconstruction … . The function of the narrative is to create a social myth conducive to social cohesion, not to describe society. … Mottahedeh is not unaware of these qualities in his sources … but is, in general over-sanguine in accepting as social fact the implications of literary narrative.[12]

Similarly, Vajda's encyclopaedic and historical approach to the collation of *ijāzas* is questioned, as 'even simple conclusions about for example a core curriculum

[10] 1981: Sachedina, 577.

[11] 1988: Hawting, 131.

[12] 1981: Mottahedeh, 364.

are blurred by doubts related to fictitious transmissions, *ijāzas* conferred by letter, and "global *ijāzas*" covering a number of works not obviously studied'.[13] With regard to J.-C. Vadet's contribution to the collection *La Notion d'Autorité au Moyen Âge*, the attempt to demonstrate that there was an inevitability about the triumph of Ashʿarism by citing late Ashʿarī sources elicits the response '... hmm'. Students of Calder will recognise this comment not as a burble of satisfaction at a point well made, but as Calder's code: 'there is an unjustified and dubious leap of reasoning here which should be as obvious to you as it is to me.' Regarding Stern's posthumously published *Studies in Early Ismāʿīlism*, Calder writes:

> The aims ... which inspire Stern and unify these disparate articles are 'history proper' and 'the early history of Ismāʿīlism' in particular, and the technique is to apply 'the critical method' in the extrapolation of the useful from the useless. ... The reader must ... be uneasily conscious that the formulation of questions alone dictates the categorization of material as either 'chaff' or 'grain'. ... . The historical methodology of separating chaff from grain is no methodology at all: it leaves everything to question. ... In fact the nature of the works exploited by Stern remains largely unknown, for he makes little attempt to find out the aims or intentions of the writers.[14]

Calder's mild criticism of Morgan's *Medieval Persia 1040–1797* also concerns (primarily) the historian's recognition of the sources employed in a narrative's construction. With regard to literary conventions (such as hyperbole, 'invective', and the *topoi* of praise literature) and in the course of a generally positive review, Calder writes:

> The intelligent historian struggles with these [literary conventions] all the time and it seems a pity the intelligent reader should still be tricked into thinking that history is simply (still!) the art of narration.[15]

He admires Morgan's narrative skills, but feels that there is something underhanded in not recognising the problematic nature of the sources. Calder's criticism, then, is that simple historical narrative is, to an extent, dishonest; and (a point to which I return later), a key criterion of scholarly quality at whatever level (from introductory to advanced) is intellectual honesty.

Calder, unsurprisingly for those who know his published work, was suspicious of the simple use of literary sources to extrapolate historical fact – and for him, chronicles were, primarily, literary artefacts. This does not mean his views can always be neatly folded in with other sceptics (Crone, Cook and Hinds are subjected to rigorous criticism). But as Burton rightly notices (though in a

[13] 1985: Vajda, 202.

[14] 1987: Stern, 133 and 134.

[15] 1989: Morgan, 153.

critical manner),[16] the primary influence on Calder's intellectual development was his tutor, John Wansbrough, and this is readily apparent in the reviews surveyed here. Calder directly references Wansbrough in six reviews, either in laudatory terms or exhorting his readers to consult Wansbrough's work (or both).[17] In his review of *Early Muslim Dogma*, Calder sets up the alternative accounts of Cook and Wansbrough as to the dating of particular theological documents. He consistently (and self-consciously) argues for Wansbrough's position:

> ... for my own part, I find that only Wansbrough's work provides a coherent background for understanding the emergence of documents of this kind. ... [18] It is a merit of [Wansbrough's] work – and for many it will be an exasperating one – that for some time to come studies of early Islamic theology may well be read (as perhaps is all too evident in this review) as footnotes to his monumental scholarship.[19]

In later reviews, Calder describes Wansbrough's work as among 'the finest studies' of the emergence of the notion of Qurʿan and Sunna as normative; he describes a collection of papers as 'disappointing' because 'almost eight years after the publication of John Wansbrough's *Qurʿanic Studies*, so few [of the contributors have] realised that this major work, like it or not, demands a response, at numerous substantive and methodological levels'.[20] Those of us who were taught by or knew Calder often approach his writings with a similar intellectual excitement (perhaps even deference), which others cannot always perceive as justified. It is instructive to see that Calder was similarly excited by the insights he gained from his own teacher (and, to no less an extent, his teacher's teachers).[21] Apart from Wansbrough, Calder's affection for his teachers is expressed directly in various comments within the reviews.[22]

[16] Burton, 'Rewriting the Timetable of Early Islam', *Journal of the American Oriental Society*, 115;3 (1995): 453: 'Of the three intellectual predecessors informing Calder's thinking, Goldziher, Schacht, and Wansbrough, it is the third influence which emerges as the strongest.'

[17] 1980: McDermott, 366; 1983: Lazarus-Yafeh, 188; 1983: Cook, *passim*; 1986: Leaman, 106; 1987: Martin, 546 – unavoidably since the work under review concerns Wansbrough; 1990: Rippin, 335.

[18] 1983: Cook, 184.

[19] 1983: Cook, 187

[20] 1990: Rippin, 335. Calder's own response can be found in his 'History and Nostalgia: Reflections on John Wansbrough's *Sectarian Milieu*', in *Islamic Origins Reconsidered: John Wansbrough and the Study of Islam*, ed. H. Berg (Berlin: Mouton de Gruyter, 1997), 47–73.

[21] Calder also betrays the influence of his teacher in his regular citation of Wolfson: see 1980: McDermott, 366; 1982: Gimaret, 349; 1985: Platti, 319; 1987: Walzer, 548; 1988: Gimaret and Monnot, 622. In the last of these, Calder mentions that he is surprised that Wolfson is not referenced in the work!

[22] 1987: Walzer, 549: Walzer is described as 'a friend to generations of scholars and students.' Father McCarthy's translation of al-Ghazālī's *al-Munqidh* (1982: McCarthy, 124–5) 'reflects the modesty and charm of a fine teacher'.

Calder's other major methodological position was an emphatic rejection of the believer validation thesis. The clearest example of this is his review of R. Martin's collection *Approaches to Islam in Religious Studies* (which begins, 'In this volume 12 scholars approach Islam, mostly from a great distance').[23] The studies are, Calder argues, characterised by a 'debilitating irenic sentimentality' in which the experience of the individual Muslim takes precedence over scholarly rigour. In his response to Cantwell Smith's principle that 'anything I say about Islam as a living faith is valid only insofar as Muslims can say "Amen" to it', one can sense Calder's anger:

> There is no reason for a scholar, *qua* scholar, to look favourably on the principle, no matter how qualified. There are other principles of greater concern to scholarship (coherence, rationality, precision, argument) and they, in their context, matter more.[24]

Concerning Fazlur Rahman's piece he writes:

> While superficially recognising that non-Muslims (the nice ones – 'unprejudiced, sensitive and knowledgeable') may achieve an intellectual understanding of Islam, he too would prefer them to be controlled. … [25]

Rahman's control is the requirement that scholars of Islam first recognise that the Qurʿan and Sunna are normative (not just for Muslims, but for scholarship on Islam generally). It was such restrictions on a field that had yet to achieve any secure standing in academe which enraged Calder, and on which he regularly commented. Jim Morris's work on Mulla Sadrā, Calder describes as excellent, but notes:

> I am less sympathetic to the lengthy introductions and notes which undervalue … rational objective thought. That [Morris] is himself committed to the transcendent viewpoint does not absolve him from interpretive responsibility. A believer may analyse with precision and discrimination the types and categories of mystic experience. … [26]

Morris writes that 'with [transcendent experience] the meaning and function of Sadrā's concepts will appear quite plainly; without it his discussion will appear either confusing, atomistic or simply meaningless'. Calder refuses to accept that in order to understand Sadrā, one must 'experience' the transcendent:

> This kind of comment … is not only unhelpful but untrue. The structure, order, the fundamental notions and the basic intentions of this work can be understood (and criticized) without drawing on any experience of the transcendent.[27]

[23] 1987: Martin, 545.

[24] 1987: Martin, 546.

[25] 1987: Martin, 546.

[26] Elsewhere, Calder does recognise the difficulties inherent in describing mysticism: 'The analysis and elucidation of a mystic theology so as to render it – for those who are not mystics – accessible is a notoriously difficult task.' 1982: Böwering, 331.

[27] 1983: Morris, 150.

Chittick's account of Ibn 'Arabī's thought is 'a personal vision, built from immersion in and loyalty to [Ibn 'Arabī's] theological system. This is both a strength and weakness.'[28] 'It is a strength, I suspect, because the task of understanding Ibn 'Arabī is of such difficulty that a personal commitment to the truth of the message is an almost indispensable aid in maintaining one's concentration whilst reading the *Futūḥāt*. It is a weakness because such commitment tends to eschew grounding the ideas within a particular, developing and historical context.' In like manner, when non-Muslim scholars are tempted to argue for or against particular Muslim positions, Calder considers such an approach inappropriate.[29] Alternatively, on the revisionist side, he sees the work of Cook, Crone and Hinds as in part motivated by their own 'polemic'.[30] We return here to Calder's idea of scholarship, both in Islamic studies and in academia generally: evidence-based, textually grounded, rigorous, avoiding banal generalisations and available for dissection by all, regardless of personal commitment. The notion may seem now a little 'un-deconstructed' and overly scientific, and Calder's critics may argue he failed to live up to these ideals. Calder was, I think, aware that in many ways, his approach might be termed (negatively) as orientalist, but considered such a criticism to be (in his view) polemic rather than descriptive comment: it indicated the field's immaturity.[31] Burton complained that Calder's tone grated; he was overly influenced by Wansbrough's 'unproven speculations, hypotheses, innuendoes, and pointers' and was 'theory-driven'.[32] However, in his reviews, Calder called for a sympathetic account of the Muslim literary tradition. Lazarus-Yafeh's great strength, for example, is in 'the sympathy and sensitivity with which she, a believer, approaches the problems of other believers, problems which she recognises as shared'.[33] In any account of the classical texts, their authors and the ideas contained within them, the primary aim is to do justice to the sources within a modern academic framework. The scholars of the past were to be viewed as sophisticated intellectuals rather than petty casuists. The arcane topics and tortuous reasoning of classical Muslim theology and law is not irrelevant in a modern

[28] 1997: Chittick, 549.

[29] Calder criticises Ormsby for embarking on a defence of al-Ghazālī 'which is unnecessary' (1986: Ormsby, 212). Calder criticises Leaman for describing Saadya Gaon's account of objective moral principles as 'unconvincing' (1986: Leaman, 106). There are numerous other examples.

[30] See 1983: Cook, 181: 'there can be little doubt that the polemical impulse found in early Muslim dogma derives from *Hagarism* … '.; 1987: Crone and Hinds, 357: 'I am inclined to characterize the arguments of chapter 3 and 4 [of *God's Caliph*] as based on selective citation and partial misreading of sources.'

[31] Indeed, Arjomand explicitly describes Calder's work as 'a good illustration of orientalist bias', Arjomand, 'Political Ethic and Public Law', in *Religion and Society in Qajar Iran*, ed. R. Gleave (London: Routledge, 2002), 37, n. 18.

[32] Burton, 'Rewriting the Timetable', 455.

[33] 1983: Lazarus-Yafeh, 188.

context, but instead (in Calder's view) provides a means of understanding the tradition from which modern expressions of Islam have emerged. Calder was, in fact, not at all hostile to the classical tradition of Muslim scholarship as a stereotypical orientalist might be. In fact, he admired the brilliance of the scholars, 'the elegance' of classical argumentation,[34] the 'genuinely creative' aspects of religious literature,[35] and perhaps even the magnificence of a well-rounded argumentation. He speaks of the pleasure of reading Ibn Sīnā and Farābī (!) and criticises writers who have failed to convey this to the reader of English.[36] For example, he praises Frank for capturing the pleasure of reading Ghazālī in his own prose.[37] While Weiss's monumental *The Search for God's Law* had been a "toil" for its author; Calder argues that the crisscross patterns of debate within Āmidī's *al-Iḥkām* 'evoke intricacy and beauty', just like a well-designed carpet:[38]

> Achieved mastery of a precisely defined discipline [such as *uṣūl al-fiqh*] permits a kind of literary pleasure which Weiss has not here rediscovered. It was available to Muslim scholars because they participated in an educational system which eased the toil through established patterns of listening and learning at a relatively early age. It may be available to Weiss, precisely now, when he has finished the toil.[39]

When one turns to the subfields within Islamic Studies, Calder's comments reflect not only his own erudition, but also his intention to use the form of a book reviews as a spur to future scholarship. His reviews in the areas of Shīʿism, theology and law can be used to demonstrate this – though his reviews in Sufism, philosophy, history and the general scope of Islamic Studies could equally serve the purpose.

In his reviews on works relating to Twelver Shiʿism, he emphasised that the Imam was not always a distant, eschatological figure. In examining McDermott's excellent work on al-Shaykh al-Mufīd, Calder gently suggests that the relationship between the belief in a sinless Imam in occultation and the Imam's role as a legal authority might have been 'brought out' more clearly.[40] Islamic messianism, explored by Sachedina, 'does not adequately reflect … that the Imam's function as related to authority, epistemology and soteriology was always a contemporary one not necessarily linked to the eschaton'.[41] Calder views the collection of Imāmī

[34] 1987: Walzer, 548.
[35] 1981: Sachedina, 577.
[36] 1995: Goodman and Netton, 123.
[37] 1998: Frank, 132.
[38] He refers to the notion of a carpet as a metaphor for jurisprudence, which has 'a patterned beauty which appeals as instantly to the intellect as a Persian carpet does to the eye'. Calder, *Studies*, 243.
[39] 1996: Weiss, 557.
[40] 1980: McDermott, 366.
[41] 1981: Sachedina, 577.

Shīʿī writings by ʿAllāmah Tabātabāʾī as containing fine sentiments, but lacking in anything which is specifically Shīʿī or even Muslim'.[42] His remarks on Algar's selection of Khomeini's writings and declarations (*Islam and Revolution*) indicate their utility, but also their general demagoguery and bitterness – there is not much explicitly Shīʿī here (but there is much implicitly so, in Khomeini's call for *velāyat-e faqīh*). Calder chastises contributors to Kramer's volume for being too easily drawn to the sensational and to naming Shīʿī scholars of minor importance who happen to play a role in particular political events. It means, he argues, that major figures, like Āyatallāh Khūʾī, remain understudied and ignored (they are too dry and hide-bound for social scientists and modern historians). Calder rightly recognises that it is scholars such as Khūʾī who not only commanded the greatest respect, but also had the potential to effect political change if they so wished. He is also critical of historians who judge the wisdom or otherwise of the political actions of Shīʿī scholars – an example of the breach of scholarly detachment criticised elsewhere in his reviews and mentioned earlier. Calder's review of Momen's *Introduction to Shiʿi Islam* also demonstrates his eagerness to ensure that in the political clamour following the Iranian Revolution, less attention grabbing Shīʿī scholars – such as Khūʾī – gain appropriate recognition. Within the review is Calder's hallmark warning concerning simplistic use of sources, but he generally considers Momen's achievement as characterised by '[A]n unpretentious style, interpretive clarity and basically sound judgment.'[43] Concerning Kohlberg's *Variorum* collection, he praises the detailed and the thorough scholarship, but criticises the absence of a synthetic approach (it was this element he praised in Momen's *Introduction*). Furthermore, he is left dissatisfied with Kohlberg's credibility when faced with the sources (for Kohlberg, 'the happy discovery in 1699 of a manuscript written 700 years earlier scarcely raises an eyebrow; the historian's desire to explain is not clearly separated from the tradition's need for justification'.[44]). What emerges from these scattered comments is Calder's concern that the study of Shīʿism in academia not be derailed by the Iranian Revolution and the emergence of an avowedly political expression of the faith. It is crucial that the study of Shīʿism takes seriously the juristic heritage from which modern (and one might say, transient) political figures have emerged.

Calder's infamous critical review of Arjomand's *Shadow of God and the Hidden Imam* elicited a robust response from Arjomand and perhaps deserves a little more comment.[45] The continued popularity of Arjomand's work, considered an influential contribution to the study of Shīʿism in Iran, perhaps makes

[42] 1981: Tabātabāʾī/ Chittick, 576.
[43] 1985: Momen, 1110.
[44] 1993: Kohlberg, 363.
[45] See 'Arjomand to Editor', 383.

Calder's criticism misjudged. The debate over Karakī's death date mentioned by Calder and expanded on by Arjomand in his reply has probably been settled in Arjomand's favour; thought the authenticity of the *farmān* is in no way assured by determining that it was *possible* that Karakī had authored it. In any case, Calder's objection to Arjomand's thesis was not based solely on this point, but rather involved what Arjomand made of the evidence. Calder considered the *fiqh* tradition as reflecting Imāmī Shīʿī thinking; Arjomand was willing to take a broad corpus as his evidence base (including chronicles and mirror literature). Calder viewed *fiqh* literature as primarily a self-contained, seminary-based discipline, not without social comment, but not controlled solely by political and social factors.[46] Arjomand, Calder complained, mixed up the types of sources he was investigating, and the result was a work that failed to condition conclusions with an awareness of the literary nature of the sources consulted.[47]

On Ismāʿīlī Shīʿism, and following his general literary approach, Calder (almost casually) throws out the suggestion that the portrayal of early Ismāʿīlism as highly centralised (and therefore dangerous) was in fact a 'diffuse historiographical and heresiographical device, adopted and honed by the Fatimids to affirm and bolster their political authority'.[48] This suggestion has been explored by a number of subsequent scholars, and Calder's remarks seem now almost prescient given the subsequent development of Ismāʿīlī studies.

Calder sums up his characterisation of the *kalām* tradition nicely:

> A limited number of structural themes permitting an indefinite but not infinite number of intellectual responses constitutes the subject matter of mediaeval Islamic Theology.[49]

He is less satisfied, however, with the overconcentration on Ghazālī in Western scholarship. While he accepts McCarthy's translation of *al-Munqidh min al-Ḍalāl* as a useful teaching aid, Calder wonders whether Ormsby, Watt, Morelon and Frank are a little too enamoured with this scholar's accomplishment, giving the impression that to study Islamic theology is, in a sense, to study Ghazālī:

> It is pertinent if churlish to note that fame in the West, consolidated by the works of numerous translators and commentators, gives [Ghazālī] an almost disproportionate weight in our assessment of the Islamic intellectual tradition.[50]

[46] I have briefly mentioned the distinction between Arjomand's and my approach (which I humbly present as an extension of Calder's own) in *Religion and Society in Qajar Iran*, 5.

[47] Calder's complaint is also about Arjomand's style and prolific use of Weberian terminology without carefully determining a word's meaning. In this criticism, Calder was not alone. See, for example, *BSOAS* 50, 383 (sociological sections are 'for the most part, virtually incomprehensible').

[48] 1987: Stern, 134.

[49] 1980: McDermott, 365.

[50] 1983: Morelon, 210.

This may be part of the reason for Calder's excitement over Gimaret's contribution to the field in *Théories de l'Acte Humain en Théologie Musulmane* – it takes a broader picture of Muslim theological writings. Naturally, he also recognises Van Ess's fundamental contribution to the study of Islamic theology.[51] Calder's detailed analysis of Cook's *Early Muslim Dogma* has already been mentioned, and is (or should be) required reading for those interested in the development of early Muslim thought. Calder considers Cook to be paralysed by 'methodological despair' as he recognises the limitations of his own method and hedges his bets over the dating and central impulse of the documents he is analysing. Both here and in his review of Crone and Hinds' *God's Caliph* Calder reveals his deep dissatisfaction with the *Hagarism* project, and on this he is, most likely, influenced by Wansbrough. Critics of the 'revisionists' rarely recognise that they disagree with each other almost as regularly as they (in concert) turn on naive approaches to traditional accounts. *Ikhtilāf* is both within as well as between *madhāhib*.

In his specialised field (Islamic law), his reviews are few. However, the positions known from his other works are clearly in evidence:

> Peters' attempt to encapsulate the juristic heritage is fair as far as it goes, but it is necessary to point out that the mediaeval academic discipline of *fiqh* was a tortuous, subtle and uncertain science which never achieved the stasis implied in Peters' survey.

Similarly, Saleh's work on *Unlawful Gain and Legitimate Profit in Islamic Law* is, for Calder, problematic because it aims to describe what mediaeval jurisprudence has recognised as indescribable – namely the Sharīʿa of God. Saleh is, in Calder's view, 'fighting against' the *fiqh* tradition and attempting to construct a 'valid and sensible corpus' on which a legal system might be grounded. Calder is of the opinion that such a project will always be ultimately unrewarded.[52] Amin's *Law and Justice in Contemporary Yemen* is, in Calder's view, hampered by the author's tendency to see the codification of the Sharīʿa as a simple process. Indeed, the very notion of 'Islamic law', so easily bandied around, is for Calder unsatisfactory:

> The concept of Islamic law – quite unknown to the Islamic intellectual tradition – is a Western invention, now adopted as a calque in most modern Islamic languages, which cannot deal with the finer distinctions that might be expressed by the concepts of *fiqh* and *sharīʿa*.[53]

It is precisely those authors who recognise the difficulty in translating the Muslim juristic tradition into a Western language – namely Johansen and

[51] 1983: *La Notion*, 343.
[52] 1990: Saleh and Johansen, 362.
[53] 1991: Amin, 115.

Weiss – and who valiantly attempt to preserve the character of legal discussions in pre-modern Islam whom Calder considers to be making significant contributions to the field.

In his reviews, Calder is drawn to authors who use language in a subtle manner, and frustrated with those whom he considers careless. Calder's complaint was, once again, that a casual use of language does not do justice to the writings of classical Islam:

> There is a problem when a writer whose prose has an easy casualness tries to presents the thoughts of a writer whose every word merits (perhaps demands) focussed attention.[54]

An author of one contribution in a collection Calder was reviewing 'mentions that … Muhammad Abduh … "!returned (!) to a common sense (!) of rational simplicity and directness (!)"! Can this kind of thing survive a symposium on hermeneutics? Obviously yes'.[55]

To craft one's language when discussing classical Islamic thought is, in Calder's view, a measure of respect for the author one is studying. It is almost as if, for Calder, sloppy use of language is not merely a stylistic defect, but carries with it moral considerations: One is failing to treat the texts under analysis with the same care employed by the authors of those texts. This is, of course, a neglect of a scholarly responsibility; but more than that; there is a laziness in grandiose but imprecise expression which indicates a peculiarly modern arrogance (perhaps even, an 'orientalism'): The intricate discourse of the past is described with an idleness of idiom in the present, and that, Calder seems to have thought, constituted an injustice. The presence of this quality in the works he was reviewing usually prompted positive comment. Indeed, in his resolutely positive review of *Arabic Thought and Islamic Societies*, Calder considered al-Azmeh's style 'so remarkable that it threaten[ed] to become itself the major characteristic of the book'. There follows a series of lengthy citations to indicate al-Azmeh's linguistic dexterity, ending with Calder describing the book as a *tour-de-force*.[56]

It is, then, no surprise that Calder's reviews are characterised by a careful use of language, and the witty (and at times barbed) turn of phrase found elsewhere in his published oeuvre. Apart from the examples thus far, the following passages stimulate further thought:

> The historian's desire to describe the social structure of a mediaeval society – depict the manners which were conducive to social stability and cohesion – is not easily resisted even when the available sources are notoriously intractable.[57]

[54] 1995: Goodman and Netton, 122.
[55] 1990: Rippin, 334. The punctuation is, of course, Calder's.
[56] 1988: Al-Azmeh, 128.
[57] 1981: Mottahedeh, 363.

One (of several) paradoxes in the Christian doctrine of the Incarnation is that, if it does not in some degree compromise the immortal, immutable and impassible by subjecting it to suffering, change and death, it will not quite suffice for redemption and salvation.[58]

[Crone and Hinds] clearly feel that plausible history is its own justification and literary forms cannot hide the truth from discerning common sense. I believe them to be wrong.[59]

When Crone and Hinds stated in a recent work, 'Given that the caliph's exercise of power could not be controlled, the opponents of Umayyad absolutism had two courses of action to them' … the reader wondered not so much at the truth of statement, but the very possibility of that kind of perception.[60]

[T]he major intellectual traditions of Islam (juristic, theological, mystical) deny (explicitly or implicitly) that the book is an all-sufficient guide and demonstrate the need for creative reinterpretation.[61]

Fundamentalist thought may frequently be oppositional, but oppositional thought is not necessarily fundamentalist.[62]

Place the single word *discuss* after these gobbets, and one has exemplary examination questions for the advanced undergraduate student.

When describing classical Muslim theological discussions on *jabr* and *qadar*, Calder remarks that 'It is not the winning [of the argument] that counts, but the taking part'.[63] This, I think, was also (partially) Calder's attitude towards the 'discipline' (if it can be called this) of Islamic studies. 'Taking part' means understanding both the nature and extent of the scholarly task ahead of us. Islamic studies has, of course, moved on since Calder's death, and today scholarly concerns are (perhaps) even more acutely affected by political pressure. Politicians demand 'relevance' in Islamic studies (perhaps) more than in most other humanities disciplines. Calder, I believe, would have resisted such calls: not because he championed irrelevance, but because he would not have wanted academic exploration to be restricted by a particular conception of what was (and what was not) relevant. Both in his teaching and in his research writings, Calder encouraged a rigorous study of the Muslim intellectual tradition which was simultaneously critical, judicious and sensitive. Though many of his specific conclusions have been subject to (at times, convincing) criticism, Calder was not arguing only for his own version of the development of Muslim jurisprudence. Rather, he was attempting to inculcate habits of scholarship in the study of Islam; these habits, so well developed in more mature disciplines, were under threat from extraneous

[58] 1985: Platti, 318.
[59] 1987: Crone and Hinds, 375–6.
[60] 1988: Hawting, 131.
[61] 1991: Burrell, 368.
[62] 1991: Burrell, 368.
[63] 1982: Gimaret, 350.

constituencies. In the current climate, more than previously, there is a need for the 'precise description and a generous concern for detail'[64] to which Norman's reviews bears witness.

The Book Reviews of Norman Calder

I have made every attempt to find all of Norman's reviews, but cannot be certain the following list (arranged chronologically, and then by journal in each year) is comprehensive.

1980

Martin J. McDermott, *The Theology of al-Shaikh al-Mufīd (d. 413/1022),* in *Bulletin of the School of Oriental and African Studies, University of London* 43;2 (1980): 365–6.

1981

R. P. Mottahedeh, *Loyalty and Leadership in an Early Islamic Society,* in *Bulletin of the School of Oriental and African Studies, University of London* 44;2 (1981): 363–4.

'Allāmah Ṭabātabāī (ed. and trans. William C. Chittick), *A Shi'ite Anthology,* in *Bulletin of the School of Oriental and African Studies, University of London* 44;3 (1981): 576–7.

Abdulaziz Abdulhussein Sachedina, *Islamic Messianism: The Idea of the Mahdi in Twelver Shi'ism,* in *Bulletin of the School of Oriental and African Studies, University of London* 44;3 (1981): 577–8.

1982

Daniel Gimaret, *Théories de l'Acte Humain en Théologie Musulmane,* in *Bulletin of the School of Oriental and African Studies, University of London* 45;2 (1982): 349–50.

R. J. McCarthy, *Freedom and Fulfillment: An Annotated Translation of Al-Ghazālī's* al-Munqidh min al-Ḍalāl *and Other Relevant Works of al-Ghazālī,* in *Journal of Semitic Studies* 27;1 (1982): 124–5.

Gerhard Böwering, *The Mystical Vision of Existence in Classical Islam: The Qur'ānic Hermeneutics of the Sūfī Sahl Al-Tustarī (d.283/896),* in *Journal of Semitic Studies* 27;2 (1982): 331–2.

[64] 'Precise description and a generous concern for detail are the beginnings of scholarship. I am not recommending methodological naivety but only after a student has some familiarity with what lies before him can he assess what tools may help him to describe, analyse and explain it.' (1987: Martin, 546).

1983

James Winston Morris, *The Wisdom of the Throne: An Introduction to the Philosophy of Mulla Sadra,* in *Bulletin of the School of Oriental and African Studies, University of London* 46;1 (1983): 149–50.

Régis Morelon, *Al-Ġazālī, Le Livre du Licite et de l'Illicite:* Kitāb al-Ḥalāl wa-l-Ḥarām, in *Bulletin of the School of Oriental and African Studies, University of London* 46;1 (1983): 210.

Ayatallah Khomeini (ed. and trans. Hamid Algar), *Islam and Revolution: Writings and Declarations of Imam Khomeini,* in *Bulletin of the School of Oriental and African Studies, University of London* 46;1 (1983): 210–11.

La Notion d'Autorité au Moyen Âge: Islam, Byzance, Occident (Colloques Internationales de La Napoule), in *Bulletin of the School of Oriental and African Studies, University of London* 46;2 (1983): 342–3.

M. Cook, *Early Muslim Dogma,* in *Journal of Semitic Studies* 28;1 (1983): 180–7.

H. Lazarus-Yafeh, *Some Religious Aspects of Islam: A Collection of Articles,* in *Journal of Semitic Studies* 28;1 (1983): 187–8.

R. Peters, *Islam and Colonialism: The Doctrine of Jihad in Modern History,* in *Journal of Semitic Studies* 28;2 (1983): 380–1.

1984

Fadlou Shehadi, *Metaphysics in Islamic Philosophy,* in *Bulletin of the School of Oriental and African Studies, University of London* 47;3 (1984): 558–9.

1985

Georges Vajda (ed. Nicole Cottart), *La transmission du Savoir en Islam, (VIIe-XVIIIe siècles),* in *Bulletin of the School of Oriental and African Studies, University of London* 48;1 (1985): 202.

S. M. Stern (ed. F. W. Zimmermann), *Medieval Arabic and Hebrew Thought,* in *Bulletin of the School of Oriental and African Studies, University of London* 48;1 (1985): 202–3. S. M. Stern (ed. F. W. Zimmerman), *History and Culture in the Medieval Muslim World,* in *Bulletin of the School of Oriental and African Studies, University of London* 48;3 (1985): 613–14.

L. Pouzet, *Une Herméneutique de la Tradition Islamique: Le Commentaire des Arbaʿūn al-Nawawīyah de Muḥyi al-Dīn Yaḥyā al-Nawawī (m.679/1277),* in *Journal of Semitic Studies* 30;2 (1985): 320–1.

E. Platti, *Yaḥyā b. ʿAdī, Théologien Chrétien et Philosophe Arabe. Sa Théologie de l'Incarnation,* in *Journal of Semitic Studies* 30;2 (1985): 318–20.

M. Momen, *An Introduction to Shiʿi Islam – The History and Doctrines of Twelver Shiʿism,* in *Times Literary Supplement,* 4305 (1985): 1110.

1986

Eric L. Ormsby. *Theodicy in Islamic Thought: The Dispute over al-Ghazālī's 'Best of All Possible Worlds'*, in *Bulletin of the School of Oriental and African Studies, University of London* 49;1 (1986): 211–2.

Gabriel R. Warburg (ed.), *Studies in Islamic Society: Contributions in Memory of Gabriel Baer*, in *Bulletin of the School of Oriental and African Studies, University of London* 49;2 (1986): 429.

Oliver Leaman, *An Introduction to Medieval Islamic Philosophy*, in *Journal of Semitic Studies* 31;1 (1986): 105–7.

1987

S. M. Stern, *Studies in Early Ismāʿīlism*, in *Bulletin of the School of Oriental and African Studies, University of London* 50;1 (1987): 133–4.

Richard C. Martin, *Approaches to Islam in Religious Studies*, in *Bulletin of the School of Oriental and African Studies, University of London* 50;3 (1987): 545–6.

Richard Walzer, *Al-Fārābī on the Perfect State: Abū Nasr al-Fārābī's* Mabādiʿ Ārāʿ ahl al-madīna al-fāḍila*: A Revised Text with Introduction, Translation and Commentary*, in *Bulletin of the School of Oriental and African Studies, University of London* 50;3 (1987): 548–9.

P. Crone and M. Hinds, *God's Caliph: Religious Authority in the First Centuries of Islam*, in *Journal of Semitic Studies* 32;2 (1987): 375–8.

S. A. Arjomand, *The Shadow of God and the Hidden Imam – Religion, Political Order and Societal Change in Shiʿite Iran from the Beginning to 1890*, in *Middle Eastern Studies* 23;1 (1987): 124–5.

1988

Aziz al-Azmeh, *Arabic Thought and Islamic Societies*, in *Bulletin of the School of Oriental and African Studies, University of London* 51;1 (1988): 128–9.

G. R. Hawting, *The First Dynasty of Islam: The Umayyad Caliphate A.D. 661–750*, in *Bulletin of the School of Oriental and African Studies, University of London* 51;1 (1988): 131.

Daniel Gimaret and Guy Monnot (trans.), *Shahrastani: Livre des Religions et des Sectes. I.*, in *Bulletin of the School of Oriental and African Studies, University of London* 51;3 (1988): 621–2.

1989

David Morgan, *Medieval Persia 1040–1797*, in *Bulletin of the School of Oriental and African Studies, University of London* 52;1 (1989): 153–4.

Martin Kramer, *Shiʿism, Resistance and Revolution*, in *Bulletin of the School of Oriental and African Studies, University of London* 52;2 (1989): 364–5.

1990

A. Rippin (ed.), *Approaches to the History of the Interpretation of the Qurʾān,* in *Journal of Semitic Studies* 35;2 (1990): 333–5.

Nabil A. Saleh, *Unlawful Gain and Legitimate Profit in Islamic Law: Riba, Gharar and Islamic Banking* and Baber Johansen, *The Islamic Law on Land Tax and Rent: The Peasants' Loss of Property Rights as Interpreted in the Hanafite Legal Literature of the Mamluk and Ottoman Periods,* in *Journal of Semitic Studies* 35;2 (1990): 361–5.

1991

R. M. Burrell (ed.), *Islamic Fundamentalism,* in *Bulletin of the School of Oriental and African Studies, University of London* 54;2 (1991): 367–8.

S. H. Amin, *Law and Justice in Contemporary Yemen: People's Democratic Republic of Yemen and Yemen Arab Republic,* in *International Journal of Middle East Studies* 23;1 (1991): 114–5.

1992

Marvin Fox, *Interpreting Maimonides: Studies in Methodology, Metaphysics and Moral Philosophy* and Oliver Leaman, *Moses Maimonides,* in *Bulletin of the School of Oriental and African Studies, University of London* 55;2 (1992): 319–20.

1993

Etan Kohlberg, *Belief and Law in Imāmī Shīʿism,* in *Bulletin of the School of Oriental and African Studies, University of London* 56;2 (1993): 361–3.

1995

L. E. Goodman, *Avicenna* and Ian Richard Netton, *Al-Farabi and His School,* in *Bulletin of the School of Oriental and African Studies, University of London* 58;1 (1995): 121–3.

1996

Bernard G. Weiss, *The Search for God's Law: Islamic Jurisprudence in the Writings of Sayf al-Dīn al-Āmidī,* in *Bulletin of the School of Oriental and African Studies, University of London* 59;3 (1996): 556–7.

1997

William C. Chittick, *Imaginal Worlds: Ibn al-ʿArabī and the Problem of Religious Diversity,* in *Bulletin of the School of Oriental and African Studies, University of London* 60;3 (1997): 549.

1998

Richard M. Frank, *Al-Ghazālī and the Ashʿarite School,* in *Bulletin of the School of Oriental and African Studies, University of London* 61;1 (1998): 131–3.

Principal Sources Used

Ḥanafī Texts

Haddādī. *al-Jawhara al-nayyira*. Istanbul: Matba'a Mahmūd Beg, 1884; repr. Multan: Maktaba-ye Haqqāniyya, n.d.
Ibn 'Ābidīn. *Majmū'a rasā'il Ibn 'Ābidīn*. n.p., n.d.
Ibn 'Ābidīn. *Radd al-muhtā.*, Beirut: Dār al-Fikr, 1979, IV.
Ibn Nujaym. *al-Baḥr al-rā'iq*. Cairo: al-Matba'a al-'Ilmiyya, 1310/1892–3, I.
Kāsānī. *Badā'i' al-ṣanā'i' fi tartīb al-sharāi'*. Beirut: Dār al-Kitāb al-'Arabī, 1982, I, VII.
Laknawī. *Al-Fawāid al-bahiyya*. Beirut: Dār al-Ma'rifa, n.d.
Marghinānī. *al-Hidāya*. Cairo: Muṣṭafā al-Bābī al-Halabī, 1970, V.
Mawṣilī. *al-Ikhtiyār li-ta'līl al-mukhtār*. Beirut: Dār al-Ma'rifa, 1975, IV.
Nasafī. *Kanz al-daqāiq*, text in commentary on *Kanz* by Zayla'ī, *Tabyīn al-ḥaqā'iq*. Beirut: Dār al-Ma'rifa, 1975, III.
Qāḍīkhān. *Fatāwā*, in margin of *al-Fatāwā al-hindiyya*. Bulaq: al-Maṭba'a al-Kubrā al-Amīriyya, 1310/1892–3, I.
Qudūrī. *Matn*. Cairo: Muṣṭafa al-Bābī al-Ḥalabī, 1957.
Sarakhsī. *Mabsūṭ*. Beirut: Dār al-Ma'rifa, 1986, IX.

Shāfi'ī Texts

Nawawī (ed. Mohammed Tahar). *Les Quarante Hadiths*. Paris: Deux Océans, 1980.
Nawawī. *Majmū'*. Cairo: Maṭba'a al-'Āṣima, 1966, I.
Nawawī. *Majmū'*. Cairo: Maṭba'a al-Imām, 1969, VI.
Nawawī. *Minhāj al-tālibīn*. Cairo: Muṣṭafā al-Bābī al-Ḥalabī, 1338/1919–20, I.
Nawawī. *Rawḍa al-ṭālibīn*. Beirut: al-Kitāb al-Islāmī, n.d., I.
Nawawī. *Sharḥ Muslim*. Cairo: al-Maṭba'a al-Miṣriyya, 1349/1929–30, I.
Ramlī. *Nihāyat al-muḥtāj*. Beirut: Dār al-Kutub al-'Ilmiyya, 1993, I.
Subkī. *Fatāwā*. Beirut: Dār al-Ma'rifa, n.d., II.
Zarkashī. *Tashnīf al-masāmi' bi-jam' al-jawāmi'*. Cairo: Maktab Qurṭuba, 1998, IV.

Encyclopaedic Works

Ibn Ḥajar al-ʿAsqalānī. *al-Durar al-kāmina*. Dār al-Kutub al-Ḥadītha, 1966, III.
Shawkānī. *al-Badr al-ṭāliʿ*. Cairo: Maṭbaʿa al-Saʿāda, 1348; 1929–30, I.
Subkī. *Ṭabaqāt al-Shāfiʿiyya al-Kubrā*, Cairo: ʿĪsā al-Bābī al-Ḥalabī, n.d., VIII, X.

Index

For EU product safety concerns, contact us at Calle de José Abascal, 56–1°,
28003 Madrid, Spain or eugpsr@cambridge.org.

www.ingramcontent.com/pod-product-compliance
Lightning Source LLC
LaVergne TN
LVHW011522200926
848484LV00001B/110

* 9 7 8 0 5 2 1 1 1 0 8 0 8 *